*Lectures on the Will to Know*

*Also in this series:*

*Forthcoming in this series:*

# MICHEL FOUCAULT

## *Lectures on the Will to Know*

### LECTURES AT THE COLLÈGE DE FRANCE

### 1970-1971

### and

## *Oedipal Knowledge*

Edited by Daniel Defert
General Editors: François Ewald and Alessandro Fontana

English Series Editor: Arnold I. Davidson

TRANSLATED BY GRAHAM BURCHELL

palgrave
macmillan

Liberté · Égalité · Fraternité
RÉPUBLIQUE FRANÇAISE

This book is supported by the
French Ministry of Foreign Affairs,
as part of the Burgess programme
run by the Cultural Department of
the French Embassy in London.
(www.frenchbooknews.com)

First published 2013 by
PALGRAVE MACMILLAN

Palgrave Macmillan in the UK is an imprint of Macmillan Publishers Limited,
registered in England, company number 785998, of Houndmills,
Basingstoke, Hampshire RG21 6XS.

Palgrave Macmillan in the US is a division of St Martin's Press LLC,
175 Fifth Avenue, New York, NY 10010.

Palgrave Macmillan is the global academic imprint of the above companies
and has companies and representatives throughout the world.

Palgrave® and Macmillan® are registered trademarks in the United States,
the United Kingdom, Europe and other countries

ISBN 978–1–4039–8656–6

This book is printed on paper suitable for recycling and made from fully
managed and sustained forest sources. Logging, pulping and manufacturing
processes are expected to conform to the environmental regulations of
the country of origin.

A catalogue record for this book is available from the British Library.

A catalog record for this book is available from the Library of Congress.

10  9  8  7  6  5  4  3  2  1
22  21  20  19  18  17  16  15  14  13

Printed and bound in Great Britain by
CPI Antony Rowe, Chippenham and Eastbourne

# CONTENTS

# FOREWORD

MICHEL FOUCAULT TAUGHT AT the Collège de France from January 1971 until his death in June 1984 (with the exception of 1977 when he took a sabbatical year). The title of his chair was "The History of Systems of Thought."

On the proposal of Jules Vuillemin, the chair was created on 30 November 1969 by the general assembly of the professors of the Collège de France and replaced that of "The History of Philosophical Thought" held by Jean Hyppolite until his death. The same assembly elected Michel Foucault to the new chair on 12 April 1970.[1] He was 43 years old.

Michel Foucault's inaugural lecture was delivered on 2 December 1970.[2] Teaching at the Collège de France is governed by particular rules. Professors must provide 26 hours of teaching a year (with the possibility of a maximum of half this total being given in the form of seminars[3]). Each year they must present their original research and this obliges them to change the content of their teaching for each course. Courses and seminars are completely open; no enrolment or qualification is required and the professors do not award any qualifications.[4] In the terminology of the Collège de France, the professors do not have students but only auditors.

Michel Foucault's courses were held every Wednesday from January to March. The huge audience made up of students, teachers, researchers and the curious, including many who came from outside France, required two amphitheatres of the Collège de France. Foucault often complained about the distance between himself and his "public" and of how few exchanges the course made possible.[5] He would have liked a seminar in which real collective work could take place and made a number of attempts to bring this about. In the final years he devoted a long period to answering his auditors' questions at the end of each course.

This is how Gérard Petitjean, a journalist from *Le Nouvel Observateur*, described the atmosphere at Foucault's lectures in 1975:

> When Foucault enters the amphitheater, brisk and dynamic like someone who plunges into the water, he steps over bodies to reach his chair, pushes away the cassette recorders so he can put down his papers, removes his jacket, lights a lamp and sets of at full speed. His voice is strong and effective, amplified by the loud-speakers that are the only concession to modernism in a hall that is barely lit by light spread from stucco bowls. The hall has three hundred places and there are five hundred people packed together, filling the smallest free space ... There is no oratorical effect. It is clear and terribly effective. There is absolutely no concession to improvisation. Foucault has twelve hours each year to explain in a public course the direction taken by his research in the year just ended. So everything is concentrated and he fills the margins like correspondents who have too much to say for the space available to them. At 19.15 Foucault stops. The students rush towards his desk; not to speak to him, but to stop their cassette recorders. There are no questions. In the pushing and shoving Foucault is alone. Foucault remarks: "It should be possible to discuss what I have put forward. Sometimes, when it has not been a good lecture, it would need very little, just one question, to put everything straight. However, this question never comes. The group effect in France makes any genuine discussion impossible. And as there is no feedback, the course is theatricalized. My relationship with the people there is like that of an actor or an acrobat. And when I have finished speaking, a sensation of total solitude ... "[6]

Foucault approached his teaching as a researcher: explorations for a future book as well as the opening up of fields of problematization were for-mulated as an invitation to possible future researchers. This is why the courses at the Collège de France do not duplicate the published books. They are not sketches for the books even though both books and courses share certain themes. They have their own status. They arise from a specific discursive regime within the set of Foucault's "philosophical activities." In particular they set out the program for a genealogy of knowledge/

power relations, which are the terms in which he thinks of his work from the beginning of the 1970s, as opposed to the program of an archeology of discursive formations that previously orientated his work.[7]

The course also performed a role in contemporary reality. Those who followed his courses were not only held in thrall by the narrative that unfolded week by week and seduced by the rigorous exposition, they also found a perspective on contemporary reality. Michel Foucault's art consisted in using history to cut diagonally through contemporary reality. He could speak of Nietzsche or Aristotle, of expert psychiatric opinion or the Christian pastorate, but those who attended his lectures always took from what he said a perspective on the present and contemporary events. Foucault's specific strength in his courses was the subtle interplay between learned erudition, personal commitment, and work on the event.

♠

With their development and refinement in the 1970s, Foucault's desk was quickly invaded by cassette recorders. The courses—and some seminars—have thus been preserved.

This edition is based on the words delivered in public by Foucault. It gives a transcription of these words that is as literal as possible.[8] We would have liked to present it as such. However, the transition from an oral to a written presentation calls for editorial intervention: at the very least it requires the introduction of punctuation and division into paragraphs. Our principle has been always to remain as close as possible to the course actually delivered.

Summaries and repetitions have been removed whenever it seemed to be absolutely necessary. Interrupted sentences have been restored and faulty constructions corrected. Suspension points indicate that the recording is inaudible. When a sentence is obscure there is a conjectural integration or an addition between square brackets. An asterisk directing the reader to the bottom of the page indicates a significant divergence between the notes used by Foucault and the words actually uttered. Quotations have been checked and references to the texts used are indicated. The critical apparatus is limited to the elucidation of obscure points, the explanation of some allusions and the clarification of critical points. To make the lectures easier to read, each lecture is preceded by a brief summary that indicates its principle articulations.

For this year, 1970-1971, we do not have recordings of Foucault's lectures. The text is therefore based on his preparatory manuscript. In the "Course Context," Daniel Defert explains the criteria employed to edit the text.

The text of the course is followed by the summary published by the *Annuaire du Collège de France*. Foucault usually wrote these in June, some time after the end of the course. It was an opportunity for him to pick out retrospectively the intention and objectives of the course. It constitutes the best introduction to the course.*

Each volume ends with a "context" for which the course editors are responsible. It seeks to provide the reader with elements of the biographical, ideological, and political context, situating the course within the published work and providing indications concerning its place within the corpus used in order to facilitate understanding and to avoid misinterpretations that might arise from a neglect of the circumstances in which each course was developed and delivered.

The *Lectures on The Will to Know*, delivered in 1970-1971, and *Oedipal Knowledge*, are edited by Daniel Defert.

♠

A new aspect of Michel Foucault's "œuvre" is published with this edition of the Collège de France courses.

Strictly speaking it is not a matter of unpublished work, since this edition reproduces words uttered publicly by Foucault. The written material Foucault used to support his lectures could be highly developed, as this volume attests.

This edition of the Collège de France courses was authorized by Michel Foucault's heirs who wanted to be able to satisfy the strong demand for their publication, in France as elsewhere, and to do this under indisputably responsible conditions. The editors have tried to be equal to the degree of confidence placed in them.

FRANÇOIS EWALD AND ALESSANDRO FONTANA

---

* [There are, however, no summaries for the lectures given in 1983 and 1984; G.B.]

1. Michel Foucualt concluded a short document drawn up in support of his candidacy with these words: "We should undertake the history of systems of thought." "Titres et travaux," in *Dits et Écrits, 1954-1988*, four volumes, eds. Daniel Defert and François Ewald (Paris: Gallimard, 1994) vol. 1, p. 846; English translation by Robert Hurley, "Candidacy Presentation: Collège de France" in *The Essential Works of Michel Foucault, 1954-1984, vol. 1: Ethics: Subjectivity and Truth*, ed. Paul Rabinow (New York: The New Press, 1997) p. 9.
2. It was published by Gallimard in May 1971 with the title *L'Ordre du discours*, Paris, 1971. English translation by Ian McLeod, "The Order of Discourse," in Robert Young, ed., *Untying the Text* (London: Routledge and Kegan Paul, 1981).
3. This was Foucault's practice until the start of the 1980s.
4. Within the framework of the Collège de France.
5. In 1976, in the vain hope of reducing the size of the audience, Michel Foucault changed the time of his course from 17.45 to 9.00. See the beginning of the first lecture (7 January 1976) of *"Il faut défendre la société." Cours au Collège de France, 1976* (Paris: Gallimard/Seuil, 1997); English translation by David Macey, *"Society Must be Defended." Lectures at the Collège de France 1975-1976* (New York: Picador, 2003).
6. Gérard Petitjean, "Les Grands Prêtres de l'université française," *Le Nouvel Observateur*, 7 April 1975.
7. See especially, "Nietzsche, la généalogie, l'histoire," in *Dits et Écrits*, vol. 2, p. 137; English translation by Donald F. Brouchard and Sherry Simon, "Nietzsche, Genealogy, History" in *The Essential Works of Michel Foucault 1954-1984, vol. 2: Aesthetics, Method, and Epistemology*, ed. James Faubion (New York: The New Press, 1998) pp. 369-392.
8. We have made use of the recordings made by Gilbert Burlet and Jacques Lagrange in particular. These are deposited in the Collège de France and the Institut Mémoires de l'Édition Contemporaine.

# Translator's Note

THE TEXT OF THIS volume of Michel Foucault's Collège de France lectures is based on Foucault's preparatory manuscripts for his 1970-1971 course. Inevitably this creates particular difficulties for the reader as well as for the translator. The presentation of this text in English translation differs from the French in two respects.

First, the French edition included the manuscript pagination in the margin to the left of the text. This has been omitted from the English translation. In the French edition, except where a page break corresponds with a new paragraph or section, the precise point at which one page ends and another begins is not indicated. This lack of precision inevitably increases with a translated text. Without the original manuscript or an accurate copy ready to hand, the manuscript pagination is of no use to the English reader and is an unnecessary hindrance to smooth reading. (I note that the Loeb Classical Library indicates the pagination of the source text alongside the original Greek or Latin, but omits it from the accompanying English translation.)

Second, the French edition left the many Greek terms and quotations in Foucault's lecture manuscripts in the original Greek script. In this translation all Greek terms are transliterated, following the practice of the French editors of the already published volumes of Foucault's lectures. In his "Course Context," Daniel Defert refers to B. Knox recalling that when he published his *Oedipus at Thebes* in 1957 he had shocked the academic profession by transliterating Greek terms. It is perhaps worth quoting in full what Knox said in his Preface to a later edition of his book: " ... my decision to transliterate my frequent citations from the Greek text was an expedient scorned by the profession at that time.

Whitman, for one, complained that some transliterated sentences had the 'unhallowed look of jabberwocky.' This was true, but because *the use of Greek script would have made it next to impossible for the Greekless reader to follow an argument based on a demonstration of the repetition of key words*, it was a blemish I was prepared to accept" (my emphasis; G.B.).*

With regard to the translation itself, the 1970-1971 lectures belong to the period in which Foucault was developing and working out a distinction between *connaissance* and *savoir* which will be set out in Part IV, chapter 6 of *The Archeology of Knowledge* and in varying versions subsequently. Put very crudely, *savoir* refers to the domain of practices and discourses which are constitutive of *connaissance* as a rule-governed relation between subject and object of knowledge.† Both *connaissance* and *savoir* are translated in English by "knowledge," and no satisfactory or generally accepted English equivalents have been found to mark the distinction Foucault wants to make. Both are translated as "knowledge" here, followed by the appropriate French word where it was necessary to mark the distinction.

---

* B. Knox, *Oedipus at Thebes* (New Haven: Yale University Press/London: Oxford University Press, 1998), "Preface to the New Edition," p. x.
† The distinction is, of course, discussed in the lectures themselves and in Daniel Defert's "Course Context."

# 9 December 1970

*Shift of the theme of knowledge (*savoir*) towards that of truth.*
*Elision of the desire to know in the history of philosophy since*
*Aristotle. Nietzsche restores that exteriority.* ∿ *Internal and*
*external reading of Book I (A) of the* Metaphysics. *The*
*Aristotelian theory of knowledge excludes the transgressive knowl-*
*edge of Greek tragedy, sophistic knowledge, and Platonic recollec-*
*tion.* ∿ *Aristotelian curiosity and will to power: two morphologies*
*of knowledge.*

THE WILL TO KNOW is the title I would like to give to this year's lectures. To tell the truth, I think I could also have given this title to most of the historical analyses I have carried out up until now. It could also describe those I would now like to undertake. I think all these analyses—past or still to come—could be seen as something like so many "fragments for a morphology of the will to know."*

In any case, in one form or another, this is the theme that I will try to deal with in the years to come. Sometimes it will be taken up in specific historical investigations: how was knowledge of economic processes established from the sixteenth to the eighteenth century; or how was the knowledge of sexuality organized and deployed from the seventeenth to the nineteenth century. Sometimes, and no doubt less often, it will be examined directly, as such, and I will try to see to what extent it is

---

* *The Will to Know (*La Volonté de savoir*) will in fact be the title of the first volume of the* Histoire de la sexualité (Paris: Gallimard, 1976).

possible to establish a theory of the will to know that could serve as the basis for the historical analyses I have just referred to.

So in this way I would like to alternate concrete investigations and theoretical punctuations, but in an irregular way, according to requirements.

It is one of these punctuations that I would like to mark this year, at the same time as beginning an historical investigation in a seminar, which may continue for several years. The general framework for the seminar will be penality in nineteenth century France. The precise point of the analysis will be the insertion of a discourse claiming scientific status (medicine, psychiatry, psychopathology, sociology) within a system—the penal system—which previously was entirely prescriptive; I should say *almost* entirely prescriptive, because we need only think of the role of doctors in the witchcraft trials of the sixteenth and seventeenth centuries to see that the problem goes back much further than the nineteenth century. So the point of the analysis will be this insertion; the privileged material will be psychiatric expertise in penal matters and, finally, the aim of the research will be to identify the function and assess the effect of a discourse of truth in the discourse of law.

As for the lectures, last week[1] I hastily indicated *the game*[2] I would like to play: it will involve seeing whether the will to truth exercises a role of exclusion in relation to discourse—to some extent, and I mean only to some extent—analogous to the possible role played by the contrast between madness and reason, or by the system of prohibitions. In other words, it will involve seeing whether the will to truth is not as profoundly historical as any other system of exclusion; whether it is not as arbitrary in its roots as they are; whether it is not as modifiable as they are in the course of history; whether like them it is not dependent upon and constantly reactivated by a whole institutional network; and whether it does not form a system of constraint which is exercised not only on other discourses, but on a whole series of other practices. In short, it is a matter of seeing what real struggles and relations of domination are involved in the will to truth.

This is how I have characterized the theme of these lectures.

It is easy to see the series of questions which I have the impression of having blithely passed over with these few indications. And to start with, when we speak of will to truth (are we speaking of the will that chooses truth rather than falsity, or of a more radical will that lays down and imposes the truth/error system?), is it a question of the will to truth or of the will to know? And between these two notions, what about the notion that we cannot fail to come across when we analyze either of the others—I mean: knowledge (*connaissance*)?* So, the interplay between these three notions—knowledge-*savoir*, truth, and knowledge-*connaissance*—has to be established.

Another question, also of a semantic order: what should we understand by will? What distinction is to be made between this will and what we understand by desire in expressions like desire for knowledge (*connaissance*), or desire to know (*savoir*)? What relationship is to be established between the expression isolated here, "will to know (*savoir*)" and the more familiar expression "desire to know (*connaître*)"?

As in most investigations of this kind, it will be possible to resolve these semantic questions completely only at the end of the journey.[3] At least we will regularly need to mark out the ground and put forward some bridging definitions.

But there are other problems. To start with: how was it that the historical study of certain bodies of knowledge (*connaissances*), or [of certain] kinds of knowledge (*savoirs*), of certain disciplines, of certain discursive events, led to this question of the will to know? For we have to acknowledge that few historians of science have felt the need to resort to it until now. What makes this notion necessary or indispensable?

Inadequacy of the instruments of historical analysis provided by epistemology.

Second problem: relations between will to know and forms of knowledge-*connaissance*: at the theoretical level; at the historical level.

Third major problem: is it really reasonable to pick out the notion of will as central for an analysis of kinds of knowledge (*savoirs*) which tries to avoid reference to a founding subject? Is this not another way of once again reintroducing something like a sovereign subject?[4]

Fourth problem: if it is a matter of discovering a sort of great assertive (albeit anonymous) will behind the historical phenomena of knowledge, will this not return us to a sort of autonomous and ideal history

---

* See "Translator's note" above, p. xv.

in which the will to know itself determines the phenomena in which it manifests itself? How would this differ from a history of thought, consciousness, or culture? To what extent is it possible to articulate this will to know on the real processes of struggle and domination which develop in the history of societies?

And finally we see what is at stake, I won't say the fifth problem, but the one that runs through all those I have referred to—and I should not even say problem, but open wager that I am not sure of being able to take up, [it being a matter of seeing]:

—whether, through the history of true discourses, we can bring to light the history of a certain will to the true or false, the history of a certain will to posit the interdependent system of truth and falsity;

—whether, second, we can show that this historical, singular, and ever renewed activation of the system of truth and falsity forms the central episode of a certain will to know peculiar to our civilization;

—and finally, whether we can articulate this will to know, which has taken the form of a will to truth, not on a subject or on an anonymous force, but on real systems of domination.

—Then, to sum up all these steps, each of which is very lengthy and complex, we will have put the game of truth back in the network of constraints and dominations. Truth, I should say rather, the system of truth and falsity,[5] will have revealed the face it turned away from us for so long and which is that of its violence.

It has to be said that philosophical discourse is of little help in this investigation. Undoubtedly, there is hardly a philosophy which has not invoked something like the will or desire to know (*connaître*), the love of truth, etcetera. But, in truth, very few philosophers—apart, perhaps, from Spinoza and Schopenhauer—have accorded it more than a marginal status; as if there was no need for philosophy to say first of all what the name that it bears actually refers to. As if placing at the head of its discourse this desire to know (*savoir*), which it repeats in its name, was enough to justify its own existence and show—at a stroke—that it is necessary and natural: All men by nature desire to know ... Who, then, is not a philosopher, and how could philosophy not be the most necessary thing in the world?

Now what I would like to show this evening, through an example, is how, right from the start of a philosophical discourse, this desire to know, which philosophy nonetheless appoints to explain and justify its existence, is elided.

The example is taken from the first lines of Aristotle's *Metaphysics*.

Next week, I would like to show how Nietzsche was the first to release the desire to know from the sovereignty of knowledge (*connaissance*) itself: to re-establish the distance and exteriority that Aristotle cancelled, a cancellation that had been maintained by all philosophy.

23 [December], I would like to see what it *should* cost thought to pose the problem of the [will*] to know.

\*     \*     \*

A well-known, quite banal passage whose initial marginal position in the *Metaphysics* seems to keep to the edge of the work: "All men by nature (*phusei*) desire to know; the proof of this is the pleasure caused by sensations, for even apart from their usefulness, we enjoy them for themselves, and visual sensations more than the others."[6]

In fact, this passage can be read from within the œuvre: each of its elements gets its meaning, value, and functions from Aristotle's philosophy; there is not one which cannot be justified by it. Despite its almost marginal character, this transparent text can be re-enveloped within the œuvre. It can be read internally. But it is also open to an external reading: we can identify an operation here concerning philosophical discourse itself. And not only that of Aristotle, but philosophical discourse as it has existed in our civilization.[7]

[...†]

I would like to say that Aristotle's text—which is something of a liminal text—is, like others occupying a similar position and performing analogous functions, a "philosophical operator"; with elements internal to the system, and entirely interpretable on the basis of the system, it

---

\* The manuscript has: truth (*vérité*).
† Manuscript page [13] crossed out.

concerns the possibility and justification of the whole system, its origin
and necessary birth; and beyond the system itself, it concerns and acts on
the status of philosophical discourse in general:

—a philosophical operator: the text in which Descartes[8] sets out
his desire to arrive at the truth, lists the reasons for doubting, and
excludes the possibility of he himself being mad;
—a philosophical operator: Spinoza's text in *On the Improvement of
the Understanding*,[9] on the desire for a new life, the uncertainty of
the goods one possesses, the uncertainty of arriving at an eternal
and perfect good, and the discovery of this good in [the happiness
of] the true idea.

No doubt we could also recognize what could be called "epistemological operators" in some scientific texts: they concern the very possibility of the discourse within which they are set, and by this we should
understand not the possibility of its axioms or postulates, the symbols
employed and their rules of use, not that which makes possible the
coherence, rigor, truth, or scientific character of the discourse, but that
which makes possible its existence. I am thinking, for example, of the
beginning of Saussure's *Course of General Linguistics*; or of the text by
Linnaeus on the structure of the sexual apparatus of plants[10] (inasmuch
as it founds the possibility of a taxonomic description, a description
whose object is precisely its own condition of possibility—namely that
structure itself).

Let us return to Aristotle's text. [To] the first sentence: All men by
nature desire to know.[11] This entails, quite clearly, three theses:

1. there is a desire that is focused on knowledge,
2. this desire is universal and is found in all men,
3. it is given by nature.

a. Aristotle will give proofs of these theses. Now these proofs, or
rather this proof is presented as a *sēmeion*. This term, *sēmeion*, should not
be translated exclusively as "sign." Generally it refers to proof, evidence,
to that which demonstrates. In philosophers and orators it is a traditional way of introducing any proof (*sēmeion*: which shows, as is shown

by). However, in Aristotle, this expression introduces a very particular type of reasoning. It does not involve reasoning from the cause, but from the example, the particular case. The particular case is subsumed under a still hypothetical general principle; and the truth of the particular case establishes the truth of the general principle. This is the enthymeme (at any rate, one of its possible structures).[12]

It is by no means immaterial that the proof that all men desire knowledge is presented as an enthymeme.

b. The proof is that sensations give pleasure and among them, visual sensations—and that they give pleasure in themselves independently of any relationship to utility.

Now this proof, or rather this particular case, involves three moves that maybe cannot be completely superimposed on the move that allows one to descend quite simply from the general to the particular.

α—We go in fact from knowledge, *eidēnai*, to sensation, *aisthēsis*, and finally to visual sensation. How can sensation, with its pleasure, be an example of the desire to know?

β—Second move: the desire to know was inscribed in nature, *phusei*, it is now presented as the pleasure of the sensation taken in itself, i.e., apart from any *utility*, and from any action, as it is said later—as if the non-utility of the sensation was inscribed in nature.

γ—We go from desire, *oregontai*,[13] a traditional term in Aristotle, to pleasure. But pleasure is not designated by the traditional *hēdonē*, but by a word—*agapēsis*—which is fairly rare in Aristotle and which, in particular, does not enter into his traditional theory of pleasure.

*Agapēsis*, which refers rather to the fact of paying one's respects to something or someone, bringing to it the attachment one owes it, willingly according it that which is rightfully due to it, and being satisfied with this other thing, recognizing that it has fulfilled its obligations to oneself. *Agapēsis* refers to the satisfaction of order. The pleasure (*agrément*) you take in something that is agreeable to you.

So we have a thesis
an argument in the form of an enthymeme,
a triple shift in this argument.

A—First question: how is sensation, with its specific pleasure, a satis-factory example of the natural desire to know?

Three things must be proven:

—that sensation really is a knowledge;
—that sensation is accompanied by pleasure;
—that the pleasure one gets from sensation really is bound up with what makes it a knowledge.

First proposition: sensation really is a knowledge. See the passages in *On The Soul*,[14] which say:

—that sensation is an activity (a shared action of sensing and sensible);
—that it is an activity of the sensitive soul;
—that the result of this activity is to actualize the quality, *poion*, of something. Sensation is the action of qualitative knowledge.

Second proposition: sensation is in fact accompanied by pleasure. See the passage in *Nicomachean Ethics*, X, 6,[15] which says:

—that pleasure should not be considered as the same thing as activity, that it is different;
—but that nevertheless it accompanies activity when this is deployed in the proper way;
—and moreover that there are as many distinct pleasures as there are specific activities of sensation;

Third proposition: what makes sensation knowledge is in fact what brings about the pleasure of the sensation.

And here there are two series of justifications: one is implicit in the text of the *Metaphysics*, the other is at least partially present in it.

The implicit justification is found in the *Nicomachean Ethics*. There are things which seem pleasant to sick people and which are unpleas-ant to people in good health, and conversely. Now, only things pleasant to healthy people are truly pleasant, they alone procure true pleasures, because only such sensations actualize the real qualities of the object.

Pleasure is connected with the very truth of the knowledge. And where there is no knowledge there is no real pleasure.

The explicit justification in this text is more curious, although we [find] it in many other of Aristotle's texts, and it is this: there is one sense which gives more to knowledge than the others, and it is the sense that procures the most pleasure. This is the sense of sight.

The reason why sight gives more to knowledge than the other senses is that through the specific qualities it perceives (color, light), sight additionally enables one to grasp some common sensibles [sensible qualities common to all the senses] (like rest and movement, number, unity; *On The Soul*),[16] and in making unity perceptible, it enables one to distinguish, through sensible qualities like color, the individuals which have them.

Hence the text from the *Metaphysics*: Sight is the sense that "discloses the most differences."[17]

The reason why sight, more laden with knowledge than the other senses, equally gives more pleasure, is that the other pleasures of the senses (like touch or taste) are unlimited, open to intemperance, and consequently turn into disgust (*Eudemian Ethics*). The pleasure of sight stays within its own limits, it remains a true pleasure.

[ ... *]

[Another] move: [from given by] nature to the absence of utility; or again from sensory pleasure in general to the specifically human pleasure man can take in his own sensations.

B—The first question raises a question in fact: if all the sensations give some pleasure and in proportion to their activity of knowledge, why do not animals, which have sensations, desire to know? Why does Aristotle seem to attribute the desire to know to all men, but only to men?

The reason is the generic differences which characterize man and enable him, unlike animals, to take pleasure in useless sensation.

a—The first set of these differences are still found in sensation on the border [of] animality and humanity:

—memory produced by sensation, but only in some animals;
—listening, hearing. A frequently repeated theme in Aristotle is that hearing is not found is some animals (ants and bees). For

---

* Manuscript page [22] crossed out.

Aristotle understands by hearing a phenomenon of considerable scope, since at one end it concerns hearing inarticulate sounds (*tōn psophon*) the text says; but it also involves the capacity to understand language and, and at a still higher level, to receive an education.

With memory, the property of being intelligent (*phronimos*) appears; and with this hearing the ability and disposition to learn appears, the ability to be a disciple; the fact of being "*mathētikos*" (disciplinable).

b—The second set of differences distinguishing man from the sensitive animal is *tekhnē* (art) and *epistēmē* [science].

Both are capable of being taught, as the same book of *Metaphysics* will say (I (A), 981b): so it is these that pass through hearing. They are also characterized by the fact that they bring with them a universal judgment arrived at on the basis of a "multitude of notions which come from experience"* (*ek pollōn tēs empeirias ennoēmatōn*), that is to say, they depend upon memory. Finally, they have this particular feature of often being less effective than experience. Experience can recognize cases and grasp opportunities; art and science lay down general principles but do not provide the rules, schema, and principle of their application.

c—Finally, the third difference separating human nature from the sensitive animal is the presence of *sophia*: *sophia* is knowledge of the cause, which is comprised in knowledge of essence in its universal aspect.

Now this knowledge of causes is the supreme knowledge; it is of use only to itself, it is free and has no other end than itself; it is not ordered by reference to any utility.

Being the end for itself, it is the end of all knowledge, that towards which knowledge is headed.

Extending somewhat the thought [of the first lines] of the *Metaphysics* we establish a correlation between two principles. On the one hand, there is a mode of knowledge specific to man and which is not at all that of sensation; it is knowledge that to start with has for material (for material cause) the images of memory and articulate sounds; for

---

* French translation, 981a: experimentals (*expérimentales*); English, p. 1552: "from many notions gained by experience one universal judgment about similar objects is produced."

form (or formal cause) *tekhnē* and *epistēmē*; and for end and final cause, wisdom, *sophia*. On the other hand, at each level the bonds of utility become looser: we see this through the example of bees and ants, for whose lives hearing is not necessary; *tekhnē* and *epistēmē* are less useful than experience; finally, through a final reversal, *sophia* has no other end than itself.

So we must now say that the famous "satisfaction that we take in useless sensations" is not so much, or not only a particular case of the great and general desire to know to be found everywhere in nature, but that it is above all—in following the thread of this analysis—the still rudimentary model, the miniscule paradigm of a knowledge with no other end than itself.

Man no doubt remains at the level of what is useful for life so long as he remains at the animal level of sensation. But if he nevertheless finds satisfaction in sensations that are not directly useful, this is because there is already emerging the act of a knowledge which will not be subordinate to any utility, since it is in itself its own end.

*We might have been surprised that proof that the desire to know given to all men by nature is found in the satisfaction of useless sensations (even though sensations are naturally useful). This is because the nature in question was in reality a certain nature of man destined to a knowledge without any other end than itself. And it was this final end that already drew to itself the simple activity of sensing (*sentir*) and made it already pleasant, when, it was released for a moment from proof of utility.

And it is now easy to answer the third question concerning the third move: why does Aristotle advance the pleasure, the *agreeableness* we find in sensations as proof that "all men desire to know"?

The key to this move is undoubtedly in the use of the word *agapēsis*. What accompanies all activity, provided it takes place in appropriate conditions, is the pleasure called *hēdonē*. On the other hand, what accompanies the higher activity of virtue and contemplation is something else: happiness, *eudaimonia*.

Now what specific pleasure accompanies sensation when it is the paradigm of contemplation, when it enjoys its own uselessness and is

---

* Three quarters of manuscript page [28] suppressed.

also already the image of theory? It is undoubtedly not *hēdonē*, which can accompany any sensation whatever; nor is it *eudaimonia*, which implies continuity, habit, *exis*. It is accompanied by a specific category of *hēdonē*, which is like the sign, the paradigm of the future happiness of theory. It is accompanied by *agapēsis*. Just as useless sensation is the paradigm of future contemplation, so the agreeableness that doubles it already delineates the future happiness: *agapēsis*.

Duality, therefore, of this word *agapēsis*, as if it pointed to the material of sensory and animal pleasure already taking the generically human form of happiness.

*So, in Aristotle's text there are not so much ambiguities as superimpositions of sense:

—when Aristotle speaks of nature (*phusei*), he means nature in general but also the generic difference of man as opposed to animals;
—when he introduces a proof calling it *sēmeion*, he designates the example as a particular case of a general principle as well as the paradigm of something to come;
—when he employs the term *agapēsis*, he means the pleasure of the sensation as well as something which heralds the happiness of contemplation.†

Through these superimpositions, Aristotle manages, on the one hand, to inscribe the desire for knowledge in nature, to link it to sensation and the body, and to give it a certain form of sensual pleasure as correlate; but on the other hand, and at the same time, he gives it status and foundation in the generic nature of man, in the element of wisdom and a knowledge with no other end but itself and in which pleasure is happiness.

As a result, body and desire are elided; the movement leading to the great serene and incorporeal knowledge of causes is in itself already, at

---

* Added by the editor on the basis of a preserved fragment of the lecture delivered. The manuscript has only this schema:

| nature | example | pleasure |
|---|---|---|
| *phusei* | *sēmeion* | *agapēsis* |
| differentiation | paradigm | happiness |

† End of transcription of the oral presentation.

the level of sensation, the obscure will to accede to this wisdom, it is already philosophy.

Thus philosophy, performing the role of supreme knowledge—knowledge of first principles and final causes—also has the role of enveloping all desire to know from the start. Its function is to ensure that what is really knowledge coming from sensation, from the body, belongs already, by nature and according to the final cause that directs it, to the realm of contemplation and theory. Its function is also to ensure that, despite appearance, desire is neither anterior nor exterior to knowledge, since knowledge without desire, a happy knowledge and pure contemplation is already in itself the cause of that desire to know that trembles in the simple agreeableness of the sensation.

If we now stand back a bit from this text, we can identify some massive events which it presupposes or makes possible.

1. To be able to say that man naturally desires to know and that this desire is foreshadowed in the pleasure of the sensation presupposes exclusion of the theme of a transgressive, forbidden, fearsome knowledge.

Now it is this theme that we find constantly in Greek tragedy and especially [in] Aeschylus and Sophocles. The tragic hero is far from naturally desiring knowledge.

In the first place, in fact, if he desires knowledge it is not because he is moved by a natural impulse inscribed in his nature from the moment of sensation. It is because a word has been uttered from afar and above—an enigmatic word, with double meaning, which he does and does not understand, which reassures him, but nevertheless troubles him.

In *The Persians*,[18] it is the queen's dream, the ghost of Darius. In *The Women of Trachis*,[19] it is the Centaur's prophecy to Deianeira: Heracles will be affected by magic contact "so that he will never prefer any other woman" (569). In *Oedipus*, of course, it is the reported rumor.

Now, this knowledge that is desired (because it is at once obscure and promising) is a fearsome knowledge:

a—In fact, it is jealously and greedily held back by the gods: "The ways of divine thought go to their end through thickets and thick shadows which no gaze can penetrate" (Aeschylus, *The Suppliants*, 93).[20]

b—it blinds the very ones it concerns: a knowledge which watches and whose gaze dazzles those on whom it fixes. Oedipus does not look at the secret but the secret looks at him, it does not take its eyes off him, and seeks to capture him by finally striking him. It blinds the very ones it concerns, to the point that when the gods give up a little of their secret, the hero is the only one not to recognize this knowledge drawing nearer and threatening him, whereas the public and the Chorus already know. This is what happens to Ajax:[21] he has been misled by Athena, and everyone knows this; but he does not see this fearsome presence at his side, he does not see the great figure who is destroying him, and he implores her: "I ask of you only to be at my side and always allied, as you are now."

c—Finally, it is a knowledge that kills. The hero does not resist it when it swoops down on him. The flash of light and death merge.

The Aristotelian themes of a knowledge which goes from pleasure to happiness, of a knowledge towards which one is carried by a natural impulse, through the intermediary of words that teach and do not prophesize, and a memory without forgetfulness or enigma—are all opposed to tragic knowledge.[22] Elsewhere, a bit further on in the *Metaphysics*, Aristotle says: The gods are not jealous.[23]

2. In saying that man naturally desires to know and that this desire to know is already driven by the impulse towards theoretical happiness, Aristotle rules out the sophistic or Socratic-sophistic question: "Why do we desire to know?"

The question arose in multiple forms, [to wit]:

—if we desire to know out of virtue or because we already have a good nature, then why learn? We know already;

—or: if we desire to learn for bad reasons (so as to get the upper hand over others, or to win unjust cases), then we will have to change in order to learn, or the fact of learning will change the one who learns. In short, the subject of knowledge will not be

the same as the subject of desire. *Euthydemus*: to teach is to kill[24]—
and behind all this emerges the big question that philosophy has
not ceased to conceal precisely inasmuch as its birth may not be
entirely foreign to it: can knowledge be sold? Can it, on the one
hand, be closed up on itself like the precious object of greed and
possession? And, on the other hand, can it enter into the game
and circulation of wealth and goods?

For if knowledge is a thing we desire, why would it not be a good like
others, entering like them into the universality of money?

Aristotle rules out this question by placing the desire to know well
before the completion of knowledge, at the lowest level, [that] of sensation; by seeing to it nevertheless that this desire belongs already to
knowledge, since it is in sensation that knowledge first appears. Desire
is enclosed within knowledge, but knowledge is not given entire with
desire.

*Still through this assertion of the natural character of the desire
to know, [Aristotle] rules out the Platonic theme of memory and the
supercelestial world.

On the one hand, in Aristotle the desire to know is foreshadowed at
the level of and in sensations; the desire to know is not linked to the
project of getting free from them and going beyond them in order to find
a truer reality. Quite the reverse, if there is a danger, it is that one does
not get free of them. On the other hand, memory, which is indeed indispensable to the desire to know (*connaître*) in the whole of its movement,
is linked to sensation, since it is its persistence and trace. The desire to
know (*savoir*) does not move away from *phantasia*,[25] it is inscribed in it
and depends on it.

Nevertheless, we see that in ruling out the Platonic theme, Aristotle
resolves the same problem as Plato; at least, he complies with the same
theoretical requirement. Namely: to ensure that the will to know is not
founded on anything other than the precondition of knowledge itself; to
ensure that the desire to know is enveloped entirely within knowledge;
to ensure that knowledge has already absorbed it from the start and
that, on its first appearance, it thus gives it its place, its law, and the

---

* Three quarters of manuscript page [37] crossed out.

principle of its movement. Plato satisfied this requirement through the myth of recollection: even before you know, even before you desire to know, you knew, you had already known.

We are accustomed to reading the theory of recollection as not only the correlate of the transcendence of ideas, but also as a way of connecting knowing and desiring to know to each other. Actually, this theory should be read as a way of lodging the desire to know within knowledge.

By placing the *mnēmē* in the very tracks of sensation, Aristotle completely changes the arrangement, but he makes it play the same role: in its nature, action, and power, the desire to know is not outside the knowledge it desires.

The Aristotelian text thus presupposes the exclusion of three themes: that of tragic knowledge (*savoir*), that of learning-commodity, and that of knowledge (*connaissance*)-memory. But like [Plato*], albeit in a different way, he seeks to protect knowledge from the exteriority and violence of desire. The desire to know is no more than a game of knowledge in relation to itself, it does no more than show its genesis, delay, and movement; desire is knowledge deferred, but made visible in the impatience of the suspense in which it is held.

The consequence of this envelopment, and much more in Aristotle than in Plato, is that knowledge (*savoir*) and desire are not in two different places, possessed by two subjects or two powers, but that the one who desires knowledge is already the one who possesses it or is capable of possessing it; and it is without violence, appropriation, and struggle, without commerce too, but by the simple actualization of his nature, that the one who desires to know will indeed end up knowing: a single subject goes from desire to know (*savoir*) to knowledge (*connaissance*), for the good reason that if knowledge were not there as precedence (*précédence*)[†26] of the desire, the desire itself would not exist.

And conversely, the desire to know is in its nature already something like knowledge, something belonging to knowledge. It cannot want knowledge for something other than itself since it is starting from

---

* The manuscript: the latter.
† Unclear. It could also be read: *providence*.

knowledge that it wishes to know. Knowledge is at once its object, its end, and its material. This is why:

—on the one hand, in the diversity of desires, there will be that singular, separate, and serene desire that we will call curiosity, the desire to know for the sake of knowing, etcetera;
—and, on the other hand, we will not acknowledge any violence, will to domination, or force of exclusion and rejection in this desire. The game of exteriority of desire and knowledge is replaced by a mutual belonging of each to the other, the envelopment of the first by the second, and something like a co-naturalness.

Hence we understand:

α—the need to lodge both of them in a same agency—same soul, same subject, same consciousness;
β—the scandal in making will and desire emerge outside knowl-edge, as Nietzsche and Freud have done;
γ—the difficulty of thinking philosophically a will to know (*savoir*) that would derive in advance from the unity of a knowing (*connaissant*) subject.

In order to fix the vocabulary, let us say that we will call knowledge-*connaissance* the system that allows desire and knowledge-*savoir* to be given a prior unity, reciprocal belonging, and co-naturalness. And we will call knowledge-*savoir* that which we have to drag from the inte-riority of knowledge-*connaissance* in order to rediscover in it the object of a willing, the end of a desire, the instrument of a domination, the stake of a struggle.

*Let's stand back a bit again. For centuries there has existed a theme the banality of which induces weariness, which is that ultimately every-one is a bit of a philosopher.

It is a theme immediately dismissed by philosophical discourse in order to develop the theme that philosophy is a specific task, set back

---

* According to the notes of an auditor, this page of the lecture was not delivered.

and at a distance from all others, and irreducible to any other. But it is a theme no less regularly taken up again by philosophical discourse in order to assert that philosophy is nothing other than the movement of truth itself, that it is consciousness becoming aware of itself—or that the person who wakes up to the world is already a philosopher.

But we should note that this theme, ever dismissed and taken up again, of a philosophy linked to the first movement of knowledge in general, is a theme which would have appeared very foreign to the first Greek philosophers. But more importantly we can see the function it performs: there is already contemplation in the crudest and most physical knowledge; it is this contemplation, then, that will lead to the whole movement of knowledge according to its specific logic or the necessity of the object it contemplates. As a result, desire is elided along with its effectiveness. Desire is no longer cause, but knowledge that becomes cause of itself (on the basis of the idea, or of the sensation of obviousness, or of the impression, no matter)—cause of itself and of the desire directed towards it.

And as a consequence, the subject of desire and the subject of knowledge are one and the same. The sophistical problem (the person who does not yet know and desires cannot be the person who knows and no longer desires) is erased. The strange discussion of the *Euthydemus* in which the Sophist says: "If you want your friend to learn, he must no longer be the same, he must die," this ironic irruption of death between the subject of desire and the subject of knowledge, can now be erased, for desire is no more than the scarcely perceptible quivering of the subject of knowledge around what he knows. The old millennial theme of "everyone is more or less a philosopher" has a precise and ascribable function in Western history: it is a matter of no more or less than sealing up the desire to know in knowledge itself.

1. In the inaugural lecture of 2 December, published with the title *L'Ordre du discours* (Paris: Gallimard, 1971); English translation by Ian McLeod, "The Order of Discourse," in *Untying the Tex*, ed. Robert Young (London: Routledge and Kegan Paul, 1981).

2. By placing at the outset the metaphor of the game, employed by Nietzsche in *The Birth of Tragedy* and then becoming one of his key concepts, is Foucault evoking Eugen Fink who frees Nietzsche from the Heideggerian interpretation through his usage of the game? See E. Fink, *Das Spiel as Weltsymbol* (Stuttgart: W. Kohlhammer, 1960); French translation by H. Hilderbrand and A. Lindenberg, as *Le Jeu comme symbole du monde* (Paris: Minuit, 1966). It is not a matter of strategic game, of game of truth—to which Foucault will resort later. (See "Course Context," below, pp. 272-275: "Foucault's game," where it is Deleuze who is called in.

3. The true end of the journey may well have been the lecture of 6 January 1982. See M. Foucault, *L'Herméneutique du sujet. Cours au Collège de France, 1981-1982*, ed. F. Gros (Paris: Gallimard-Seuil, coll. "Hautes Études," 2001), pp. 18-20; English translation by Graham Burchell, *The Hermeneutics of the Subject. Lectures at the Collège de France, 1981-1982*, English series editor Arnold I. Davidson (New York and Basingstoke: Palgrave Macmillan, 2005), pp. 16-19.

4. Here Foucault completely shifts the stake of his research away from the more epistemological one given in his candidacy presentation to the Collège de France in "Titres et travaux" (1969), in *Dits et Écrits, 1954-1988*, four volumes, ed. D. Defert and F. Ewald, with the collaboration of J. Lagrange (Paris: Gallimard, 1994); See vol. 1, no. 71, pp. 842-846; re-edition in two volumes (Paris: Gallimard, "Quarto," 2001), vol. 1, pp. 870-874; English translation by Robert Hurley, "Candidacy Presentation: Collège de France" in *The Essential Works of Michel Foucault, 1954-1984, vol. 1: Ethics: Subjectivity and Truth*, ed. Paul Rabinow (New York: The New Press, 1997) pp. 5-10.

5. Marcel Detienne had recently described the antithetical couple formed by *Alētheia*, Greek truth, and *Lēthē*, oblivion, which he distinguished from the couple described by W. Luther in *Wahrheit und "Lüge" im ältesten Griechentum* (Leipzig: R. Noske, 1935), updated in 1954 and 1958. See Marcel Detienne, *Les Maîtres de vérité dans la Grèce archaïque*, Foreword by Pierre Vidal-Naquet (Paris: Maspero, 1967) pp. 45-49; English translation by Janet Lloyd, *The Masters of Truth in Archaic Greece* (New York: Zone Books, 1999) pp. 63-67. (See "Course context" below, pp. 269-270).

6. Aristote, *La Métaphysique*, Book A, 1, 980a 21-24, ed. and trans. J. Tricot (Paris: Vrin, 1948) two volumes, vol. 1, p. 1; English translation by W.D. Ross, *Metaphysics*, in Aristotle, *The Complete Works of Aristotle (The Revised Oxford Translation)*, Vol. Two, ed. Jonathan Barnes (Princeton: Princeton University Press, 1984), p. 1552: "All men by nature desire to know. An indication of this is the delight we take in our senses; for even apart from their usefulness, they are loved for themselves; and above all others the sense of sight." This quotation is absent from the manuscript and from the transcription of the session in which Foucault read it.

7. In the lecture of 6 January 1982, Foucault describes Aristotle: "the philosopher whom we have recognized as the founder of philosophy" (*L'Herméneutique du suject*, p. 19; *The Hermeneutics of the Subject*, p. 17).

8. See the text at the start of the *Meditations* quoted in M. Foucault, *Histoire de la folie à l'âge classique* (Paris: Plon, 1961) pp. 55-56; English translation by Jonathan Murphy and Jean Khalfa, *History of Madness* (London and New York: Routledge, 2006) pp. 44-46, which became the object of a polemic with Jacques Derrida from 1963 to 1972; see J. Derrida, *L'Écriture et la Différence* (Paris: Seuil, 1967) pp. 61-97; English translation by Alan Bass, *Writing and Difference* (Chicago: University of Chicago Press, 1980) pp. 31-63.

9. Foucault is referring here to §5 of *Traité de la réforme de l'entendement*, a much more Cartesian than Stoic passage, despite some parallels, on which Foucault had previously written many notes in the Charles Appuhn edition (Paris: January, 1929); English translation by R.H.M. Elwes as *On the Improvement of the Understanding* in Spinoza, *Works*, vol. II (New York: Dover Publications, 1955). He refers to this passage again in the lecture of 6 January 1982, *L'Herméneutique du sujet*, p. 29; *The Hermeneutics of the Subject*, p. 27.

10. Ch. Linné, *Système sexuel des végétaux*, trans. N. Jolyclerc (Paris: Ronvaux, Imprimeur, Year VI, 1798) vol. 1, pp. 19-20; See M. Foucault, *Les Mots et les Choses* (Paris: Gallimard, 1966) ch.

5, §VII: "Le discours de la nature"; English translation by A. Sheridan as *The Order of Things* (London: Tavistock, 1970) ch. 5, §VII, "The discourse of nature."
11. See above, p. 5 and note 6. Gilles Deleuze had already offered a Nietzschean commentary of this presupposition in *Différence et Répétition* (Paris: PUF, 1968) pp. 172-173; English translation by Paul Patton, *Difference and Repetition* (London: Athlone Press, 1994) pp. 131-132: "There is no point in multiplying the declarations of philosophers, from 'Everybody has by nature the desire to know' to 'Good sense is of all things in the world the most equally distributed,' in order to verify the existence of this presupposition ... When Nietzsche questions the most general presuppositions of philosophy, he says that these are essentially moral, since Morality alone is capable of persuading us that thought has a good nature and the thinker a good will, and that only the good can ground the supposed affinity between thought and the True ... As a result, the conditions of a philosophy which would be without any kind of presuppositions appear all the more clearly: instead of being supported by the moral Image of thought, it would take as its point of departure a radical critique of this image and the 'postulates' it implies." Foucault gave an account of this commentary. See "Ariane s'est pendue" (1969), *Dits et Écrits*, vol. 1, no. 64, pp. 767-771; "Quarto" ed., vol. 1, pp. 795-799; and "Theatrum philosophicum" (1970) in *Dits et Écrits*, vol. 2, no. 80, pp. 75-99; "Quarto" ed., vol. 1, pp. 943-967; English translation by Donald F. Brouchard and Sherry Simon (amended by the editors) as "Theatrum philosophicum" in *The Essential Works of Michel Foucault, 1954-1984, vol. 2: Aesthetics, Method, and Epistemology*, ed. James Faubion (New York: The New Press, 1998).

This passage not only indicates the subterranean dialogue struck up between *Difference and Repetition* and these lectures of 1970, but the continuation of Deleuze's text shows that he himself enters into dialogue with *The Order of Things*. We note that this passage also refers to Martin Heidegger, *Was heißt Denken?* (Tübinger: M. Niemeyer, 1954); French translation by A. Becker and G. Granel, *Qu'appelle-t-on penser?* (Paris: PUF, 1959); English translation by J. Glenn Gray, *What is Called Thinking?* (New York: Harper and Row, 1968).
12. The different kinds of enthymeme—or "oratorical arguments"—are described by Aristotle in *Rhetoric*, Book 1, 2, 135a et seq. and I, 23: the enthymeme is the substitute of the syllogism, which is a dialectical reasoning. See L. Robin, *Aristote* (Paris: PUF, 1944) p. 53 et seq., and p. 289.
13. *"Pantes anthrōpoi tou eidenai oregontai phusei"*. See above, p. 5 and note 6.
14. Aristote, *De Anima* III, 2, 425b, 26 et seq.; English translation by J. A. Smith, Aristotle, *On The Soul*, in *The Complete Works of Aristotle*, Vol. One, p. 677. See L. Robin, *Aristote*, pp. 182-193.
15. Aristote, *Éthique à Nicomaque*, X, 6, ed. and trans. J. Voilquin (Paris: Garnier, 1940), an edition particularly annotated by Foucault; English translation by W.D. Ross revised by J.O. Urmson, Aristotle, *Nicomachean Ethics*, in *The Complete Works of Aristotle*, Vol. Two, pp. 1859-1860.
16. Aristote, *De Anima*, II, 6, and III, 1, 425a; Aristotle, *On The Soul*, pp. 665, 676.
17. Aristote, *La Métaphysique*, A, 1, 980a 21, p. 2): "of all our senses, sight is the one that makes us acquire most knowledge, and that discloses to us the most differences"; English translation, p. 1552: "sight ... most of all the senses, makes us know and brings to light many differences between things."
18. Aeschylus, *The Persians*, trans. S. G. Benardete in *The Complete Greek Tragedies. Volume 1: Aeschylus* ed. David Grene and Richard Lattimore (Chicago and London: University of Chicago Press, 1959), 680 et seq., pp. 243-250.
19. Sophocles, *Les Trachiniennes*, ed. and trans. P. Masquerary (Paris: Les Belles Lettres, 1942) 569, see also 555-575; English translation by Michael Jameson as *The Women of Trachis*, in *Sophocles II*, ed. David Grene and Richard Lattimore (Chicago and London: University of Chicago Press, 1969), pp. 92-93.
20. See Aeschylus, *Les Suppliantes*, ed. and trans. P. Mazon (Paris: Les Belles Lettres, 1923) 93; English translation by S. G. Benardete as *The Suppliant Maidens* in *Aeschylus*.
21. Sophocles, *Ajax*, trans. John Moore, in *Sophocles II*, 70 et seq., p. 10.
22. This sentence gets its full meaning when brought together with Nietzsche's: "Ich erst habe das Tragische entdeckt," F. Nietzsche, *Der Wille zur Macht*, §1029, in *Nietzsches Werke*, XVI, 377 (Leipzig: C. G. Naumann, 1901 [1899]) XVI, 377, quoted by Ch. Andler in *Nietzsche, sa vie et sa pensée*, vol. VI: *La Dernière Philosophie de Nietzsches. Le renouvellement de toutes les valeurs* (Paris: Bossard-Gallimard, 1931) p. 358; English translation of Nietzsche by Walter Kaufmann and R.J. Hollingdale, *The Will to Power*, ed. Walter Kaufmann (New York: Vintage Books, 1968) p.

531: "*I have been the first to discover the tragic.*" See also *The Twilight of the Idols* in *The Twilight of the Idols and The Anti-Christ*, trans. R. J. Hollingdale (Harmondsworth: Penguin, 1990) "What I owe to the ancients," §5, p. 121: "the *tragic* feeling, which was as much misunderstood by Aristotle as it especially was by our pessimists ... *Birth of Tragedy* was my first revaluation of all values: with that I again plant myself in the soil out of which I draw all that I will and *can*—I, the last disciple of the philosopher Dionysos—I, the teacher of the eternal recurrence ... "

23. Aristote, *La Métaphysique*, A, 2, 983a, vol. I, p.10: "It is not permissible that the divinity be jealous"; Aristotle, *Metaphysics*, p. 1555: "the divine power cannot be jealous." (The transcription of Foucault's lecture adds: "anti-tragic expression par excellence.")

24. Platon, *Euthydème* in *Œuvres complètes*, ed. and trans. L. Robin (Paris: Gallimard, 1971) vol. 1, p. 577, 283d: "since your intention is that he [Clinias] not be the man he is at present [M.F. writes: the same] ... is your intention not quite simply that he perish?"; English translation by W. H. D. Rouse, *Euthydemus*, in Plato, *The Collected Dialogues*, ed. Edith Hamilton and Huntington Cairns (Princeton: Princeton University Press, Bollingen Series LXXI, 1961), p. 397: "Since you want him no longer to be one that he is now, you want him to be destroyed, it seems!"

25. Imagination is treated above all in *On the Soul*, III, 3.

26. P. Aubenque, in *Le Problème de l'Être chez Aristote* (Paris: PUF, 1966²), p. 54, writes: "the distinctive feature of the syllogism is to depend upon an antecedent truth ... *precedence* of the truth to itself rather than vicious circle" (emphasis added).

# two

# 16 DECEMBER 1970

*For an analysis of the de-implication of knowledge and truth.* ∿
*Obscure primacy of the truth in Aristotle in which desire, truth,*
*and knowledge form a theoretical structure. Spinoza, Kant, and*
*Nietzsche seek to disrupt this systematicity.* ∿ *Freeing oneself*
*from the "old Chinaman" of Königsberg, but killing Spinoza.* ∿
*Nietzsche gets rid of the affiliation of truth and knowledge.*

LAST WEEK, I TRIED to analyze an apparently quite commonplace passage from Aristotle. It concerned the desire to know and its natural character. But, by studying the terms a bit more closely, we saw that this natural desire to know was shown first of all by a *pleasure* taken in a *useless sensation*. A triple displacement revealed two things:

1. There was knowledge at the root of the desire, even before it manifests itself and starts to function. A knowledge that is still sensory, of course, but a knowledge nonetheless, a knowledge already there on the basis of which the desire could unfold.

So that knowledge was prior to the desire for it; and this desire was itself nothing other than a sort of inner retardation of knowledge with regard to itself, a desire correlative to the period that retarded knowledge in order to arrive in one go at its true nature, namely, contemplation.

2. But this triple displacement also showed something else. In fact, in Aristotle's text we saw:

—that if the sensation could be considered as a legitimate example of knowledge, the reason for this was that it had access to
truth—to things themselves in their specific qualities.

We also saw:

—that if one could take a certain form of pleasure (*agapēsis*) in the
sensation, this was because the sensation was capable of presenting itself to us as the advance figure of contemplation, that is to say
of knowledge of truth in itself.

Finally we saw:

—that this pleasure was linked to the very uselessness of the sensation, that is to say, to the fact that the role of the sensation is
not merely to serve animal life and its needs, but that it can have
access itself to the truth.

In short, underneath the text that spoke of a sort of natural desire to
know and seemingly prior to any knowledge, beneath this text, there
were two operations: one that reintroduced knowledge underneath
desire and at its very source; and the other, even more hidden, that
introduced truth as a third element between desire and knowledge. All
the arguments and proofs found in Aristotle's other texts, and by which
this triple displacement can be justified, presuppose that sensation and
its pleasure are connected with truth.

If there is desire to know in general, and if knowledge can give rise to
something like desire within its own movement, it is because everything
already takes place in the realm of truth.

Truth as guarantee and foundation of the desire to know.

Now I think that ultimately this is the most important point: in
order to effectuate the transition from desire to knowledge, there is,
there had to be truth:

—it is because it is already a question of truth in the desire that the
desire can be desire for knowledge;

—conversely, it is because the relationship to truth is fundamental that the desire for knowledge already belongs, in itself, at its root, to the domain of knowledge; finally,

—it is because the relationship to truth commands both knowledge and desire that they can have only one and the same subject. The subject of knowledge and the subject of desire can be considered the same, since they have the same relationship to truth.

Truth thus plays three roles: it assures the transition from desire to knowledge; on the other hand, and as if in return, it founds the precedence of knowledge over desire; and it gives rise to the identity of the subject in desire and knowledge.

Now this interplay of truth in relation to desire and knowledge is what constitutes the strong point of this whole systematicity.

If, in Western philosophy until Nietzsche, desire and will were never able to rid themselves of their subordination to knowledge, if the desire to know was always doubled by the precondition of knowledge, the reason is this fundamental relationship to truth.

That is why we can say that Spinoza had already gone to the furthest limit: at the highest point of this theoretical structure, at the point where he was closest to getting outside it and overturning it.

[Look at] the beginning of *On the Improvement of the Understanding*: ["I finally resolved to inquire whether there was some object that was a true good, capable of communicating itself, and by which the soul, renouncing everything else, could be affected solely, a good of which the fruit of its discovery and possession would be an eternity of continuous and sovereign joy."*];[1] it is not a question of a desire to know here, as in Aristotle, but of a desire for happiness—for an eternal happiness which nothing could compromise (and of which nothing is yet said about it pertaining to the realm of knowledge). Now it is in this search for happiness, or rather in examination of the conditions under which one could find this happiness, in the examination of its uncertainties or of its certainty, that the true idea, the happiness peculiar to the true idea, is discovered (and through the game of this search itself). It is starting from there that the resolution to seek to know is set out. Truth is thus nominated as that

---

* This quotation does not appear in the manuscript of this lecture.

which founds knowledge as well as the desire to know. It is on the basis of the truth that all the other elements are set out and ordered.

We can see: all of the apparent arrangement of the Aristotelian text is overturned. Here there is adequation of happiness and the true idea; on the basis of which the will to know and knowledge are deployed. In Aristotle, there is natural desire to know discreetly indicated by the little happiness of not very useful sensations. But in fact, for Aristotle's text to be able to hold up, contemplation (contemplation of the truth, and contemplative happiness) had to emerge already and be inscribed at least potentially in sensory happiness and the desire to know.

Spinoza names in plain language, and in order, what makes classical metaphysics possible.[2]

Now it is in fact this will-knowledge-truth relationship that is at stake in Nietzsche.[3]

As a first approximation, Nietzsche's texts can (and should) be read as an attempt to free the desire to know from the form and law of knowledge.

a—This involves showing that there is a desire at the root of knowledge, at the historic point of its sudden emergence, and that this desire has no kinship with knowledge. No relatedness at the level of ends, or by origin or nature.

It is not related by origin, since, if you like, knowing is living—because one is forced into movement, it is detestation [*detestari*]. There is no affiliation at the level of ends, since one knows in order to dominate, to get the upper hand, not in order to know.

b—It involves showing that throughout its history and development knowledge has not been guided by the internal necessity of what is known, or by the ideal genesis of the forms of knowledge, but by a rule of will—which is asceticism.

c—Finally it involves showing that spread out behind the very act of knowledge, behind the subject who knows in the form of consciousness, there is the struggle of instincts, partial selves, violence, and desires.

Of course, all of this is in Nietzsche's texts, and abundantly so.[4] But all this effort to get through to the other side of knowledge, this effort to break through its limits and find oneself outside in relation to it, is in great danger and risks remaining precarious.

In fact, how is it possible to know this other side, this outside of knowledge? How is it possible to know knowledge outside knowledge? Should we suppose a truth outside of knowledge and on which we could depend in order to define the limits of knowledge from the outside? But how could we have access to this truth if not on the basis of this knowledge from which it is a matter of getting out?

Either what we say about knowledge is true, but this can only be from within knowledge, or we speak outside of knowledge, but then nothing allows us to assert that what we say is true.

At the outer bounds of Nietzschean discourse, but still looming over it, we see the threat of Kant.[5]

The Kantian dilemma is inevitable, unless... Unless we get rid of the affiliation of truth and knowledge; unless knowing is not by nature, destination, or origin knowing the truth; unless the truth is not that which is given (or denied) to knowledge, not that which has a common site with knowledge, making it possible to say just as easily that knowledge has access to the truth, or that the truth is irremediably separate from it.

Only if truth and knowledge do not belong to each other by right will one be able to pass to the other side of knowledge without falling into the paradox of a both unknowable [and] unknown truth.*

(Differences from Kant:

ideology
—inaccessible truth
—and limited knowledge.)

I think all the Nietzschean analysis of the desire, instinct, and will to know, irreducible to knowledge itself, is doubled by the work that makes it possible to de-implicate truth and knowledge; just as the Aristotelian reduction of the desire to know to knowledge recounted, in the background, the alliance of knowledge and truth.

---

* Manuscript: both unknowable unknown.

It is this de-implication of truth and knowledge—condition of possibility and guiding thread for an analysis of the will to know - that I would like to analyze this evening. But two comments before beginning:

a—the existence of this work behind the scenes may explain the boldness and naivety with which Nietzsche, in order to pass to the other side of knowledge and undertake its critique, employs huge doses of knowledge borrowed from the sciences: biology, history, philology.[6] This use of knowledge would itself immediately fall under the critique if the de-implication of knowledge and truth were not carried out at the same time, or rather if it did not itself carry out this de-implication, but in a different direction.

Nietzsche's positivism is not a moment of his thought which has to be overcome; it is not a superficial level whose depth one might discern by looking down from above; it is a critical act in accordance with two orthogonal directions: one addressed to the outside of knowing; the other addressed to the untenable vacancy (*non-lieu*) of knowledge and truth.[7] So we should not pass over this positivism, as if treating it with tact. What is most important will take place right within this positivist critique.

b—The second comment concerns Nietzsche's relationship to Kant and Spinoza. Kant is the danger, the tiny daily peril, the network of traps; Spinoza is the great other, the sole adversary.

In fact, Kant is the trap laid for every critique of knowledge. He asserts that we will never be able to pass to the other side; or that in passing to the other side we will let the truth escape; and that our discourse will inevitably be dogmatic since it will pass itself off as true without possessing, to guarantee it, knowledge of the truth.[8]

But Spinoza is the adversary, since, from *On the Improvement of the Understanding* to the last proposition of the *Ethics*, he is the one who names, founds, and renews the affiliation of truth and knowing in the form of the *true idea*.

Spinoza is for Nietzsche the philosopher par excellence because he is the one who links truth and knowledge in the most rigorous way. To avoid the trap of Kant one has to kill Spinoza. One will escape the critique and the "old Chinaman of Königsberg"[9] only by having undone that affiliation of truth and knowledge to which Spinoza has the right to give his name since it is he who thought it through from end to end—from the first postulate to the final consequence.

Spinoza is the condition of Kant. One can avoid Kant only after having freed oneself from Spinoza.[10] Naivety of the skeptics, of the neo-
Kantians,[11] of Kant himself,[12] who thought he could escape Spinoza
through the critique. Naivety of those who thought they could escape
the idealism of philosophical discourse by resorting to Spinoza.[13]*

---

* The notes taken at the lecture by Hélène Politis indicate that at this point a long discussion of
Nietzsche began, continued in the following lecture of 23 December. It no longer appears in the
manuscript. Its main points are found in a lecture given in Canada. See the "Lecture on Nietzsche"
below, pp. 202-223.

1. Spinoza, *Traité de la réforme de l'entendement*, in *Œuvres*, trans. Ch. Appuhn (Paris: Garnier, 1929) vol. 1, §1, p. 224 (edition annotated by Foucault, probably in the 1950s); English translation by R.H M. Elwes, *On the Improvement of the Understanding*, in *Works of Spinoza*, vol. II (New York: Dover Publications, 1955) p. 3: "I finally resolved to inquire whether there might be some real good having power to communicate itself, which would affect the mind singly, to the exclusion of all else: whether, in fact there might be anything of which the discovery and attainment would enable me to enjoy continuous, supreme, and unending happiness."

2. In his edition of Spinoza, Appuhn emphasizes that according to Spinoza science is not Stoic contemplation, but active, Cartesian, Baconian, it transforms things, the body, the soul; the sage is not absorbed in the Great All but seeks to assimilate it—Generation of truth by thought.

3. "I am completely surprised, delighted. I have a *precursor*, and what a precursor! I scarcely knew Spinoza. To have had now the desire to read him, *voila de l'instinct*. To start with, the general tendency of his philosophy is the same as mine: to make knowledge the most powerful passion. Then I find myself again in five essential points of his doctrine ...: he denies free will, purpose, the moral order of the universe, altruism, evil" (postcard to Franz Overbeck, Sils, 30 July 1881, quoted in *La Vie de Frédéric Nietzsche d'après sa correspondance*, ed. G Waltz (Paris: Rieder, 1932) letter 147.

4. In the "Course Summary" (see below, p. 227), Foucault refers only to *The Gay Science* (1883). His preparatory notes refer to *Human, All Too Human*. But from the 1950s, he made notes on all of Nietzsche's texts. In "La vérité et les formes juridiques" (1974, *Dits et Écrits*, vol. II, no. 139, pp. 538-646, see p. 543 et seq.; "Quarto," vol. I, pp. 1406-1490, see p. 1410 et seq.; English translation by Robert Hurley, "Truth and Juridical Forms" in *Essential Works of Foucault 1954-1984, vol. 3: Power*, ed. James Faubion (New York: The New Press, 2000), see p. 6, Foucault mentions "On Truth and the Lie in an Extra-Moral Sense," written in 1873, "if not in the middle of Kantianism then at least in the middle of neo-Kantianism," which would have been the starting point for his reflection here.

5. "The metaphysicians. I am speaking about the greatest misfortune of modern philosophy, about Kant." F. Nietzsche, *Œuvres philosophiques complètes*, XIV: *Fragments posthumes (début 1888-début janvier 1889)*, ed. G. Collin and M. Montinari, trans. J.-Cl. Hémery (Paris: Gallimard, 1977) p. 283.

6. Charles Andler recalls the authors studied by Nietzsche in these different domains in *La Dernière Philosophie de Nietzsche*. Foucault is no doubt referring to the function given here to the works of contemporary historians.

7. All of this discussion on the meaning of the Nietzschean enterprise is to be set against Heidegger's text, *What is Called Thinking?*

8. See F. Nietzsche, *Twilight of the Idols*, p. 50, "How the 'Real World' at last Became a Myth": "3. The real world, unattainable for the moment, undemonstrable, cannot be promised, but even when merely thought of a consolation, a duty, an imperative. (Fundamentally the same old sun, but shining through mist and scepticism; the idea grown sublime, pale, northerly, Königsbergian)." See also F. Nietzsche, *La Volonté de puissance*, ed. and trans. G. Bianquis (Paris: nrf/Gallimard, 1947-1948), vol. 1, Book 1, ch. 2, p. 90: "The will to find the truth": "The weak point of Kantian criticism has gradually become visible even to rather dull eyes: Kant no longer had the right to make his distinction between 'phenomenon' and 'thing-in-itself,' he deprived himself of the right to persevere in this old distinction since he repudiated as illicit the conclusion that goes back to the phenomenon: the *cause* of the phenomenon, in conformity with his idea of causality to which he attributed a strictly *intra-phenomenal* value"; English translation by Walter Kaufmann and R.J. Hollingdale, *The Will to Power*, ed. Walter Kaufmann (New York: Vintage Books, 1968) p. 300: "The sore spot of Kant's critical philosophy has gradually become visible even to dull eyes: Kant no longer has a right to his distinction 'appearance' and 'thing-in-itself'—he had deprived himself of the right to go on distinguishing in this old familiar way, in so far as he rejected as impermissible making inferences from phenomena to a cause of phenomena—in accordance with his conception of causality and its purely intra-phenomenal validity."

9. F. Nietzsche, *Beyond Good and Evil*, trans. R.J. Hollingdale (Harmondsworth: Penguin, 1973) §210, p. 122: "Even the great Chinaman of Königsberg was only a great critic." Foucault returns to Nietzsche's relationship to Kant in "La vérité et les formes juridiques"; "Truth and Juridical Forms," which is a summary of the major themes of these lectures.

10. See especially, *Twilight of the Idols*, "Morality as Anti-Nature" §4; *Beyond Good and Evil*, §21.

11. This overview of the history of philosophy seems to refer to the interpretations which oppose Heidegger in *Kant and the Problem of Metaphysics*, trans. James S Churchill (Bloomington and London: Indiana University Press, 1962) and the neo-Kantians. On this point, see J. Vuillemin, *L'Heritage kantien et la révolution copernicienne* (Paris: PUF, 1954).

12. Notably, *Critique of Judgment*, §72, 73, 80.

13. This allusion could be aimed at Althusser, who is referred to implicitly at several points in these lectures.

# three

# 6 JANUARY 1971*

*The Sophists:[†] their appearance and their exclusion.* ∽ *History of philosophy in its relations to the truth according to Aristotle. Philosophical discourse cannot have the same status as poetic discourse.* ∽ *The historical mode of existence of philosophy set for centuries by Aristotle.* ∽ *The existence of philosophy made possible by the exclusion of the Sophists.* ∽ *The Sophist as figure. Sophism as technique.* ∽ *Sophistics manipulates the materiality of words.* ∽ *The different roles of Plato and Aristotle in the exclusion of the Sophists.*

I STARTED WITH TWO models of analysis. In one (which seems to me to characterize the philosophical tradition), the will to know (*savoir*) comes from a prior knowledge of which it is at once the deployment, the dislocation, and the inner retardation.

In the other model, knowing must be analyzed as pure event at the surface of processes which do not themselves belong to the order of knowledge-*connaissance*;[‡] we call knowledge-*savoir* the set of these events. As for knowledge-*connaissance* (that is to say the subject-object relation), this will be an effect internal to knowing. An effect that it has not been possible to avoid but that maybe is not necessary. Finally, truth is

---

* Concerning the lecture of 23 December, see above, p. 28, note*; see also the "Lecture on Nietzsche" below, pp. 202-223.
† Title of the lecture manuscript. The initial capital letter given to the word "Sophists" in Foucault's text has been respected.
‡ This is developed in the "Lecture on Nietzsche," below, pp. 202-214.

not that which is in principle linked to knowledge (*connaissance*), but both exist in a relation to each other of both support and exclusion. The undertaking then is this. Is it possible to do a history whose reference would not be a system of subject and object—a theory of knowledge-*connaissance*—but that would be addressed to the events of knowledge-*savoir* and to the effect of knowledge-*connaissance* internal to these events? The problem is one of gauging the possibility of reversing the traditional configuration that posits knowledge-*connaissance*—as form or faculty—as precondition and then the events of knowledge-*savoir* as singular acts[1] that actualize this faculty and may in some cases modify its form.

This is precisely what I would like to do first of all with regard to the Sophists. To analyze the appearance and then the exclusion of the Sophists, as an event of knowledge-*savoir* which gave rise to a certain type of assertion of the truth and to a certain effect of knowledge-*connaissance* which then became normative form.

I will leave problems of method to one side; I will come back to them at the end of this first inquiry. Today, as point of departure for this analysis, I would like to take what appears to me to be the final point of outcome of the history of the sophistic: what we could [call] its act of exclusion.

And then, starting from that point, I will try to go back to the sophistic itself.

I do not think we have to go to Plato to find this act of exclusion, not even to *The Sophist* (which provides its definition however), but to Aristotle[2]—in the *Sophistical Refutations*, and in some passages in the *Analytics* and the *Metaphysics*.

To take the measure of this act of exclusion we should perhaps start with this text from the *Metaphysics*:

"...as for sophistic, it is only an apparent philosophy without reality ( ...*ē de sophistikē phainomenē, ousa d'ou*)."[3]

and compare it with Aristotle's analyses a bit before, in Book I (A), of the philosophies that preceded him.

How are the analyses of earlier, Platonic and pre-Platonic philosophies conducted in Book I (A)?

We know that Aristotle seeks confirmation of his own theory of causes: if the philosophers prior to him have found a fifth cause, it is he, Aristotle, who will be mistaken; if they have not discovered it, Aristotle's own conviction is confirmed.

So the philosophers are therefore already in some way in the element of the truth. But how, and what is the relation of these different philosophical discourses to the truth?

1. First of all, philosophies are distinguished from each other by each having grasped one or several elements of the truth (of causes, primary natures, substances, or accidents). The singular identity of each philosophy is determined by its differential relation to the truth (Thales because he named Water as material cause, Anaxagoras because he sought the efficient cause). In short, the formal cause of a philosophy is constituted by a certain relation to the truth.

2. Then, the specific development of a philosophy or the transition from one philosophy to another is imposed by the constraint of the truth:

> "At this point, reality itself marked out the way and forced them to investigate further."[4]
>
> "After them, and when such principles, once discovered, were shown to be insufficient to generate the nature of things, philosophers, forced once more ... by the truth itself, turned to a different causal principle" (Heraclitan Fire, the *nous*, of Anaxagoras and Hermotimus of Clazomenae).[5]

So let us say that the truth is the efficient cause of change or movement in philosophical discourse.

3. But there is more. The object of philosophy is first principles and it is these that the first philosophers already sought in their way. Now one passage [in the *Metaphysics*] teaches us:

> "The principles of eternal Beings are necessarily true par excellence, for they are not only sometimes true, and there is no cause of their being; on the contrary, they are the cause of the being of other beings. Thus, a thing has as much truth as it has being."[6]

Stating the principles of things, philosophers express Being itself.

We can therefore say that the truth is indeed the material cause of philosophy. The principles expressed in it are, through themselves, that which has most being and most truth.

4. Finally, let us not forget that philosophy is the science that does not arise from need, but from wonder,[7] that is to say from that which allows one to recognize one's own ignorance and to want to escape it by the sole effect and the sole good of knowledge:

> "... if it was to escape ignorance that the first philosophers devoted themselves to philosophy, it is clear that they pursued science with a view to knowing and not for any utilitarian end."[8]

The truth is therefore the final cause of philosophy. (Moreover, at II ($\alpha$), 1, 993b 21 he expressly says so: the end of speculation is truth.)

But given these conditions, how is it that philosophy is not true? How is it that it contains errors? How is it that there are philosophies which are incompatible with each other?

It is, Aristotle says, because philosophers conduct themselves "like badly trained soldiers conduct themselves in combat, thrusting in every direction and often landing lucky blows, but without any science."[9]

What the philosopher lacks is precisely the science of these principles, the science of that truth which both guided them and constrained them; what they lacked was the system of first principles and the four causes.

The philosopher is in the truth: he is there by right, from the outset. It is the truth that is substantially present in that of which he speaks; it is the truth that acts in an efficient way in the development of philosophy; it is the truth that shapes the singularity of each philosophy; it is the truth that serves as the end of all the aims of philosophy. The philosopher is guided by the quadruple causality of the truth.

But there is the margin of chance, of blindness and silence which surrounds all these first philosophies. They derive from the necessity of the truth which operates as their quadruple cause. But since they do not know these four causes, they speak of them unknowingly and unintentionally, like novice soldiers who give blow for blow but do not understand the strategy of the battle in which they are nevertheless caught up and which surrounds them. Hence the famous metaphor of the arrow and the door:

" ... with truth ... it is as the proverb says:
Who will not put the arrow in a door?"[10]

And yet, if sticking the arrow in such a large target is inevitable, it is only by chance that one hits this or that point.

*Conclusion*

This history of philosophy, which Aristotle recounts as a movement of both constraint and chance in the element of a truth which is both hidden and manifested in it, has, in its singularity, a triple importance.

1. Aristotle separates philosophical discourse from a number of techniques of interpretation and analysis. He thereby separates it from all those other discourses which fall within the domain of these techniques of interpretation and analysis.

a—In saying that the truth is both said and not said by the philosopher (said and not said in the form of stammering), Aristotle was still close to the methods of interpretation used by grammarians in their commentaries on the poets. Symbolic or allegorical methods pointing out what was deliberately hidden by Homer behind the figure of Nestor or Ulysses.[11]

But there is a difference however—and a crucial one—which is that for Aristotle the equivocation of the said and the not-said, this distance without gap which means that the truth is both hidden and present in the philosopher's words, this light that is shadow, is not the effect of an oracular kind of intentional secret or prudent reserve. If philosophers do not speak the truth, this is not because their indulgence wishes to protect men from its terrible face; it is because they lack a certain knowledge (*savoir*).

But we need to add straightaway that this lack is not the same as that kind of ignorance with which some commentators (like, precisely, the Sophists) charged the poets. The philosopher's dimension, according to Aristotle's analysis, is that of a knowledge/non-knowledge (*savoir/non-savoir*), which is neither that of the secret nor that of ignorance, which is characterized neither as a double game nor as a gap in knowledge (*connaissance*). What is involved is a certain lack constitutive of the very relation to the truth. What the philosopher does not and cannot say is precisely that which determines the truth he utters.

Philosophical discourse therefore has to escape allegorical exegesis as much as positivist critique. Philosophical discourse can no longer have the same status as poetic discourse.

b—In showing a certain interplay in every philosophical discourse between chance, the blindness of an individual oeuvre, and then the constraint of the truth, the law it imposes, the progression it traces, Aristotle detaches philosophical discourse from any political type of hold (or, since the difference is scarcely marked in this period of Greek history, any judicial or rhetorical hold).

Whatever the philosopher says, in his philosophical discourse at any rate, he will be in the truth, even if he is himself a man of little virtue or a bad citizen; something of the truth will pass into his discourse, and, on the other hand, his discourse will never completely die out, it will never be completely erased in the history of the truth; in one way or another it will forever recur in it. The philosopher is someone who is never completely driven out or who is never completely killed. There is no philosophical ostracism. The victories discourse may win against him, the jousts in the course of which he may be vanquished, do not affect that part of truth which is delivered in his discourse.

Certainly, the philosopher is no longer the *theios anēr* Hesiod spoke about,[12] and who rightfully said what is necessary (what is necessary = both the truth and the just in one); but no more is he the man of rhetorical and political *agōn*.

That part of the truth he has not said is always dominant in him, but he is never vanquished or excluded. Thus, in this both mythical and rationalized history of philosophy recounted in the *Metaphysics*, Aristotle isolates and excludes from other discursive practices a discourse in which the truth is cause and in which the truth is at stake. He radically separates it from poetical and mythical speech, and he separates it also from that rhetorical and political debate in which [philosophical discourse] was still partly engaged in Plato. It means for him a mode of historical connection and affiliation with no equivalent or counterpart in other discourses.

2. The second reason why Aristotle's analysis is important [is] that it set the historical mode of existence of philosophy for centuries, and no doubt up to the present.

Of course, there have been a great many variations and there may not have been many histories of philosophy resembling—in the form of analogy—Aristotle's. But if we do not find the model imitated by others in this Aristotelian analysis, we do however find their possibility.

The history of philosophy is always organized in terms of an interplay between the individual œuvre and an historical destination of the truth. The history of philosophy is always plotted through named individualities; it has worked, always at a certain level, with units which are and can only be designated by proper names. And in comparison with these units and the proper names which designate them, units like empiricism, pantheism, or rationalism are abstract constructions.

The history of philosophy has always been conceived as basically a dispersion of individualities. But if these individualities are valid as philosophical moments, it is because, in one form or another, the truth itself gave itself to them; or something of the truth spoke through them. Even their error was brought by the truth.

So that we always find that the truth is, by right, thought by every philosophical work (and by the fact that it is a philosophical work). But the unthought of every philosophy ensures that this thought of the truth is at the same time evasion, forgetting, oversight, and incompletion of the truth.[13]

With regard to each singular œuvre, every new philosophy has to think the unthought of a different philosophy. The history of philosophy thus conceives of philosophies as existing in a reciprocal relation of repetition and commentary: each has to think the unthought of others which defines their singular relation to the truth.

The task that the history of philosophy has ceaselessly set itself is still very close to what Aristotle proposed when he said:

"In a sense, they [= philosophers] manage to say and not say ... "[14]
   "We may say, in a sense, that they [= principles] have all been stated before us, and, in another sense, that none of them have."[15]

A number of principles are thus assured for the history of philosophy:

—That of interiority, or of the inaccessibility of philosophy from outside. Since it is in the element of the truth and since its discourse always brings with itself a fundamental and ineradicable relation to the truth, no discourse, no practice that is not philosophical can really affect it.

—That of the return to ... and going back over itself: since philosophy has in some way always already said what it has to say, where will it find what it now has to say if not in itself; if not by thinking what was still unthought in the thought already thought; if not by taking what has already been said as both the object of thought and the subject of repetition?

We can see: this perpetual precedence of philosophical discourse in relation to itself, this right or necessity for philosophy to think what has already been thought, this elimination of all exteriority, is the form Aristotle gave to the historicity of philosophy in Book I (A) of the *Metaphysics*;[16] it is also the form Aristotle gave to the interplay of knowledge and desire right at the start of this same Book I (A).

Finally, we can say that the theory of knowledge and the form given to the history of philosophy have corresponded to each other constantly throughout history. It was a question of eliminating the outside. The outside in the theory of knowledge was desire, or at least what was symbolized by desire. The outside in the history of philosophy is what is represented or symbolized by the Sophist and by everything that the figure of the Sophist took with him.

If I have stressed this passage from Aristotle, it is because it seems to me to define and prescribe a certain interiority of philosophy, because it seems to me to reject a certain outside of philosophical discourse: an outside whose elimination makes possible the very existence of philosophy; an outside on which philosophical discourse obscurely depends.

And if we accept that science had its origin within philosophical discourse, we can see what is at stake in the problem posed. The act that, by exclusion, defined an outside of philosophical discourse and tied philosophy and truth together in a certain mode, must in fact characterize our will to know. It is that act that has to be uncovered.

3. Now if this text is interesting for what it contains—the possibility of a history of philosophy—it is no less interesting for what it excludes. And

what it excludes appears in another text, the last book of the *Topics*, the *Sophistical Refutations* (which was no doubt one of the first; see Kneale[17]). For it is mainly there (as well as in a few other texts) that the Sophists appear in Aristotle. Now the way in which Aristotle speaks about them and the place he accords them has a completely different meaning [from that] which he gave to the pre-Socratic philosophers.

The first thing to note is that there is not much explicitly about the Sophists. There is little about the Sophist figure in general. Apart from allusions, there is little about the Sophist profession, about teaching for payment, about the political and moral off-handedness, the hasty and encyclopedic knowledge with which their contemporaries and successors so often reproached them.[18]

There is discussion of sophistics, of sophisms, of sophistical arguments, refutations, and discourses. It is as if the great Socratic and Platonic debate with the Sophists was closed; as if all that remained of the Sophist was no more than the abstract danger of sophistical arguments—arguments which are in danger of coming up in any discussion.

It is all as if sophism and the Sophists had been separated from each other; as if this couple, which is still difficult to separate in Plato, had now been well and truly divided; as if the Sophist had been driven out and sophism, on the other hand, included and mastered. However, we should note straightaway that sophism is not integrated simply and without difficulty into the general category of faulty reasoning or errors of reasoning. It is not even part of the dialectical discussions. It occupies a marginal and singular place. And yet this very inclusion is uncertain: the victory over sophism may not be absolutely clear or decisive.

And this slight difficulty which we recognize in Aristotle is far from disappearing whenever Western philosophy has to concern itself with sophisms—even very long [after] the memory of the unbearable Sophists has been forgotten.

Thus in the scholastic tradition:[19]

1. sophistical discussion is part of school exercises alongside other logical games.

—There were the *insolubilia*,[20] when one could deduce the contradictory of a non-necessary proposition; e.g.: *Dico falsum*.

—There were *sophisms* which could equally be demonstrated to be true or false, e.g.:

*logica est scientia*—because it is acquired through science.

*logica non est scientia*—because it is only *modus sciendi* (quoted by Wallerand in the works of Siger de Courtrai).[21]

But the sophism exercise had to be concluded with the teacher's intervention showing the source of the illusion of necessity; he had to dispel the chimera and demonstrate the good solution.

Whereas insolubles were monstrosities or difficulties inherent to logic, sophisms were only temporary effects which one had to be able to dispel.

2. Buridan, in his *Commentarii* on the *Sophistical Refutations*, distinguishes:

—the *disputatio doctrinalis*,[22] which must lead to exact science;
—the *disputatio dialectica*, which must reduce the uncertainty of some assertions;
—the *disputatio tentativa*, which must stress the students knowledge;
—the *disputatio sophistica*, in which one was not concerned about the truth.

And even after scholasticism, when, in Baldwin's *Dictionary of Philosophy*, Peirce defines the most serious, most philosophically problematic form of sophism, he presents it as an argument whose conclusion is inadmissible even though logical rigor has *apparently* been respected.[23]

So, what is this concern of philosophy for these arguments which are semblances, which are not concerned with the truth, and which are, momentarily, linked to illusory effects? Why give space to this shadow play? Is it so difficult to get rid of what is often only crude craftiness and trickery?

Why spend so much time concerning oneself with what does not exist? Why this concern for what is presented as only pretence, theater, and dishonest struggle? Why does a discourse which should deal only with truth and falsity still need to exercise this moral police? What is this ethical game of the honest and the dishonest when we should say only true or false?

In order to answer we no doubt need to examine Aristotle's analysis; we should consider that moment when, for the first time, and in the absence of the Sophists, sophisms were refuted.

Now we should note that throughout the text Aristotle establishes a difference of kind between sophisms and faulty reasoning.

Thus, at 176b 30 [of *Sophistical Refutations*], in the general category of faulty reasoning, Aristotle distinguishes between faulty reasoning and what is not real reasoning; "for there is faulty reasoning, either if a false conclusion has been reached, or if the reasoning, while not being a real reasoning, nevertheless appears to be so."[24]

Aristotle describes faulty reasoning, *o pseudēs sullogismos*, a little later in the text. He also analyzed it in the *Prior Analytics* (II, 2). There is faulty reasoning either when the conclusion is true but has been reached from false premises, or when the conclusion is false.

And this form of faulty reasoning is subdivided in turn; the conclusion may be false either because a premise is false, or because the two premises are true but the conclusion has not been deduced properly.

Opposite this faulty reasoning, Aristotle places sophistical reasoning, which on a number of occasions he says only appears to be reasoning.

Beginning of the text [*Sophistical Refutations*]:

"That some reasonings (*sullogismoi*) are genuine, while others seem to be so but are not, is evident."[25]

The Sophist is not someone who is intentionally or unintentionally mistaken. The difference between the Sophist and the ignorant (or stupid) is not the difference between an intentional error (into which one falls in order to trip up one's adversary) and an unintentional error (of which both interlocutors are victims). The Sophist should not be interpreted as someone who uses error as a trap and uses faulty reasoning as a crafty weapon. He occupies a different dimension from that of true or faulty reasoning; he is on the side of the semblance of reasoning. He occupies the dimension of shadow and reflection; he occupies a reasoning mirage, but he does not really reason. And this invalidation, produced not by error but by semblance, affects not only the Sophist's reasoning moreover, it affects all his wisdom, his *sophia*:

> "for Sophistic is an apparent wisdom but without reality, *esti gar ē sophistikē phainomenē sophia ausa d'ou*),"[26]

and Aristotle [continues]—we will have to return to this in more detail—:

> "and the Sophist, a man who makes financial profit from an apparent but unreal wisdom), it is clear that for them [= for "some people"] it is necessary ... to seem to perform the work of wisdom, rather than to do so really without seeming to."[27] (See also 171b.)

Money is at the heart of this semblance: it is the reason for it and no doubt its symbol as well. The problem is knowing what this semblance of reasoning, what this other side of true or faulty reasoning, this enigmatic element opposed to the no less enigmatic reality of reasoning, is.

How can the semblance of reasoning arise?

At first sight, if we follow Aristotle's analysis, the listing of all these forms of apparent reasoning give the impression of immense heterogeneity, from the crudest trick to some still fairly crude logical games:

—There are sophisms which arise from simple homonymy, *manphanein*.[28]

—There are even worse sophisms which arise from the employment of two words with different pronunciation but the same spelling; and then there are sophisms which pose, for us at least, real grammatical or logical problems (see the employment of *outos*).

Or again, included among sophistic techniques are the use of propositions to which one cannot answer yes or no (to which one cannot assign a truth value), and then techniques like those that consist in speaking very quickly, or in reversing the order of questions, or in hiding the one really important question among all the others one asks.

In this proliferation of techniques, Aristotle's proposed classification does not seem to be much help, at least at first sight, since he does not divide it up according to their form or their principle, but according the effect obtained:

—sophisms which appear to refute;
—sophisms which appear to reveal the interlocutor's error;
—sophisms which appear to subject him to a paradox;
—sophisms which appear to make him commit a solecism;
—sophisms which appear to make him fall into verbiage.

Now a passage at the beginning of the *Sophistial Refutations* gives a general explanation of sophisms. To tell the truth, this explanation is rather strange. It presents itself as almost general, and yet it only concerns a quite small category of sophisms. This is it:

"Refutation is a reasoning that leads to contradiction of the conclusion. Now the sophists do not do this, but only appear to do so, for several reasons: one of these, which is the most natural and most common, is that which stems from the names given to things. In fact, since it is not possible to bring the things themselves into the discussion, but instead of the things we have to make use of their names as symbols, we suppose that what happens in the names happens in the things as well, as in the case of pebbles with regard to calculating. Now there is no complete resemblance between names and things: there are a limited number of names, as well as of the plurality of definitions, whereas there are an infinite number of things. Consequently, it is inevitable that several things are signified by the same definition and by ... the same name."[29]

Let us leave to one side the extension that must be given to this text. One thing that is clear here is the location of the sophistical effect. It is made possible by the fact that it is not things themselves which are *manipulated* in the discourse, but their verbal symbols. Precisely, their name.

But if this symbolization makes the sophism possible, it does not explain it. The sophism does not take place in the dimension in which words are signs. It takes place in a certain difference between names and things, between the symbolic elements and the elements symbolized. In what does this difference consist?

It does not consist in that by which words produce an effect of mean-ing, whereas things do not. No more does it consist in the difference [between] *phusis* and *nomos*, between the natural character of things and the conventional character of words.

It consists in the fact that there a finite number of names and an infinite number of things, that there is a relative scarcity of words; that we cannot establish a bi-univocal relation between words and things. In short, the relation between words and what they designate is not iso-morphic to the relation that enables one to count.

In other words, it is a characteristic peculiar to the materiality of words—their scarcity—that gives rise to the sophism. The Sophist is someone who makes use of the same word, the same name, the same expression in order to say two different things, such that he says two things in the very same thing said.

And if we now recall the definition of the syllogism: "a reasoning in which, certain premises being assumed, a conclusion other than what has been assumed necessarily follows from these premises" (*Prior Analytics*, Book I, 1, 24b 18)[30] (and if we recall what the refutation of a syllogism is: a reasoning that contradicts the conclusion of the previous reasoning),[31] we can see that the sophism does not consist in saying something new by virtue of a logical constraint and on the basis of less agreed premises, but in taking the same thing said from the same statement, in their material identity, even though the interlocutors do not have the same premises in mind and this due to the conjunction, the confusion, the resemblance, the identity of the names that designate the things. Because of this random superimposition due to the fundamental scarcity of words.

We can draw a conclusion from this, which is that the sophism is not a defective category of reasoning, it is not reasoning at all: or rather, it is the inverted image of reasoning; where in reasoning there was identity of agreed premises, in the sophism there is difference; where there was logical necessity, there is de facto scarcity and chance; where there was a new proposition, there is repetition of the thing said; and finally, where there was the constraint of truth and the conviction of the other, there is the trap by which the adversary is caught in the thing said—in the materiality of the thing said.

But an objection appears straightaway: in Aristotle's text, the material scarcity of words seems to account for only some and not all sophisms.

It accounts for sophisms that are due to the existence of synonyms (for example a single word, *manphanein*, to say to learn and to understand), or amphibologies[32] (*"Je souhaite la capture de l'ennemi"*\*), or ambiguities due to stress (in written texts).[33]

In short, it accounts for what Aristotle calls refutations linked to the discourse itself, but not for the others. Moreover, Aristotle says that this scarcity of names is "one of the most natural and frequent reasons" (*Sophistical Refutations*, 165a 5),[34] but only one of the reasons.

But if we look at the whole classification of sophisms proposed by Aristotle, we see that, either directly or indirectly, it is always the materiality of discourse that is brought into play in its different aspects. Beyond sophisms of scarcity (a single written or spoken word, a single expression to say different things), there are:

- Sophisms of dissociation. Discourse is made up of a succession of words, and once this sequence has been established we can separate and group them at will:

A,B,C —————— A and B,C
    AB and C

E.g.: 5 being (2 and 3), we say that 5 is even because it is 2 and odd because it is 3 (166a 33).

- Sophisms of permutation. Discourse is made up of elements which in certain conditions may take the place of each other:
  Socrates is white
  white is a color
  therefore Socrates is a color.

- Sophisms of association. Discourse is composed of elements forming a group which makes sense; but a sub-group disassociated from the first also makes sense:
  The Indian is black
  But the Indian is white as regards his teeth
  Therefore the Indian is black and white.[35]

- Sophisms of confusion. Some successive and distinct elements of discourse can be joined together:
  Is A a man and B a man?

---

\* [The two possible meanings in French are wanting the enemy's capture and wanting capture by the enemy; G.B.]

Yes.

Then striking A and B one strikes a man [one man] and not two.

• Sophisms of precedence. Discourse is an indefinite sequence of propositions; at any rate, it is a sequence which can always be extended as far as one likes in such a way that the interlocutor cannot actualize it from end to end and make it simultaneous.

Thus, by discussing at such length one can get someone to think that a proposition has been demonstrated whereas it is [not]:

—either because it is precisely what is to be demonstrated (petitio principii);

—or it is false (but one does not notice that it is false).

This is how Aristotle includes speaking very quickly in the series of sophisms, overwhelming the adversary in a flood words and disrupting the natural order of questions.

• Sophisms of indefinite multiplication. This is the game of succession and permutation.

• Sophisms of repetition. There are things which have already been said and which one can repeat as they have been said.

Thus, there are sets of phrases already uttered on one and the same subject. And by leading the discussion on to one of these subjects, one can always repeat this set of nevertheless contradictory propositions.

E.g.: on what is preferable, nature or the law.

• Sophisms of grammar. Discourse is a set of elements some of which relate both to things and to discourse itself. Between the elements of discourse there are (grammatical) links which do not represent or are not isomorphic to the relations between things. There are grammatical constraints or freedoms with no equivalent in things.

Thus, the grammar of the neuter and the demonstrative.

We can see: Aristotle's analysis of sophisms is situated entirely at the level of the materiality of discourse. The sophism is a tactic internal to this materiality. But we can also see that this specific materiality of discourse, which at first sight appeared as numerical inequality of words and things, as scarcity of names, now appears according to more numerous dimensions:

> —in the first place it is not only the scarcity of words but the necessary succession and possible displacements of the elements of discourse in relation to each other—linear characteristic;
> —more broadly, it is the fact that every statement is inserted within an immense and, in truth, never completely controllable series of previous discourse—serial characteristic;
> —more broadly still, it is the fact that discourse is formed from a number of real events (of *things said*)[36] which, once produced, cannot be changed. What's said is said. You said it, too bad for you—event characteristic;
> —finally it is the fact that this materiality of discourse is linked to struggle, rivalry, to the situation of combat between men who are arguing—strategic characteristic.

We now contrast the syllogism and the sophism in the following way:

1. The syllogism is characterized by premises which have been "assumed" in the sense that they have been granted, acknowledged rightly or wrongly as true—agreed. The sophism is characterized by phrases which have been assumed in the sense that they have actually been said. Acknowledged or not, really agreed or not, matters little: they are things said.
2. The syllogism develops entirely between two limits: agreement on the premises, the necessary truth of the conclusion. The sophism operates in the unlimited series of previous statements.
3. The syllogism is subject to the constraint of the concept, that is to say, of what is signified by names. The sophism is deployed as a free tactic at the level of words themselves, independently of what they signify.
4. The syllogism produces an effect of truth (sanctioned by the interlocutors' agreement). The sophism produces an effect of victory (sanctioned by the fact that the interlocutor can no longer speak without contradicting himself).

On this basis, we can understand:

—that the sophism is pseudo reasoning (*faux raisonnement*) (and not merely faulty reasoning (*raisonnement faux*)).

Strictly speaking it is non-reasoning, it is not reasoning at all. The operation of reasoning takes place at the level of what is signified (concepts); the operation of the sophism takes place at the level of the materiality of the symbols; and what is produced at the level of the signified thereby is only the shadow of a real operation (which takes place at the level of the materiality of the symbols).

There is no doubt that the metaphor we find at the beginning of the *Refutations* should be taken in the strict sense: "just as ... those who are not clever in manipulating their counting pebbles are deceived by those who know how to use them, so it is with arguments" (165a 14-15).[37] Second consequence:

—that the sophism is resolved by the introduction of difference.

It is difference, in fact, that on the one hand enables one to construct the concept, to master and organize the ideality of meaning, to divide species and genus, to distinguish subjects and attributes; in short, to construct a whole universe of meaning on the basis of which one will be able to formulate true or false statements. But it is also difference that, by breaking them up or controlling them, will block the identity of the thing said, the displacements or confusions of elements of discourse, and the indefinite rhapsody of their succession.

Aristotle shows the role of difference throughout the chapters in which he lists the means for escaping sophisms. We constantly have to distinguish, he says.

Through the thought of difference[38] one can neutralize the materiality of discourse (and all those identities, confusions, repetitions which ultimately have their origin in scarcity); through the thought of difference one can get over the materiality of discourse, dispel the shadow of reasoning which plays on its surface, organize reasoning on the basis of the concept and its ideal necessity, and in return render discourse transparent to that necessity (and, thereby to its own materiality). The *logos*, in its unfolding, will be able to exist on the same level as conceptual necessity.

Difference, by which the material reality of discourse is eliminated, is the condition of apophantic judgment as the field of the truth or error of propositions.

The third consequence is that we can see from this in what and why the sophistic can never coincide with the plane of apophantic judgment. The sophism is never really declarative. There can be apophantic judgment only on condition that the materiality of discourse is first neutralized and then that this discourse is dealt with in accordance with the axis of reference to what it is speaking about. It is false to say that what is, is not, and that what is not, is; it is true to say that what is, is, and that what is not, is not (see *Metaphysics*, III (B), 2, 996b 26-30).

The sophistic always remains at the level of a certain "hyletics" of discourse. It develops on the basis of real events (what has actually been said); it operates on material qualities or determinations (identity of sounds, separability of words, possible permutations of groups of words); and what it ends up with is not a true proposition which has to be acknowledged by everyone, but the silence of one of the two partners, who can no longer continue to speak and finds himself excluded from the game of this materiality. It is not a matter of leading two subjects to think the same thing by speaking the truth; it is a matter of excluding one of the speaking subjects from the discourse by transforming things at the level at which they were said.

The apophantic judgment is defined by continuity of the relation to the object; the sophistic, by exclusion of the subject.

So, in the apophantic, the materiality of discourse will be no more than a reduced and indifferent shadow. In the sophistic, reasoning will be a shadow, but not the shadow-residue, the shadow one leaves behind oneself; it will be the theatrical shadow, the double and the mime behind which one hides. And we can understand now what Aristotle means when he says that the sophism is only a semblance of reasoning: the Sophist acts as if he was reasoning whereas he only manipulates words; he takes up a position on the theatrical space of a reasoning that is only a comedy and game of masks in comparison with the materiality of discourse. And Aristotle knows full well that this materiality of discourse is only a shadow, a residue in comparison with the ideal necessity of the apophantic. So that, behind his shadow theater in which he pretends to reason, the Sophist himself, behind the scenes, delivers only the shadow of a discourse.

From this we can thus understand the great split that occurred in the history of logic:

> —a logic of the concept and difference which right from the start neutralizes the materiality of discourse. The threshold of this logic will be the individual and the conceptual;
> —a logic of discourse which will try to define the point at which the emergence of meaning and the immaterial arises from the materiality of the thing said.

The threshold of this logic will be between the materiality of discourse and the immateriality of meaning. This phase of logic unfolds from Megara[39] (and the discovery of the Liar by Eubulides) to the Stoics (and the difference between *phōnē* and *lekton*).[40]

Finally, we can see clearly how Aristotle is inscribed on the same line as that traced by Plato; but also the displacement he carries out. After all, the *Sophist* was in fact devoted to the analysis of the relations between simulation, non-being, and the Sophist. The central point of the dialogue was the demonstration that non-being could affect *logos*. The aim of the *Sophist* was to refute the sophistical argument that

> —if a thing has been said, then that thing said exists; and that
> —if that thing exists, then it is true;
> —therefore, that non-being and error can never affect discourse.

To which Plato gets the Stranger to reply that there can be a false discourse, that is to say, a discourse which says that what does not exist does exist (that Theaetetus here flies [in the air]),[41] or that what exists does not exist—which is the very definition of *logos apophantikos*.[42] And if there can be a false discourse, there can be someone who passes off false discourse as true discourse.

It needed all the great Platonic theory of being, non-being, and participation to manage to make the Sophist possible. But we can see: the Sophist is made possible by the existence of a false discourse. The false discourse is made possible because we can say of non-being—and despite

Parmenides—that it is. Now, given these conditions, the sophism is no more excluded than any false discourse: even a bit less, since it is a false discourse that can pass itself off as true.

The real exclusion of the sophism takes place with Aristotle:

—when he defines the sophism not as a faulty reasoning that has the appearance of truth, but as a semblance of reasoning that is therefore neither true nor false;

—in short, when he has the boldness to make the thing said, in its materiality, an unreal shadow that haunts the ideal reality of the *logos*.

1. On the distinction *savoir-connaissance*, see M. Foucault, *L'Archéology du Savoir* (Paris: Gallimard, 1969) ch. VI; English translation by A.M. Sheridan Smith, *The Archeology of Knowledge* (London: Tavistock Publications, 1972), Part IV, ch. 6 (See also "Translator's note" above, p. xv).

2. Aubenque, following Dupréel, has given the study of sophistical reasoning - the sophistical refutation - a decisive place for understanding Aristotle's logic and ontology. Foucault seems to follow him in the first part of his argument. See P. Aubenque, *Le Problème de l'Être chez Aristote*, ch. II, "Être et langage."

3. Aristote, *La Métaphysique*, , 2, 1004b 27, vol. 1, p. 117; Aristotle, *Metaphysics*, Book IV (Γ), 2, 1004b 27, p. 1586: "and sophistic is what appears to be philosophy but is not."

4. Ibid., Fr., A, 3, 984ba 18-20, p. 16; Eng., Book I (A), p. 1556: "but as men thus advanced, the very facts showed them the way and joined in forcing them to investigate the subject."

5. Ibid., Fr., A, 3, 984b 7-11, p. 17; Eng., Book I (A), p. 1557: "When these men and the principles of this kind had had their day, as the latter were found inadequate to generate the nature of things, men were again forced by the truth itself, as we said, to inquire into the next kind of cause."

6. Ibid., Fr., α, 1, 993b 26-32, p. 61; Eng., Book II (α) p. 1570: "Therefore the principles of eternal things must always be most true; for they are not merely sometimes true, nor is there any cause of their being, but they themselves are the cause of the being of other things, so that as each thing is in respect of being, so is it in respect of truth."

7. Ibid., A, 2, 983a 13, pp. 10-11: "wonder that things are what they are"; Eng., Book I (A), p. 1555: "wondering that the matter is so."

8. Ibid., A, 2, 982b 19-22, p. 9; Eng., Book I (A), p. 1554: "since they philosophized in order to escape from ignorance, evidently they were pursuing science in order to know, and not for any utilitarian end."

9. Ibid., A, 4, 985a 14-16, p. 20; Eng., Book I (A) p. 1558: "... as untrained men behave in fights; for they go round their opponents and often strike fine blows, but they do not fight on scientific principles."

10. Ibid., α, 1, 993b 3-5, p. 60; Eng., Book II (α), p. 1570: "since truth seems to be like the proverbial door, which no one can fail to hit."

11. For Hippias (A, 10) or Antiphon (A, 6), Nestor was a representation of wisdom and Ulysses of cunning. Both were supposed to have composed oratorical arts at Troy. See R. Scheider, G. Uhlig, and A. Hilgard, eds., *Grammatici Graeci* (Leipzig, 1878-1910; reprint, Hildesheim: Georg Olms, 1965).

12. *Theios anēr*, the poet who reveals the plans of Zeus, *Works and Days*, 293-294. Foucault is citing here M. Detienne, *Crise agraire et attitude religieuse chez Hésiode* (Brussels: Berchem, "Latomus" 68, 1963, pp. 42-51; note taken from a card of M.F.: *Alētheia* in Hesiod's poetry. These analyses are taken up by Detienne in *Les Maîtres de vérité dans la Grèce archaïque*, p. 25; *The Masters of Truth in Archaic Greece*, pp. 50-51. See also L. Bieler, *Theios Anêr. Das Bild des "göttlichen Menschen" in Spätantike und Frühchristentum* (Vienna: O. Häfels, 1935-1936) two volumes; reprinted (Darmstadt: Wissenschaftliche Buchgesellschaft, 1956, 2nd ed. 1976).

13. The privative expression *A-lêtheia* as deconstruction of the traditional notion of truth-*adaequatio* is a constant target in this lecture so as finally to be assigned to a regional genealogy. The opposition *Alêtheia/Lêthê* comes directly from M. Detienne, *Les Maîtres de vérité*, p. 51 et seq.; *The Masters of Truth*, p. 69 et seq.—a work with many annotations by Foucault. It enabled him to make a critical bypassing of Heidegger.

14. Aristote, *La Métaphysique*, A, 7, 988b 13-14, p. 35; Aristotle, *Metaphysics*, Book I (A), p. 1563: "... it turns out that in a sense they both say and do not say ... "

15. Ibid., A, 10, 993a 14-15, p. 58; Eng., Book I (A), p. 1569: "... and though in a sense they have all been described before, in a sense they have not been described at all."

16. W. Jaeger, in *Aristoteles: Grundlegung einer Geschichte seiner Entwicklung* (Berlin: Weidmann, 1932): "Aristotle was the first to establish alongside his own philosophy a conception of his personal position in history" (quoted in P. Aubenque, *Le Problème de l'Être chez Aristote*, p. 71).

17. W. and M. Kneale, *The Development of Logic* (Oxford: Clarendon Press, 1962) p. 13: "De sophisticis elenchis, an appendix to the *Topics*, which is generally regarded as one of the earliest of Aristotle's logical works."

18. H.-I. Marrou, *Histoire de l'éducation dans l'Antiquité* (Paris: Seuil, 1948); English translation by George Lamb, *A History of Education in Antiquity* (Madison: University of Wisconsin Press, 1982).

19. The *Sophistical Refutations (De sophisticis elenchis)* was the most influential of Aristotle's works of formal logic in medieval logicians. See W. and M. Kneale, *The Development of Logic*, p. 227. Eugenio Garin, in *L'Éducation de l'homme moderne, 1400-1600* (Paris: Fayard, 1968) pp. 62-64, notes: "After 1150, Aristotle, with the *Organon*, the physics and metaphysics, had a decisive weight on the Parisian university, the episcopal school breaks up. ... From the thirteenth century the Universities blossom in Europe."

20. Variants, among sophisms, of the "paradox of the Liar." See W. and M. Kneale, *The Development of Logic*, pp. 228-229.

21. According to Ch. Thurot, *Notices et extraits de divers manuscrits latins pour servir l'histoire des doctrines grammaticales au Moyen Âge* (Francfort/Main: Éd. Minerva, 1967 [1868]), p. 128, Siger de Courtrai characterized grammar by the meaningful value of the terms, "*ex parte vocis*," and logic "*per relationem ad res*," by its essential link to the object. Consequently, the philosopher, considering the essence of things, comes before the grammarian.

22. The disputations were exercises of logical skill which were part of university practices for more than three centuries. See W. and M. Kneale, *The Development of Logic*, p. 300; Buridan, *Sophismata* (Paris: printed by Jean Lamber, no date).

23. Reprinted in C. S. Peirce, *Collected Papers* (Cambridge, Mass.: Harvard University Press, 1931-1958) in eight volumes.

24. Aristote, *Organon*, (Paris: J. Vrin, 1936), vol. VI: *Réfutations sophistiques*, ed. and trans. J. Tricot (Paris: Vrin, 1969 [1939]), p. 86; English translation by W. A. Pickard-Cambridge, Aristotle, *Sophistical Refutations*, in *The Complete Works of Aristotle*, p. 301: "since false deduction has a double use—for it is used either if a false conclusion has been deduced, or if there is only an apparent deduction and no real one"; see also 165b 11-23, ibid., p. 6; Eng., p. 279.

25. Ibid., 164a 23-25, p. 1; Eng., p. 278: "That some deductions are genuine, while others seem to be so but are not, is evident."

26. Ibid., 165a 21-22, p. 3; Eng., p. 279: "(for the art of the sophist is the semblance of wisdom without the reality ... )."

27. Ibid, 165a 22-24, pp. 3-4; Eng., p. 279: "( ... and the sophist is one who makes money from an apparent but unreal wisdom); for them, then, it is clearly necessary to seem to accomplish the task of a wise man rather than to accomplish it without seeming to do so." See also 171b.

28. See above, p. 15 and p. 21 note 24, and p. 36. Reference to Plato, *Euthydemus*, 275d-277e, oratorical joust between two sophists and Clinias.

29. *Réfutations sophistiques*, 165a 4-13, pp. 2-3; *Sophistical Refutations*, p. 278: " ... a refutation is a deduction to the contradictory of the given conclusion. Now some of them do not really achieve this, though they seem to do so for a number of reasons; and of these the most prolific and usual is the argument that turns upon names. It is impossible in a discussion to bring in the actual things discussed: we use their names a symbols instead of them; and we suppose that what follows in the names, follows in the things as well, just as people who calculate suppose in regard to their counters. But the two cases are not alike. For names are finite and so is the sum-total of accounts, while things are infinite in number. Inevitably, then, the same account and a single name signify several things."

30. Aristote, *Premiers Analytiques*, trans. and ed. J. Tricot in Aristote *Organon*, vol. III, pp. 4-5. In place of reasoning (*raisonnement*) Tricot has discourse (*discours*); English translation by A.J. Jenkinson, *Prior Analytics*, in *The Complete Works of Aristotle*, Vol. One, p. 40: "a discourse in which, certain things being stated, something other than what is stated follows of necessity from their being so."

31. Cf. ibid., I, 25b 40-26a 1-2, pp. 13-14; Eng. p. 41.

32. Lalande, *Vocabulaire philosophique*, I, p. 42, points out that Greek and Latin provide many examples of amphiboly or amphibology in which the word order does not give a certain indication of what is the subject and what the complement.

33. "As for me, I consider that things are not changed only by the addition of another thing but also by the difference of stress"; Hippias, quoted by E. Dupréel, *Les Sophistes* (Neuchâtel: Éd. du Griffon, 1948) p. 141.

34. Aristote, *Réfutations sophistiques*, 165a 5, p. 2: "the most natural and common"; Aristotle, *Sophistical Refutations*, p. 278: "the most prolific and usual."

35. The color, here, does not specify the man; it is an accident not an essence. This refers to the debate between the Platonists and Peripatetics. See Aristotle, *Metaphysics*, I, 9, 1058b 10-12.

36. See Cl. Ramnoux, *Héraclite, ou l'Homme entre les choses et les mots* (Paris: Aubier-Montaign, 1959), especially ritual formulae, sacred stories, as opposed to things shown. Foucault designated in this way—"things said"—the object of *The Archeology of Knowledge* in the first version deposited in the manuscripts of the Bibliothèque Nationale.

37. *Réfutations sophistique*, p. 3; *Sophistical Refutations*, p.278: "...just as in counting, those who are not clever in manipulating their counters are taken in by the experts, in the same way in arguments..." Allusion to the use of stones/pebbles for calculating.

38. In *Difference and Repetition* Deleuze analyzed difference in Aristotle's *Metaphysics* (especially in pp. 30-34). See M. Foucault, "Theatrum philosophicum" (1970).

39. Founded by Euclid, Socrates' disciple, the Megara school is considered to be one of the first centers of logical research on the basis of everyday language. The Megarics were the first qualified in eristic. Eubulides, Euclid's successor, is thought to have formulated the "Liar's paradox" as one of the divisions of truth and falsity.

40. Beyond a theory of the voice distinct from the articulated word, the Stoics distinguished between the—incorporeal—signified (*lekton*) and the—corporeal—signifier (*phōnē*), linguistic expression, and object expressed. See Sextus Empiricus, *Adversus mathematicos*, VIII, 11-12, quoted in W. and M. Kneale, *The Development of Logic*. See also Diogène Laërce, *Vie, doctrines et sentences des philosophes illustres*, VII, 55-63, in E. Brehier, *Les Stoïciens* (Paris: Gallimard, 1962), pp. 34-37; English translation by R. D. Hicks, Diogenes Laertius, *Lives of Eminent Philosophers* (Cambridge, Mass., and London: Harvard University Press and William Heinemann Ltd, The Loeb Classical Library, 1979) vol. II, Book VII, pp. 164-173.

41. Platon, *Le Sophiste*, in *Œuvres complètes*, ed. and trans. L. Robin (Paris: Gallimard, 1970) vol. II, 263a, p. 329 ("Theaetetus, with whom I am now conversing, flies in the air") and 240e-241a, p. 294 ("...a statement will be considered false when one says of what is that it is not and of what is not that it is"); English translation by F.M. Cornford, Plato, *Sophist*, in *The Collected Dialogues*, p. 1010: "Theatetus, whom I am talking to at this moment, flies" and p. 984: "And a false statement...is to be regarded...as stating that things that are, are not, and that things that are not, are."

42. *Logos apophantikos* or declarative proposition, in Aristotle, *De interpretatione*, 4-17a2 et seq: "Not all discourse is a proposition (*apophansis*), but only discourse in which there is truth or falsity"; English translation by J. L. Ackrill, *De Interpretatione*, in *The Complete Works of Aristotle*, Vol. One, p. 26: "...not every sentence is a statement-making sentence, but only those in which there is truth or falsity." See *La Metaphysique*, vol. II, Γ, 7, 1012a 26-28, p. 154: "It seems...that Heraclitus' view, that everything is and is not, makes everything true, and that of Anaxagoras, that there is an intermediary between contradictories, makes everything false"; Eng., *Metaphysics*, p. 1598: "The doctrine of Heraclitus, that all things are and are not, seems to make everything true, while that of Anaxagoras, that there is an intermediary between the terms of a contradiction, seems to make everything false"; see too Θ, 10, 1051b 3, Fr. pp. 54-55; Eng. pp. 1660-1661.

# four

# 13 January 1971

*The sophism and true discourse.\* ⌢ How to do the history of apophantic discourse. ⌢ Logical versus sophistical manipulation. ⌢ Materiality of the statement, materiality of the proposition. Roussel, Brisset, Wolfson, today's sophists. ⌢ Plato excludes the figure of the Sophist, Aristotle excludes the technique of the sophism. ⌢ The sophism and the relation of discourse to the speaking subject.*

LAST WEEK, WE SAW how Aristotle ruled out the sophism with regard to philosophy; how he constituted a philosophical discourse which existed by right in the element of truth, and how, with regard to this discourse, sophistic practice was no more than exteriority and unreality. Shadow.

There is a tendency for historians who concern themselves with the Sophists[†] to want to revoke this measure of banishment; to reduce the distance and restore reality to sophistic discourse within philosophical discourse (Grote, Gomperz for the nineteenth century; Dupréel).[1] As if philosophical discourse alone is capable of according the Sophists seriousness and reality, which, ultimately and implicitly, amounts to a form of endorsement of the Aristotelian exclusion: "The Sophists are not guilty of what they are accused of; if they were, if they had said and done what they are charged with having said and done, we would of course leave them in the pure semblance where they have been kept; but

---

\* Lecture manuscript title.
[†] "Sophists" and not "sophists": respecting the original written form.

they too are philosophers in a certain way, they too, in a way, fall within the domain of true discourse, of discourse that tells of being, that is in being; so they are not at all lifeless and bodiless shadows lurking beyond the borders of philosophy. They have their place, their site, their reality in philosophy."

I would like to attempt a different analysis which does not strive to reduce the distance between the sophistic and philosophy, which does not reintroduce the Sophists through the little door of historical reevaluation, but which lets the distance stand as it was perceived, lets the exclusion stand as it was pronounced by Aristotle, his contemporaries, and his successors.

Rather than establish a sort of common space in which the notions and problems of the Sophists rejoin those of philosophers, I would like to try to pass to the outside: to analyze what Sophist discourse might have been in its mode of existence and functioning in the milieu of a society like Greek society. On what conditions was such a discourse able to exist and disappear? This question will mean taking up a quite different genre of analysis—no longer that of the analyses of the history of philosophy, methods that until now have served to locate the procedures of exclusion and the void they have left.

For today, I would like to remain at the level of this exclusion. To take the measure, from the point of view of philosophy, of the opposition it applies between true or faulty reasoning and pseudo argumentation. To show how, while remaining within philosophy, we can recognize, at least tentatively, a certain outside of which the Sophist is the symbol, of which he is the most menacing, stubborn, and sniggering prowler.

How does Aristotle proceed to this exclusion?

By defining the sophistic as a *phainomenē philosophia all ouk ousa*, a philosophy that has no being. Now how can it not exist and yet appear?

It can because precisely there are forms of reasoning which have the appearance of being reasoning, but which are not. The raison d'être of the non-being of this non-philosophy is in the non-being of apparent reasoning.

The *Sophistical Refutations* take us through varieties of completely heterogeneous reasoning, argumentation, difficulties, and traps. Thus:

It is those who know who learn (*apprennent*), since grammarians learn (*apprennent*) what their disciples recite to them.

"You wish for me the enemy's capture (*Tu souhaites pour moi la capture de l'ennemi*). That is to say that you wish the enemy to be captured for me, but you wish equally that the enemy captures me."

Or: "Is that which belongs to the Athenians the property of the Athenians?—Yes. —... But, man belongs to the animal kingdom?—Yes—So man is the property of the animal kingdom" [17, 176b].

Or: Coriscus[2] is different from Socrates, Socrates is a man, so Coriscus is different from a man.

Or: What one no longer has one has lost; if you have ten jacks and give away one, you no longer have ten; therefore you have lost ten jacks [see 22, 1787b].

Or yet again: asking a question without showing why one is asking it or with regard to what one is asking it. Asking a great number of questions so that the adversary no longer knows where he is, or again speaking very quickly.

Or: employing certain grammatical facts like the neuter (this) to designate a man.

Or: leading the discussion to a point where one will be able to employ a ready made argumentation prepared in advance.

Or again: when the interlocutor defends a thesis peculiar to philosophers, experts, or a few, counter him with the popular thesis, what the *polloi* say, and conversely.

Aristotle, at least to start with, does not distribute this set of rather puerile quibbles according to their form, but according to their result. This is because in fact, since they are cases of pseudo reasoning with no other reality than their appearance, they have no other principle than the effect they seek to produce. The appearance they give themselves.

Hence the classification in five terms which Aristotle proposes:

—sophisms which pretend to refute: that is to say, to prove the proposition contradictory to the one put forward by the interlocutor (refutation);

—sophisms which pretend to reveal the adversary's error (demon-strating, for example, that one of his premises is false) (error);
—sophisms which pretend to show that the adversary maintains a singular thesis that no one reasonably maintains (paradox);
—sophisms which give the impression that the interlocutor does not know his grammar and commits solecisms;
—those finally which give the impression that the adversary talks in order to say nothing, piling one word on top of another to infinity.

Under each of these large rubrics, Aristotle indicates the sophisms most often used to obtain this or that result (for example, homonymy, especially for pseudo refutation; the use of ready-made discourse for paradox; grammatical oddities for solecism).

But if now we wonder what is common to all these contrivances which give the form of reasoning to word-play, or which confuse discussions by conduct that we others would call "bad faith," it is quite easy to see that what is involved is a certain material manipulation of elements of discourse.

\* \* \*

We have tried to pinpoint and classify these manipulations independently of the classification offered by Aristotle:

—repeating and getting others to repeat the same word in its material identity, even though it does not have the same meaning (profiting, if necessary, from the ambiguities of the written form, which up until the third century did not indicate stress);
—dissociating, recomposing, extending definitively the linear series of words which form the discourse;
—calling upon and bringing into play already constituted series that it suffices to repeat word for word;
—[using\*] certain distinctive grammatical features.

---

\* Manuscript: use of.

What exactly is the difference between these manipulations, which Aristotle and philosophy judge to be illegitimate, and those put to work by true reasoning?

A—First set of differences concerning the manipulation itself and its rules:

—after all, any legitimate reasoning (from Aristotle's point of view) involves manipulations which are not that far removed from those found in the Sophists' practice: every A is B, now every B is C, therefore every A is C.

We divide the first two statements into two and substitute the end of the second for the end of the first. But a manipulation always presupposes two things:

—first of all a definition of the constituent unit of the discourse and of their composition. Subject, predicate, proposition;
—then rules of substitution of subjects for each other, of predicates, of propositions. So, categories, equivalences, subordinations.

In short, a whole grammar in the broad sense: theory of elements, of their combination, and of their substitution.

The sophism, on the other hand, does not rest on the elementary structure of the proposition but on the existence of a statement;[3] on the fact that some words have been uttered and remain there, at the center of the discussion, as having been produced and as able to be repeated, recombined according to the partners' wishes; what's said is said: not as an ideal, regular form able to receive certain types of content, but a bit like those trophies that, after a battle, warriors set down the middle and allocate, not without dispute and challenge *es meson*.[4]

What does it mean that the point of departure of the sophism is set down *es meson*, in the middle, that its communal character with regard to the partners is not due to its general form but to its position, in this place, at this moment, in this milieu?

a—That it has been brought about as an event, that is to say that it has occurred once and once and for all; that it remains as having occurred.

Now, if the different parts of this event are by no means equivalent from the point of view of the form of the proposition, [from the point of view] of the event they are homogeneous.

In the statement "5 is 2 + 3," 5, 2, and 3 are events that occur in the same way. And as a result 2 + 3 does not have to be kept inseparable.[5]

The event is divisible into as many parts as one likes and these are homogeneous with each other. There cannot be any theory of types of attribution, of rules of substitution among the elements. The only differences which apply are those:

—of the inside and the outside in relation to the game;
—of memory or oblivion.

Belonging to a certain actuality defined by the words conserved and by memory: not immutable formal differences but the fluctuating frontiers of the field of actuality.

b—but that the statement has been placed *es meson* means something else. For there to be sophistical argumentation, it is not enough to take into consideration the fact that something has been said, the fact that it was said by someone also has to be taken into account. But this needs to be studied more closely.

The attribution of a statement to a speaking subject does not refer to the meaning he wanted to give to it, to his signifying intention or his thought. If he uses the verb *manphanein*, it is not important that he wanted to say "to learn."[6] This intention does not fix the use of the word in the discussion. Even more radically: the sophistical game being played does not allow the speaking subject to refer to (grammatical or logical) rules concerning the use of words and agreed by all the participants. There is no recourse to a "meta-linguistic level of arbitration." Each subject is bound to what is said by an immediate relationship of belonging or imputation: either because he said it himself, or because he answered yes.

There is commitment of the speaking subject to what is said and not compliance with rules or intended meaning. And if the subject can maintain his assertion until the end, it remains credited to his account; he can appropriate it, he has won. If he cannot maintain it, then he loses it and he has lost. It matters little whether what he said was true or false. He has not held out. He is obliged to break with his own sentence, to relinquish the appropriation or imputation and that's it, he's excluded.

The sophism is not demonstrated, it is won or lost.

Whereas logical and legitimate manipulation, according to Aristotle, presupposes a system of anonymous, unchangeable, and common rules within which individuals place themselves in order to produce their statements and decide on recognition of a proposition as new and true, the sophism is decided at the level at which a discursive event taken from a determinate field of memory is imputable to an individual, whatever intended meaning or formal rules governed its formulation.

What is at stake beneath the apparent anarchy, bad faith, and puerility of the sophism is the reciprocal position of speaking subject and discourse (event produced, memory, imputation, maintenance or renunciation).

The triple, ordered, honest, and adult characteristic of true reasoning implies a definite, albeit very general relation between rules, subject, statement produced, and meaningful intention. This relation neutralizes the character of the statement as event.

On the other hand, a relation between subject and statement organized around the event, around its permanence and repetition, its maintained identity (without rule of internal differentiation), and its imputability (according to a form which is close to ownership as well as crime), all of this relation between subject and statement characteristic of the sophism is excluded by philosophy (and science); philosophical or scientific discourse excludes such a relation between subject and statement as formally confused, morally dishonest, and psychologically puerile. Logic, morality, and psychology see to the exclusion of the fraudulent and anarchic childishness of the sophism.

The sophism is, in the strict sense, a perversity: in the sophism, speaking subjects have an excessive connection with the body, with the materiality of their discourse, a connection which is condemned by the order of adult morality. Maybe today's true sophists are not logicians, but Roussel, Brisset, and Wolfson.[7]

B—Second set of differences concerning the effect of truth of these manipulations. This time I will begin by considering the sophism, then I will move on to legitimate reasoning.

1. From the side of the sophism. It really is often a question of truth and contradiction:

—when a proposition is asserted or agreed by the interlocutor, it is in fact asserted as true; and

—when the speaker who has formulated a statement then puts forward another one, one says to him: Stop there, you contradict yourself.

E.g., for truth: What you have not lost, you still have; you have not lost horns, therefore you have horns.

E.g., for contradiction: *Electra*.[8]

a—But when we look more closely, we see that the assertion assumed or conceded does not fundamentally concern the truth of the proposition, but the speaking subject's will to hold to what he has said. The assertion belongs to the realm of the oath rather than to that of the factual observation. The declaration does not state a fact; it does not posit a relation between the statement and an external reality that is capable of verifying the statement. It binds the speaker to what he says. It is more an assertion of faithfulness than of reality. In the sophism, to hold something to be true is an act of commitment. Hence the important fact that the sophism brings with it a bizarre, partial, restrictive, discontinuous, and shaky ontology.

In fact, the only thing the Sophist manipulates, the only being to which he addresses himself, is that of the thing said; that of the statement in its material reality. A paradoxical materiality, since it entails either sounds or letters, and hence a rareness like that of things; its linear and serial unfolding, and [nevertheless] its preservation.

Now, if words have their specific material reality, in the midst of all other things, then it is clear that they cannot communicate with these other things: they cannot signify them, or reflect them, or express them, there is no resemblance between words and the things they are supposed to speak about. At most they can be prompted, induced by these things.

But since they do not signify things, we therefore cannot have access to things through discourse. Discourse is separated from what it speaks about by the sole fact that it is itself a thing, like what it speaks about. The identity of the status of thing entails severance of the signifying relationship.

But if we cannot have access to things through discourse, of what do words speak, to what do they refer? Nothing—when we think we are talking about beings, we are talking about nothing.

But when we say that being is not, we employ words; what we say, the fact that we say it, all this exists. We bring it about that being is by the fact that we speak. And equally we bring it about that non-being is since we state "non-being." But we also bring it about that non-being is not since the words we use do not [refer] to anything and "non-being" in particular does not refer to anything, any more than the being that we accord or refuse it.

Thus, coming together around sophistical practice, we see all that pre-Socratic ontology developed by the Eleatics[9] which is precisely what is at issue in the *Sophist*, when Plato wants to overcome the Sophist. To do so he will have to overcome this ontology. But the paradoxes we find in the Sophists are not games around attribution: they do not relate to the difficulties in the connection between the affirmation of existence and the attributive statement. They found, to the exclusion of any other, the relation of the statement event to the person who makes it. This is not the ontology necessary for the truth of propositions, with its own difficulties; it is the endlessly dismantled and recommenced ontology which enables a statement to be imputed to a subject.

The apparent effect of truth which operates in the sophism is in reality a quasi-juridical bond between a discursive event and a speaking subject. Hence the fact that we find two theses in the Sophists: Everything is true (as soon as you say something, that thing exists). Nothing is true (whatever words you employ, they never express what exists).

b—We could say the same about contradiction. Apparently, the sophism makes use of contradiction to invalidate a statement. But on closer inspection something completely different is involved. Not contradicting oneself in the sophistical game is saying the *same* thing. The same thing identically, substantially. Contradicting oneself is merely saying something else, not saying the same thing. We can see that in a philosophy of the signified and of difference, one may very well say one thing, and then another, without contradicting oneself; on the other hand, in the sophistic, in which the only being is that which has been said, there are only two possibilities: either saying the same thing, or not saying the same thing (to affirm or not to affirm, which is indeed contradictory).

And we can see why sophistic ontology knows only the games of being and non-being, and sophistic logic knows only the opposition of same and different. This is why it uses all those paradoxes of pre-Socractic thought but while displacing them to the sole level of discourse.

Although the sophism may well resort to the familiar oppositions of being/non-being, contradictory/not contradictory, true/false, we need to be aware of how it does so:

—true/false functions as equivalent to agreed/not agreed.
—being/non-being functions as equivalent to said/not said
—non-contradictory/contradictory as equivalent to not-rejected/ rejected.

We can see that all these oppositions operate at the level of the existence of discourse as events in a game. And in a game culminating in the fundamental opposition victor/vanquished. The victor is he who keeps to the left side of the opposition: who repeats identically what has (actually) been said and what he has agreed can be imputed to him afterwards.

The sophism: perverse manipulation tending to establish a relation of domination.
Polemical anagram.
Such a cruel discourse.
Games of desire and power.

2. Apophantic discourse.

It has a relation to being—not at the level of its existence, where it is event, where it takes place, but at the level of *what* it says; it is an apophantic discourse because it speaks of being or non-being.

Then, it is apophantic because it is not excluded from the truth (for its non-resemblance to things) or included in it (since it is a thing); it is apophantic because: saying that something is, it happens either that the thing is (and then it is true) or that it is not (and then it is false); or again because: saying that a thing is not, either it is (and then it is false) or it is not (and then it is true).

Discourse is not apophantic inasmuch as reality and being both join together and dispute each other at the level of the event produced, but inasmuch as being and non-being is what is said to be the case in the statement, and inasmuch as truth (and error) are defined by the relation between this being that is said to be the case and being itself.

Apophantic discourse must keep the materiality and event of the statement bracketed off.

Since such is its relation to being, we can see why the true proposition excludes contradiction. In fact, let us assume that something is. The proposition will be true only if it says that this something is; it will not be true if it says that this something is not; it cannot be true therefore if it asserts both that this thing is and is not.

But, we can see, this ban on contradicting no longer concerns the material identity or otherness of the statement. It bears on the act itself of affirming or denying: we cannot at the same time affirm and deny the same thing and in the same respect.

Given these conditions it is necessary to keep clearly in mind that the *logos apophantikos* Aristotle speaks about is established in a double system of oppositions:

—it is contrasted explicitly with the prayer, order, and command [*De interpretatione*, 4, 17a 2], in short with all those formulations which cannot be reduced to true or false propositions. The *logos apophantikos* is therefore a type of enunciation which contrasts with other enunciations. The *logos apophantikos* is then a declarative statement.[10]

—It contrasts implicitly, or at any rate at another level, with statements which also have the declarative form, but which are brought into play and function at the level of their reality as event; as things produced; as things produced historically (*hic et nunc*) and by determinate subjects.

At this level, the apophantic is no longer a category of statements. It is an operation, it is an ever renewed act by which the relation of a statement to reality, to being, to truth is broken at the level of the enunciative event and transferred to what is said in the statement and the relation between what is said and things themselves.

The apophantic is what establishes a relation between the statement and being at the sole (always ideal) level of its signification. And it is through this relation established in signification that the statement can be true or false.

The apophantic then appears as an operation of the displacement of being to the ideality of signification. And it is no longer contrasted with other (non-declarative) types of statement, but to an inverse operation which consists in maintaining the relation of the statement to being at the sole level of the enunciative event. Let us call this inverse operation of the apophantic, the sophistical, eristic operation.[11]

Compared with apophantic discourse, the sophistical manipulation of statements always appears as irrelevant reasoning, as a shadow, a semblance of reasoning.

And compared with sophistical materiality, the apophantic appears therefore as a resort to ideality. Each always has the nature of shadow for the other.

Here we are no doubt at the heart of the great opposition. If the great opposition on the basis of which logic is defined is indeed the declarative/non-declarative opposition (logic, at least in its classical form, concerns itself only with the declarative), for philosophy and science, and we can say no doubt for the whole of Western knowledge (*savoir*), the opposition is between apophantic and sophistical criticism. Without doubt this opposition is not between categories of statements, but [between] levels.

We should not forget, after all, that in Aristotle the exclusion of sophisms has already taken place. If, in Aristotle at any rate, sophisms have been sufficiently mastered for them to be dealt with only at the end of the *Topics*, in appendix, in the form of catalogues of monstrosities, in the form also of formulae and remedies, in Plato, on the other hand, we know that the danger of the sophism and the Sophists is still far from being set aside. Unlike Aristotle, with Plato it is not a matter of noting that unreal shadow of philosophical discourse, but of founding philosophical discourse within and against the sophistic.[12] Now, when and how is the sophism overcome in Plato? Perhaps the sophism is never overcome, for this no doubt required the Aristotelian theory of the proposition and the theory of the categories; but Plato reckons to have subjugated the Sophist? At what point?

The victory over, or domination of, the figure of the Sophist takes place in the *Sophist*. And this victory has a double point of support in the assertion that one accedes to the truth in a discussion conducted with oneself in one's own mind,[13] and, the other point of support, connected to this, in the assertion that saying what is false, that is to say, what is not: " ... stating, about yourself ... different things as being the same, and things that are not as being, such a combination of verbs and names, is what really and truly constitutes a false discourse" (*Sophist*, 263d).[14]

On the basis of these two propositions Plato will be able to define the Sophist as the man of appearance and simulacrum.

These same two fundamental propositions are found again in Aristotle.

In the *Metaphysics*, Book IV, (Γ),[15] where he defines the true statement by the fact of saying what is, is, and what is not, is not, and in the *Posterior Analytics*, Book I, 10, 76b 24-26, when he says that the syllogism and demonstration do not deal with external discourse, but with discourse that takes place in the soul: "*o eisō logos, o en tē psukē.*"[16] And Alexander of Aphrodisias had to comment: "*ouk en tais leksesin o sullogismos ou to einai eksei all en tois sēmainomenois.*"[17] The exclusion of the materiality of discourse, the emergence of an apophantic giving the conditions on which a proposition can be true or false, the sovereignty of the signifier-signified relationship, and the privilege accorded to thought as locus of the appearance of the truth, these four phenomena are linked to each other and have given a foundation to Western science and philosophy in their historical development.

## CONCLUSION

If I have emphasized this morphology of the sophism as seen from Aristotle's point of view, the point of view that still commands us, it is because it enables us to give better definition to the historical problem to be resolved:

α—How was it that the relation between discourse and the speaking subject—at least in a determinate discursive practice—shifted in such a way as to give rise to philosophico-scientific discourse?

β—How was it that the relations of domination operating in sophistical discussions were excluded or eliminated or bracketed off—or maybe forgotten and repressed—so as to give rise to an apophantic discourse which claims to be organized by reference to being in the mode of truth?

The history of this double transformation has to be studied. It is quite probable that the Sophists were only the last episode.

1. G. Grote, *Aristotle* (London: J. Murray, 1872). Grote rehabilitated the sophists before Nietzsche, who, according to Andler, in *La Dernièr Philosophie de Nietzsche*, p. 213, adopted his conclusions (*La Volonté de puissance*, §427, 437; *The Will to Power*, §427, 437). See Th. Gomperz, *Griechische Denker: eine Geschichte der antiken Philosophie* (Leipzig: Veit & Co., 1896-1909) three volumes; French translation by A. Reymond, *Les Penseurs de la Grèce*. *Histoire de la philosophie antique* (Paris: F. Alcan, and Lausanne: Payot, 1908-1910) three volumes; Chapters V-VII of vol. 3 translated by O. D'jeranian with the title *Les Sophistes* (Paris: Éd. Manucius, 2008); T. Gomperz, *Sophistik und Rhetorik. Das Bildungsideal des εύ λέγειν in seinem Verhältnis zur Philosophie des fünften Jahrhunderts* (Leipzig-Berlin: B. Teubner, 1912); E. Dupréel, *Les Sophistes*.

2. Coriscus: a character often mentioned by Aristotle who directed the Platonic circle of Scepsis, in Troade. His son, Neleus, is said to have received Aristolte's manuscripts. See Robin, *Aristotle*, p. 11.

3. See M. Foucault, *L'Archéologie du savoir*, ch. III, pp. 140-148; *The Archeology of Knowledge*, Part III, pp. 79-87, for a lengthy elucidation of the statement in comparison with the proposition, sentence, and sign.

4. That which concerns the group set down in the middle, a political space, which distinguishes public speech from private speech outside the middle. See M. Detienne, *Les Maîtres de vérité dans la Grèce archaïque*, p. 98; *The Masters of Truth in Archaic Greece*, p. 102.

5. The sophism (*Sophistical Refutations*, 166a 30-35) that presents 5 as both even and odd does not correspond to Foucault's commentary on Aristotle.

6. This verb signifies to learn as well as to understand. Double meaning, the object of the famous verbal joust in Plato, *Euthydemus*, 275a-277d.

7. Foucault had already brought these three authors together, along with Zeno, in "Sept propos sur le septième ange" (1970) in *Dits et Écrits*, no. 73, vol. II, pp. 13-25/"Quarto" ed., vol. I, pp. 881-893. In 1970 Foucault published Brisset's *La Grammaire logique* (Paris: Tchou, 1970), and Gilles Deleuze wrote a preface to Lous Wolfson's *Le Schizo et les Langues* (Paris: Gallimard, 1970). These are different treatments of discourse as thing rather than as signifier; Foucault prefigures this type of analysis in *Raymond Roussel* (Paris: Gallimard, 1963); English translation by Charles Ruas as *Death and the Labrynth. The World of Raymond Roussel* (New York: Doubleday & Company, 1986). Deleuze evokes the same authors and their regime of signs in his *Logique du sens* (Paris: Minuit, 1969); English translation by Mark Lester as *The Logic of Sense* (London: Athlone Press, 1990) where it is a matter of "reversing Platonism."

8. Reference left in abeyance, probably accompanied by a reading by Foucault. It is likely that the reference is to Euripides, *Electra*, the most sophistical and lampoonist of the three (Aeschylus, Sophocles, Euripides): "if Apollo is insane (*insensé*), who then is wise?" If Apollo can order a parricide, this is equivalent to a sophism: one cannot be just without being unjust. [The French editor does not give the edition from which the translation of the line is taken. The English translation by Emily Townsend Vermeule in *Euripides V. Three Tragedies*, ed. David Grene and Richard Lattimore (Chicago and London: University of Chicago Press, 1968) p.51, has: "Where Apollo is ignorant shall men be wise?"]

9. Which unites two theses, the second rejected by Plato and Aristotle:
   1. Being is, non-being is not;
   2. All is one.

10. See W. and M. Kneale, "Aristotle's Theory of Meaning and Truth," in *The Development of Logic*, pp. 45-54.

11. From *eris*, dispute: "the science of disputation" (*Euthydemus*, 272b). A rather technical term, Eristics, was the name given in addition to the Megarians; see Diogenes Laertius, *Lives*, Book II, ch. 10, 106.

12. In his *La Politique d'Orphée* (Paris: Grasset, 1975) p. 99, Gilles Susong writes: "It is the rhetors and sophists who will pass on [the] discourses [of the magico-religious constellation] when broken up, whereas the philosophical sects (Orphic, Pythagorean) will develop the prototype of Platonic truth, in the rejection of deceitful appearance, *Apate*, and opinion, *Doxa*, privileging the only place where neither deception nor appearance reigns: that of the hereafter, the Other world."

   Susong appears to have followed Foucault's 1971 course, he emphasizes its convergence with Detienne's theses: "And the fact that the former took up the basic essentials of Marcel

Detienne's theses in his brilliant course is of considerable interest ... Since in fact it is in *The Masters of Truth* that a Hellenist, for the first time I think, claims to be inspired—and for main part of his approach—by Claude Lévi-Strauss, by the nodal point of his methodology, the analysis of ambiguity."

13. See Plato, *Sophist*, 263a, 264a, 264b.

14. Platon, *Le Sophist*, 263d, in *Œuvres complètes*, vol. II, p. 330; English translation by F.M. Cornford, *Sophist*, in *The Collected Dialogues*, p. 1011: "So what is stated about you, but so that what is different is stated as the same or what is not as what is—a combination of verbs and names answering to that description finally seems to be really and truly a false statement."

15. Aristotle, *Metaphysics*, Book IV (Γ), 4, 1006a 35-38 *et passim*, pp. 1589-1590.

16. [Aristotle, *Posterior Analytics*, trans. Jonathan Barnes in *The Complete Works of Aristotle*, Vol. One, p. 124: "For demonstration is not addressed to external argument - but to argument in the soul ... "; G.B.]

17. "The moderns, who follow expressions ( *tais leksesin* ) and not what they mean ( *tois sēmainomenois* ) say that the same result does not arise in the substitution for terms of their equivalent expressions." Alexander of Aphrodisias, third century C.E., second of the great Aristotle commentators, edited by M. Hayduck, Berlin Academy, 1891. See *Alexandri Aphrodisiensis* in *Aristotelis Lib. I Commentarium*, ed. M. Wallies (Berlin: Commentaria in Aristotelem Graeca, II(i), 1881) quoted in W. and M. Kneale, *The Development of Logic*, p. 158.

# five

## 27 JANUARY 1971*

> *Discourses whose function in Greek society comes from being linked to the truth. Judicial discourses, poetic discourses.* ∽ *Examination of a late document, on the threshold of Hellenistic civilization.* ∽ *Comparison with the* Iliad*: a quasi-judicial Homeric dispute. A system of four confrontations.* ∽ *Sovereignty of the judge and wild sovereignty.* ∽ *A Homeric judgment, or the famous scene of "Achilles' shield."*

### INTRODUCTION

—FORMALLY DEFINING THE SOPHISTIC by its retrospective opposition to the apophantic.

—Going back a bit, beyond the sophistic, to try to see how it was constituted.

—Going back, not to rediscover pre-Socratic thought, but in order to analyze the types of discourse institutionally linked to the truth: not what it was possible to think or say about the truth, but how the truth found its site of emergence, function, distribution, and necessary form in Greek society.

The study will focus on judicial and poetic discourse.

---

* There was no lecture on 20 January.

## I—THE FINAL STATE AND THE INITIAL STATE

1.  At one end of the process, the one closest to us, we find rules for establishing the truth which are not that far removed from our practice.

A number of juridical texts on Egyptian papyrus have been preserved concerning Greek colonies in Egypt, and in particular Alexandria. This is how testimony (in a penal or civil matter) had to be given according to the rules of this Greek procedure:

(i) The defendant or complainant writes on a tablet the name of the witness they summon, the subject of the testimony, and the thesis that the witness must support. He gives the tablet back to the magistrate.

(ii) The witness swears, according to the legal forms, that what is written on the tablets is true.

(iii) Then he testifies "on the facts he has witnessed or seen" and "does not add any other testimony."

(iv) There may be some elements in this fact that he does not know: "...let him testify for what he says he knows and let him take the oath that exempts him from testifying on facts that he says he does not know" (*Pap. Ital.*, lig. 222-233).[1]

(v) In the event of false testimony, judgment may be quashed and the false witness condemned to pay one and half times the value of the lawsuit.

So: the validity of the judgment rests—in part at least—on the truth of certain statements. If they are false, the judgment may be modified: its validity does not depend merely on its formal regularity; it does not depend merely on the fact that the case was admissible, that the procedure was followed, and the sentence was given correctly. The truth had to be told, in a quite specific way, and according to a particular grid: with regard to elements defined in advance and recognized by the magistrate as being, on the one hand, relevant to the case and, on the other, capable of truth or falsity; this truth must be told by individuals who take part in the proceedings only as bearers of truth. They do not take part because they are linked to the case by some interest or to one of the parties by blood ties or some kind of solidarity. They take part only as subjects or enunciators of truth: [an individual] is not an enunciator of truth by virtue of some authority which he possesses by nature or right, but because he has seen or heard; because he has witnessed; because he was present. And whatever he did not witness automatically falls outside the testimony.

The perception relation founds the juridical enunciation of the truth. It is what makes it possible. Testimony is organized around the experience of seeing. (From the Roman epoch to Alexandria, and maybe also before, the testimony of experts is admitted moreover: physicians, transition to knowledge [*savoir*].)

In the same epoch, Demosthenes: "The law prescribes testimony to what one knows, to acts one has witnessed; all put down in writing, so that nothing can be removed or added. With regard to hearsay evidence, the law forbids it unless the author of the words has died" (*Against Stephanos*, II, §6).[2]

This enunciation of the truth is supported by two procedures which are added to it but not identified with it:

—the oath to tell the truth, and
—punishment.

The oath refers to religious kinds of penalty and chastisement; punishment refers to penalties imposed by the courts.

Finally, enunciation of truth is taken from the system of writing. Which appears to permit:

—prior determination of the point of the testimony (what can be true or false and on what it will focus),
—fixation of the meaning of the testimony (what it will say, what it will assert to be true),
—constitution of the testimony as object, punishable in turn and liable to new proceedings. Its constitution as the object of a possible charge.

So, in the Greek procedure, enunciation of the truth is an element subject to multiple determinations.[3] Now the effect of these determinations is that the truth is not said anywhere, at any time, by anyone, and with regard to anything. The statement of the truth is limited with regard to what it speaks about. Only certain certifiable facts are capable of a true or false statement.

It is limited with regard to the subject who utters it; it must come from subjects who are not parties in the case itself, but who were its spectators. It must come from subjects who are supposed to know, who are not related to the case as parties, but whose relation to the facts of the case is one of knowledge.

It is limited with regard to its effect since, in part at least, it determines the judgment, and its falsity entails the incorrect character of the judgment; since, if false, it may entail a challenge to the judgment and a charge.

So, for statements of truth in classical Greek procedure we have a separating out of the reference, a qualification of the stating subject, and a distribution of effects.

2. Now, if we contrast this final state (on the threshold of Hellenistic civilization), with the initial state, or at any rate, the state for which we have the oldest evidence, how does the formulation of the truth appear in judicial or pre-judicial dispute?[4]

Dispute between Menelaos and Antilochos:[5]

—The chariot race. There was in fact an "overseer," Phoinix, who was positioned near the turn-post "to remember the race and bring back the truth." But he is not the one who is appealed to when the challenge is made.

—Menelaos proposes to bring the case before the "guides" of the Argives, for them to judge before all the people.

—Then straightaway he changes his mind: "I will give the judgment myself." And, "according to the rule," he proposes that Antilochos swear "by he who holds up the earth, who shakes it," that he did not impede Menelaos' chariot.

—Antilochos gives way, acknowledging his fault.

Although the term "truth" is not employed, it really is a question of truth in this procedure. But it is distributed completely differently: its location, distribution, and effects, and even more, that by which it is asserted as truth, are governed by a quite different rule.

The truth is not what one says (or the relationship between what one says and what is or is not). It is what one confronts, what one does or does not accept to face up to. It is the formidable force to which one surrenders. It is an autonomous force. But again we must really understand its nature: it is not a force of constraint, like a yoke, to which one submits. One is not morally or legally required to submit to it. It is a force to which one exposes oneself and which has its own power of intimidation. There is something in it that terrorizes. The truth is not so much a law binding men as a force which may be unleashed against them.

In the classical system, the truth is spoken by a third figure, the witness; and the latter is charged with saying what the truth is on behalf of one of the two parties.

Here, truth is the third figure. It is neither on one side nor the other. And the unfolding of the procedure does not consist in determining what side truth is on, but which of the two parties will dare to confront—or will decline to confront—the power of the truth, this fearsome focal point.

Truth does not have its seat in discourse; or it is not discourse that manifests it. One approaches it through discourse; discourse, in the form of the oath and the imprecation, designates the person who has exposed himself to its unbearable gaze.

If something is disclosed in the oath of truth, it is not what happened, it is not things themselves, but rather the defenseless nakedness of the person who agrees to being seized by it, or on the contrary the evasion of the person who tries to escape it. And yet the fact that one of the two parties agrees to expose himself in this way is not the result of a judge's action. The power of the truth is not introduced by an arbitral intervention. One of the two parties throws down a challenge to the other: will you or won't you accept the test of truth?

This means that the oath in which the truth is asserted always arises from the series of rivalries. It is a phase of the *agōn*, one of the faces of struggle.

So the nature of the relation to the truth is not different from that of the struggle itself. In a sense, it does not open out in another dimension. It is not: the quarrel being over, the truth will now begin to reveal itself. The truth is not formed in a neutral place (the judge's mind),* but in the space of the *agōn*.[6]

However, the test of truth is final with regard to the *agōn*: it is in this sense that it is singular and irreducible to all the others. What, then, is its operational force?

—If the defendant accepts the test, he is straightaway the victor;

—If he refuses it, he is straightaway defeated and the person who made the challenge is the victor.

The test of truth works without the truth having to manifest itself. It remains silent and withdrawn. It indicates itself only indirectly through the gesture, the oath, the imprecation of the person who is not afraid to approach it. But if this test is decisive, it is insofar as it brings about a displacement. It forces the one who swears into another space of *agōn*: the one that takes place with or against the gods. With his imprecation, the person who swears leaves it to the power of the gods. That is what will decide. But will it decide in the sense of the truth? In fact nothing is said about what will happen to the person who swears after the test of the oath: we know only that he is in the hands of the gods, that they may punish him or his descendants; that they may strike his goods or his body; that they may protect or severely chastise him.

The oath therefore means entry into another universe, one dominated by the power of the gods. But the gods are not bound by the truth: if the person who swears makes a false oath, he risks destruction by the gods' anger, but this is neither certain nor automatic; and if there is punishment, its time and form remain shrouded until the last moment.

Only one thing is certain: when the gods decide to punish, you won't escape their thunderbolt. So the oath does not mean entry into the invisible realm of a truth which will shine forth one day; it shifts the combat into a region where the risks are incommensurable with those

---

* Or: the subject's mind. Writing indecipherable.

of the struggle and where the laws governing these risks are absolutely hidden from human sight.

At this pre-law stage,[7] truth appears within a system of four struggles; four confrontations and four risks:

α—the struggle, violence, or fraud which gave rise to the present dispute (the chariot race in this case);

β—the confrontation which follows this first violence, the claim of the person who considers himself wronged, the two adversaries asserting their rights. This second dispute comes after and as rejoinder to the first. It may take varied forms and proceed endlessly;

γ—the challenge to make the oath of truth: dare you swear? This third dispute is one of the possibilities offered by the second: the second dispute either turns into a long series of retaliations or takes the form of this challenge, but the role of the latter is to bring it all (first and second series) to an end. It is therefore final and can take only two forms: yes or no;

δ—finally, the confrontation with the gods, which has a triple characteristic: shifting the dispute of two adversaries to just one plus the gods (the person who launched the challenge is excluded); taking the place of all the preceding confrontations; opening up a new indefinite series.

If we compare this truth to the truth at work in the classical age, we can take stock of all the differences:

α—in the classical age the truth is spoken, and in the form of the factual observation; in the archaic period it is approached in the form of the imprecation;

β—it is spoken by a witness who occupies the position of third party; in archaic law, it is launched as a challenge by one party to the other, who may accept the challenge or decline it;

γ—in classical law, the truth decides between; in Homer, it becomes the lot falling to one of the adversaries, or rather one of the two adversaries becomes its lot and prey;

δ—it is an element in the judge's decision in classical law; it makes the decision in archaic law.

There is a common point, however, which is that the truth is linked to an exercise of sovereignty; for it is insofar as he exercises authority that the judge demands the truth and imposes the sentence and its execution accordingly; in the Homeric oath, when he accepts the challenge of truth, the one who swears exposes himself to Zeus' sovereignty (shaking land and sea). But in the case of classical law, the truth is called for, formulated, and proven in the already constituted space of sovereignty; it is invited to come out in the space of the tribunal, and it is then, and only then, that it determines the point of application and the limits of that sovereignty.

In pre-law, between two adversaries who accept neither the sovereignty of one in relation to the other nor a sovereignty exercised over both, the test of truth appeals to an unlimited and wild sovereignty.

Between these two truths, the whole system of power is modified. And proof, or at least the sign, that it really is a question of power that is at stake between these two forms of judicial truth, is the fact that even in the Hellenistic age the "pre-juridical" type of oath is still found quite regularly.

We find it in cases where the adversaries want to resolve their conflict outside of the juridical apparatus offered by the organization of the State. A text[8] from 134 B.C.: "It is not we who caused your injury and we do not know who did it to you. May Ammonios and Hermocles, our brothers, swear with us that our oath is true ... [If they make this oath] let them be considered quits, if not let us resort to the epistates."[9]

In what is, to be sure, a very different form, we find again the principle of the Homeric oath: the acceptance of the oath with decisive value, at least in what concerns the adversaries. But this oath has all the same lost half of its effectiveness: since the judge intervenes if the test is refused.

The problem now is to analyze the transformation of the system of truth—judicial decision—political sovereignty.

We will study this transformation in two stages:

—the set of modifications that led to Solon;
—those that led to the classical epoch, i.e., to the epoch of the Sophists.

## II—THE FIRST GROUP OF TRANSFORMATIONS

This involves the setting up of a political-judicial organization which, in an unspecified epoch and under conditions that are not well known, is superimposed on the private ritual procedures which were no doubt typical of warrior societies, and an example of which we have seen.

We have ambiguous evidence of this archaic organization in Homer (Achilles' shield);[10] and very soon after, we see it being questioned in Hesiod.[11] The directly juridical documents are basically the Gortyn laws.

1. This is the scene of Achilles' shield: two litigants: one claims to have already paid the blood price,* the other says no. There are their supporters.

The elders give their view. Every speaker grasps the scepter. A reward of two talents of gold is promised to the one who gives the best advice.

The scene includes some important characteristics:

a—Each judge is linked to sovereignty when he speaks. To give his view is to be, for a time at least, sovereign. One speaks only from the site of sovereignty. Taking over speech and taking the symbol of sovereignty in one's hands are two concomitant and linked actions.

b—Nevertheless, we can see that this is a very limited and partial sovereignty. In fact the "tribunal" does not have to give a decisive and collective view. Each gives his view, one will be better than the others; and this opinion will have two effects: it will lead to the decision; but it will in turn be rewarded by a higher authority.

So it appears as a sort of "game," in the strict sense, between a private matter (of murder and/or debt) and a sovereignty which is only concerned with the joust.

Sovereignty intervenes only indirectly since it only judges the judges and is present only symbolically in the scepter held by the judges.

---

* [In Lattimore's translation, one has *promised* to pay the blood price in full, and the other has refused this; G.B.]

c—But there is more: the matter of the murder itself is not sub-
mitted to the judges; they do not have to say who the murderer is
and what penalty he must suffer. They have to say only whether
the blood price has indeed been paid. They have to decide on the
correct or incorrect, complete or incomplete character of the procedures which have taken place. The judges do not intervene with
regard to the offence; they intervene with regard to the application of the legal customs put to work by private individuals in
order to regulate their disputes. More precisely, with regard to the
execution.

The judges are in a secondary position. They control a juridical development the initiation and phases of which are not their
responsibility. So they do not have to tell the truth: they do not
have to establish the truth of the facts, they have to say what must
be done.

d—Supporters of the two adversaries are pressing around the
scene where the dispute unfolds, they would like to rush forward
in support of their champion, but they are held back by guards.
This presence, this pressure, on the one hand, and this prohibition, on the other, are important. It is not the individual as such
who acts in the procedure, who demands or who pays the blood
price. It is a whole group of which he is a part. It is this group,
as a whole, which will win or lose. The individual is not a subject
of right.

But what is the meaning of the fact that the supporters do not
have access to the place where justice is decided? An individualization of the law? No doubt not, but the fact that the game
of retaliation is interrupted in this place where justice is decided,
the groups stop crying out against each other. By a sort of real
metathesis, struggle ( *agōn* ) is transposed to another place which is
reminiscent of that place of athletic competition, and where there
is confrontation, competition, sentence, decision, and prize.

e—Finally, a *histōr* arrives,[12] who is not the witness, but rather
the one "who knows," who is competent, who is experienced in the
rules, customs, and the way in which disagreements are resolved.

Apart from the two partners, above, opposite, or alongside
them, we see a political power appearing which judges, and does

so in two stages (the judges are Elders and are themselves judged); a judicial competence which is imposed on them, but in the very uncertain form of the *histōr*; a judgment which decides between them but which, to tell the truth, only concerns the procedures of compensation, not the injury itself.

In the characteristics of this Homeric judgment we can see the kernel of future transformations:

—the more or less complete identification of political power and judicial power (the tiers disappear);
—the substitution of a written law for the *histōr*;
—a judgment bearing on the fact established in its truth and no longer simply on the procedure called for in the correction of this fact.

In short, the constitution of a system of discourse in which the exercise of power (the right to formulate a decision), the forced reference to writing, and the establishment of the truth, are linked to each other.
But we should not anticipate.

2. The second strata of documentation brings us face to face with the system of which we merely sense the outline in Homer, and of that which challenges it, demolishes it, and will push it aside.*

---

* Sudden cut-off. Foucault himself wrote "incomplete" on the first page.

1. Source cited in Claire Préaux, "Le témoignage dans le droit grec classique," in *Recueils de la Société Jean Bodin pour l'histoire comparative des institutions*, vol. XVI: *Le Preuve* (Brussels: Éditions de la Librairie encyclopédique, 1965) pp. 206-222.

2. Quoted in ibid. Claire Préaux appears not to challenge the attribution to Demosthenes; Louis Gernet is inclined to favor Apollodorus.

3. See Louis Gernet, "Introduction à l'étude du droit grec ancien," *Archives d'histoire du droit oriental (AHDO)*, II, 1938, pp. 281-289.

4. The concept of pre-law comes from the studies of Louis Gernet: "Droit et pré-droit en Grèce ancienne," *L'Année sociologique*, 3ᵉ série (1948-1949), Paris, 1951, pp. 21-119, where the cases reported here by Foucault are analyzed; re-published in L. Gernet, *Anthropologie de la Grèce antique* (Paris: Maspero, 1968), and in L. Gernet, *Droit et Institutions en Grèce antique* (Paris: Flammarion, coll. "Champs," 1982).

5. Homère, *Iliade*, ed. and trans. P. Mazon (Paris: Les Belles Lettres, 1938) vol. IV, XXIII/ψ, 340-592, pp. 111-121; English translation by Richmond Lattimore, Homer, *The Iliad* (Chicago and London: University of Chicago Press, 1961) Book Twenty-Three, 340-592, pp. 459-464.

6. *Agôn*: L. Gernet, "Droit et pré-droit en Grèce ancienne": "assembly brought together at the games, which gave its name to the games and then to the trial"; G. Samuel, "Les preuves dans le droit grec archaïque," in *Recueils de la Société Jean Bodin*, vol. XVI: *La Preuve*, p. 121: "designates competition in a stadium, or a trial."

7. L. Gernet, "Droit et pré-droit" p. 104: "The symbols of pre-law are essentially effective: the hand that gives or receives; the staff that asserts power or relinquishes it or confers it; the imprecatory speech, the gesture or posture equivalent to imprecation...everything that acts immediately and in virtue of its own Dunamis."

8. See Claire Préaux, "Le témoignage dans le droit grec classique" p. 221.

9. Epistates: the official, title of various "functionaries" of Greek antiquity, especially those responsible for justice.

10. Homer, *Iliad*, Book Eighteen, 497-508, Fr. p. 186; Eng. p. 388. What is described is part of the decoration of the shield forged by Hephaistos, in three circles: the universe at the centre then the town, in the first circle, and the scene of the tribunal, labor in the second circle, and pastoral life. The scene of Achilles' shield has been commented on by many authors. See J. Gaudemet, *Les Institutions de l'Antiquité* (Paris: Sirey, 1967) pp. 139-140; H.J. Wolff, R.J. Bonner, G. Smith, A. Steinwenter, G. Glotz, and L. Gernet who declare this scene: "a textbook case."

11. Hésiode, *Le Bouclier*, ed. and trans. P. Mazon (Paris: Les Belles Lettres, 1928); English translation by Glen W. Most, *The Shield* in Glen. W. Most, ed., *Hesiod: The Shield, Catalogue of Women, Other Fragments* (Cambridge, Mass.: Harvard University Press, Loeb Classical Library, 2007).

12. Homer, *Iliad*, Book Twenty-Three, 486. This passage has also been commented on by J. Gaudemet, *Les Institutions de l'Antiquité*, p. 140, who gives the word *histōr* the root *is* = *wid* (Latin: *video*; see A. Eernout and A. Meillet, *Dictionnaire étymologique de la langue latine*, Paris: Klincksieck, 1951). M. Detienne, *Les Maîtres de vérité dans la Grèce archaïque*, p. 101, n. 80; *The Masters of Truth in Archaic Greece*, p. 193, n. 73, stresses the "witness" aspect: "the *histōr* is a witness, one who *sees* and *hears*, and, as heir to the *mnēmōn*, he is also a *memorialist* [emphasis added]."

# six

## 3 FEBRUARY 1971

*Hesiod.\* ⌢ Characterization of words of truth in Homer and judicial discourse. ⌢ Greek ritual ordeal and Christian Inquisition. ⌢ Pleasure and test of truth in masochism. ⌢ Hesiod bard of* krinein *against the* dikazein *of judges-kings, eaters of gifts. ⌢* Dikaion *and* dikē *in Hesiod. ⌢ Extension of* krinein *into the Greek juridical space and new type of assertion of the truth. ⌢ Draco's legislation and reparation. ⌢* Dikaion *and order of the world.*

TWO TYPES OF JUDGMENT in the Homeric texts.

[First,] in the warrior group it is not really a matter of a judgment, but rather of a dispute which is ended by the game of the oath and challenge of truth. [Second,] in an urban or village milieu, intervention of an authority, but at the secondary level, with regard to procedures of reparation, responsibility for the initiation of which lies solely with the individuals. The authority does not see to it that reparation has been made, but that, when reparations are being made, they proceed according to the rules. These two types of procedure no doubt correspond to two types of social group and maybe to two different epochs.

Before going further, I would like to point out that the assertion of truth was present in judicial discourse from the start, or at any rate in the most archaic forms that we know. It was not added afterwards, like a

---

\* Title of the lecture manuscript.

foreign element. From the start some statements are institutionalized as having to be truthful utterances, utterances relating to the truth, utterances putting the truth into play, even less: utterances entering into an open, uncertain, perilous game with the truth.[1]

And the function of these utterances is not merely external and decorative; their operational role is decisive since it is around them, on the basis of them, that the transition takes place from the series of retaliations to the threatening vengeance of the gods.

There is no judicial discourse in which the truth is not lurking. In this sense we must endorse what Dumézil said in *Servius et la Fortune*: "As far back as we go in the behavior of our species, the 'true utterance' is a force to which few forces resist ... very early on the Truth appeared to men as one of the most effective verbal weapons, one of the most prolific seeds of power, one of the most solid foundations for their institutions."[2]

But what we have to understand is that this word of truth was not given originally and as if in the wild state; it does not have the immediate, universal, and bald form of the factual observation. We should not imagine that the judicial institution calls upon, as foundation, norm, or justification, a set of true observations which are or could be made outside this institution. Judicial discourse is not organized (finally or from the start) by reference to a statement of the truth which is prior or external to it. For judicial discourse, the relation to truth is established according to rules which are specific to it.

We have seen:

—The truth is not observed; it is sworn: oath and imprecations.
—The word of truth does not rest on what has been seen or experienced; it exposes itself to the possible future anger of the gods.
—The word of truth does not disclose what has happened; although directed at the facts, it indicates the person who takes the risk, by excluding the person who declines the risk.
—Finally, it does not found a just decision; through its specific effectiveness, it wins the day.

In the system we know today, in the system already installed in the Greek classical epoch, the truthful utterance is above all that of testimony:

it has the form of the factual observation; it rests on what has taken place and its function is to reveal it. Its model, or rather its non-verbal equivalent, is perception: showing things as if one was there, as if one was seeing them. The words of the witness are the substitute for presence.

In the system we are referring to for the Homeric period, the non-verbal equivalent for the word of truth is the ordeal,[3] the test: being exposed or exposing someone to undefined danger. Taking the oath of truth or exposing oneself to the danger of blows, the thunderbolt, the sea, wild beasts— this has the same form and the same operational property. In archaic judicial practice, the word of truth is not linked to light and looking at things; it is linked to the obscurity of the future and uncertain event.

Proof that this really is the role of the word of truth is the fact that institutionally the ordeal was used with the oath, as an alternative to it. When two adversaries were not of equal rank and the oath of one was not acceptable, he was subject to the ordeal: this was the case with women (with the test of the *rock*),[4] exposed children, and slaves. The physical danger with which one confronted them, their torture, was their oath of truth.

It is curious to see how this test of truth by the torture of slaves was preserved throughout Greek judicial practice, but gradually taking on a different role: in the fourth century it involves getting a confession from slaves who could have witnessed actions of their masters, but whose servile condition would prevent them from telling the truth.

Torture is in the service of truth-testimony, but the master has the right to refuse the test for his slave; and the refusal functions a bit like a refusal of the ordeal test; it is at any rate a bad point, a negative sign for the master's cause.

A whole history could be written of the relationships between truth and torture.

\* \* \*

Glotz has maybe said the most important thing about the Greek ordeal, but the Inquisition should be studied in this perspective.\* There, the test

---

\* The martyr keeps the truth up to and including execution and with the uncertain possibility of God coming to save him. (Note by M.F.)

of truth is complicated by the Christian behavior of confession (*l'aveu*). But the Inquisition is not purely and simply a matter of techniques for getting the confession. There is a whole network of disjunctions which support the inquisitorial test:

> —either you resist the test and do not confess to being a sorcerer; this means that the devil has enabled you to bear the unbearable; therefore you are a fiend. So you deserve another torture, until the final torture releases your soul from this carnal body and world in which the Devil reigns;
>
> —or you do not resist the test and confess; this means that you really are Satan's henchman. Therefore you deserve to be punished. Punishment which we promised you would escape if you confessed. But your confession means that you are forgiven and will die absolved, so that we are not committing a mortal sin by dispassionately sending an unrepentant sinner to God's tribunal.

It is not impossible that the autopsy of bodies, their *post mortem* torture to establish the truth of the life and disease, presented some difficulties for this very reason (for madness at any rate),[5] due to these historically highly charged relations between truth and torture.

*Masochism.* The masochist is not someone who gets his pleasure in suffering. Rather he is perhaps someone who accepts the test of truth and submits his pleasure to it: If I bear the test of truth through to the end, then I will win out over your discourse and my assertion will be stronger than yours. And the imbalance between the masochist and his partner is due to the partner posing the question in apophantic terms. Tell me what your pleasure is, show it to me; pass it through the grid of questions I put to you; let me observe it. Use of paradox.

And the masochist replies in terms of ordeal: I will always bear more than you can do to me. And my pleasure is in this always displaced, never fulfilled excess. It is not in what you do, but in this empty shadow that each of your actions casts in front of it.

To the apophantic question of his partner, the masochist retorts, not with an answer, but through an ordeal challenge; or rather, he hears an ordeal challenge and answers it: I affirm my pleasure on the far bound-ary of what you may imagine to be me.

## THE TRANSFORMATION

The core of the transformation basically consists in the appearance of a new type of judgment, procedure, and sentence alongside an earlier form.
This opposition is indicated by the existence of two words: *dikazein* and *krinein*. It is at work in a passage in Hesiod[6] in which, on the one hand, it seems to indicate the existence of two different jurisdictions, and, on the other, it seems to coincide with the opposition between good and bad justice:

> "Come, let us settle here our dispute (*diakrinōmetha neikos*) by one of those right judgments that, in the name of Zeus, really are the best of all. You have already ... seized plenty and plundered the property of others, while lavishing tributes on the kings, eaters of gifts, always ready to judge according to such justice (*basilēas dōrophagous oi tēnde dikēn ethelousi dikassai*)."[7]

Let us keep in mind several things in this passage:

a—The issue with regard to which the two justices are evoked and contrasted is a farmer's dispute over goods and property. Bad justice awards the litigants what does not belong to them; good justice, in contrast, allows each to obtain and keep what is due to him.
b—In both cases there is in fact recourse to an authority, but it seems that in the case of good justice this involves a prior agree-ment (*diakrinōmetha*) and the appeal is made to an authority one does not know; in the case of bad justice, it is made to the author-ity of kings (local leaders, heads of aristocratic families). These leaders appreciate bribes, whereas the other, good justice is carried out in the name of Zeus. [These right judgments] are, the text says, *ek Dios*: born of God. This seems to indicate an authority and, in any case, another system of guarantee.

This contrast has noteworthy analogies with what is much more clearly shown in the Gortyn inscriptions.[8]

The Gortyn law makes room for two types of judgment:

A—In one, *dikazein*, the litigants alone swear an oath—each litigant comes with his witnesses: but these are not those who know or who have seen. They are the litigant's supporters. They also swear. But they do not swear to tell the truth on the action being pleaded. Their role is not to decide between the adversaries on the basis of this third element, the truth.

They swear the same oath as the party they support; they commit themselves along with him. Like him, they expose themselves to the gods' vengeance against perjurers. But at the same time, they show the social weight of the person they accompany.

As for the verdict, it is not a free decision on the fact or right in question. It records the regularity of the procedures undertaken and followed. In particular, it is arrived at mechanically on the basis of the number of witnesses and the weight of the oath.

In a property conflict, the statement assembling *nine* witnesses will prevail. The judge is bound by these testimonies. The parties' oath wins the day (somewhat as in the scene of Menelaos' challenge), but what has disappeared here is the man to man challenge and the immediately decisive game of refusal and acceptance.

—Egalitarian confrontation is replaced by the social differentiation of individuals, of their affiliation, their clientele.
—The challenge launched at the other person (who either accepts or declines it) is replaced by confrontation between two social groups.
—Finally, the immediately decisive effect of the challenge taken up, or not, is replaced by what is in principle the mechanical decision of a third authority.

The truth, in this procedure, is therefore asserted in the oath of those who jointly swear it, in the form of the accepted risk: we expose ourselves to the gods' vengeance if we do not tell the truth. But it is also asserted in the verdict, in the form of memory: the rules have in fact been observed. And it is from this requirement of memory that corrupting gifts may divert the kings.

The god's future vengeance and the exact memory of the kings of justice.[9] Threat of the gods who remember every affront; always potentially faulty memories of those who have to recall every rule: the truth of this sort of judgment, *dikazein*, functions in the double element of this memory.

So, we have two temporal figures:

—in gods, the future memory of the present oath of men
—in kings, the present memory of the oldest rules.

The truth is not related to these two figures in the same way:

—it exposes men to the gods' future memory,
—and it rests on the kings' present memory.

These two relations do not have the same point of emergence, or the same support:

—in one case, the person who swears establishes the relation to the truth in his oath;
—in the other, the judge-king effectuates true justice in his sentence.

But in both cases, truth has the form of the unforgotten: men demand what is unforgotten from the kings, insofar as they expose themselves to the unforgotten of the gods. This truth has nothing to do with concealment and unconcealment.[10]

B—*krinein*.[11] Alongside *dikazein*, the Gortyn law makes room for another form of judgment, *krinein*. It does seem that to start with this form of judgment had an essentially vicarious role: where custom was silent or insufficient, where maybe an injury had to be assessed.

Now this judgment very quickly underwent a considerable extension to the point of becoming absolutely normal, except in cases where the first form of judgment, *dikazein*, was explicitly required (addition to the law). *Krinein* gradually occupies the whole space of Greek judicial practice. In what does it consist? It apparently consists in a simple displacement or reduplication: the judge takes the oath, either because the parties do not, or in addition to their oath.

1. What is the nature and function of this oath?

It has often been interpreted as a promissory oath (Dareste):[12] the judge commits himself to respect the law. But, apart from there not being any law in these cases, we see that according to the Gortyn law, in some cases at least, the judge must swear to the truth of the fact. But does that mean that it is an assertoric oath: I swear that this is true? (Latte).[13] In many cases (like inheritance shares), the assertoric oath would have no meaning.

It seems (Gernet) that it is above all an oath by which the judge personally exposes himself, takes the risk, and binds his destiny to the value of his own sentence. Somewhat as the amphictyons of Delphi did later before pronouncing on a dispute:[14] "Called upon to give a ruling on the goods and territory of Apollo, as far as possible I will judge the whole affair as according to the truth, without fury and without hatred, and I will not rule wrongly in any way ... And if I keep my oath, may I obtain every sort of prosperity. If I violate it, may Themis, Pythian Apollo, Leto, and Artemis, Hestia and the eternal fire kill me miserably and refuse me any salvation" (quoted in Glotz).[15]

The judge has to tell the truth and in this relation to the truth, he exposes himself to the gods' vengeance, no more or less than the litigants themselves. An assertion of truth now appears in a third position, superimposed on and superordinate to that of the parties, and it is this third enunciation which is decisive. The appearance of the judge's oath is not just a supplementary formality. It is a whole new arrangement of judicial discourse and practice.

2. What does this involve?

a—A displacement and functional retreat of the litigants' oath. Formerly, this oath exposed the litigants to the unbearable gaze of the truth and its vengeance. But we know that the oath may be true or false.

As Plato will point out later (*Laws*),* one of the two must be false. Able to be true as well as false, the oath can no longer serve as proof.

Hesiod: "The despicable will attack the good with devious words which he will support with a false oath" (*Works and Days*, 195-196); "oaths running on the tracks of crooked verdicts" (*Works and Days*, 219).[16]
Aeschylus: "I affirm that unjust claims should not triumph by oaths" (*The Eumenides*, 432).[17]

The parties are disqualified as bearers of truth. They are not exposed to the power of the truth; they retain possession of the power to speak or not speak the truth. (And it is with regard to what they swear that the judge will be able to say true or false.)

But this functional retreat is doubled by a displacement. The oath actually subsists for the parties, but it functions as the ritual institution of proceedings. The parties demonstrate by the oath that they are appealing to the judge; they indicate that they sustain contradictory theses and that they both decide to request (and to an extent agree to) proceedings.

Saying "I swear that I did not kill" and "I swear that he killed," is not stating a truth, it is instituting proceedings ritually.

In this form of judgment, swearing on oath by the parties no longer brings about the decision; its role is no longer exactly to continue and complete the rivalry of the two litigants. Its function is to transpose it onto a different stage: certainly the trial will still be a struggle (up until the classical age it will continue to be called *agōn* or *neikos*);[18] but it will have a completely different organization, since one will no longer get the better of one's adversary solely on the strength or weight of the oath, but when one has won the judge over to one's side.

The parties' swearing on oath serves ritually to open a new space of struggle where it unfolds symbolically and where it accepts the judge's sovereignty. (And what confirms this, at least negatively, is a provision of the Gortyn law: when there is no other means of judging—the other

---

* The manuscript indicates *Laws*, IX, but this book does not contain any reference to the oath. The question is evoked in somewhat different terms in Book XII, 948b-949b, and signals an evolution from the famous oaths in the names of the gods at the time of Rhadamanthus.

party defaulting or absent - the judge will leave it up to the oath of the only litigant present. The litigant's decisive oath is a last resort).

b—But the judge's oath also involves a new function of the sentence. In *krinein* the judge's sentence is not content with recording the victory of one of the adversaries, of comparing and sanctioning the opposing forces; it assigns victory. In a sense it constitutes it. But on what basis? By reference to what principle of measurement? What is it that authorizes this sentence? And what sentence will be considered to be just, good, better than the others?

1. Of course, some poetical or philosophical texts tell us. The just sentence is one in accordance with *dikē*, that states the *dikaion*;[19] more precisely, or enigmatically, that states *dikaion kai alēthēs*;[20] or, as Herodotus will say later, that gives justice, *kata to eon*.[21]

Maybe commentary on these texts could reveal the relation to truth or the relation to being (*l'étant*) on which the sentence is founded and which is manifested by this just sentence.

2. But Greek judicial practice will not doubt be a more reliable guide.

One of the principles of this judicial practice, a constant principle and one that we still find until the end of the classical age, is that every action must be brought by someone against someone; something like the prosecutor, the public prosecutor, the bench does not exist in Greek law. There must always be two partners, one of whom accuses the other, who defends himself in turn.[22]

a—In criminal trials (and this is a consequence of the first point) it is not up to the city or State or judicial authority to attack the suspect; this is a task that falls to the victim or his close relatives; in a case of murder, it is up to one of the dead person's close relatives to attack the presumed murderer. And if the heirs shirk the task, other members of the family may get up in turn, and accuse not only the criminal of his crime, but the legitimate complainant of his failing.

At the other end of the procedure, we find the same type of provision: when the sentence is reached, it is for the adversary to demand and initiate, at least symbolically, its execution. (In Athens, in the case of a double penalty, concerning both an individual and the city, the latter can demand its due only after the former has begun to demand his.)

The sentence has its place against the background of a procedure of reparation which takes place between individuals. It legitimizes, limits, and organizes reparations. It sees to it that the crime is compensated for properly. It does not constitute the criminal as a criminal. The big question in which all our penal law is entangled (is the accused truly criminal?) is foreign to Greek law; basically it knows only the question: has there really been compensation for the crime?

This is why Draco's legislation,[23] which will apply up to Demosthenes and beyond, is a legislation of reparation:

—it carefully specifies who has the right to demand reparation and to declare it sufficient or interrupt it (children and parents, brothers and sisters, cousins, descendants, father-in-law, phratry);
—it also specifies when one can exercise an immediate right of reparation (in the agora, at the palaestra);
—it specifies again whether one can exercise a right of reparation when the criminal is exiled or the victim is a slave.

On the other hand, Draco's legislation is rudimentary concerning the nature of the crime, what it is in itself:

—homicide in legitimate defense (which is already a reparation),
—murder, and
—involuntary homicide.

The purpose of the judge's sentence in criminal matters is above all to preside over the organization of reparation.

b—And in "civil" actions? As paradoxical as it may be, the sentence plays the same role.

Take the inheritance proceedings studied by Gernet:[24] when someone challenges someone else over an inheritance which he has appropriated, the two adversaries are not plaintiff and defendant, they are two symmetrical adversaries; there is not a plaintiff who has to justify his rights: there are two wrestlers who have to justify their claims against each other. There is no authority of the thing judged in these proceedings. One can always call them into question by advancing a new reason. A third claimant may always intervene. Finally, negative prescription only comes into force five years after the death of the person who was declared heir.

In proceedings concerning contracts, non-observation is always seen as an injury.

So the role of the sentence is not to declare a right belonging to a subject. It is not founded upon a subjective right; it does not have to recognize a subject of right.[25] It has to regulate the interplay of recompenses and dismissals. It is not of matter of each having their specific right recognized; it is a matter of the interplay of allocations, compensations, reparations taking place in a satisfactory way.

Greek judicial practice does not have to rely on the rights of the subject in their truth;[26] it has to rely on a distribution and reparation in accordance with the allocation and circulation of things, with their just cycle.

c—This is why, correlative to this justice of *krinein* we see the appearance of a new notion, that of *dikaion*, the just.

The *dikaion* does not exist in *The Iliad*. *Dikē* appears five times, designating the disputed action brought for judgment, and the sentence itself.[27] It appears several times in Hesiod, always linked to *dikē*, and in particular in the great passage of *Works and Days* devoted to the happiness and unhappiness of the City (255-263).[28] In this famous passage we see that a whole series of misfortunes ensue if kings do not deliver justice according to the principle of the *dikaion*—what are the misfortunes and how are they distributed?

[ ... *]

And the causality itself is modified. In Homeric *pre jure*, it was the will of Zeus that was immediately appealed to. In Hesiod, it is *Dikē*, who serves as intermediary. When the kings do not judge well, *Dikē* leaves Earth and requests the vengeance of Zeus (she takes refuge on her father's lap).

The effect of injustice is above all the absence of justice. When present, justice is both the sign and guarantee of the happiness of cities; this is the sense in which Aratos evokes the three ages:[29] the golden age in which Justice is present on the public square and at crossroads; the silver age, when she has withdrawn to the mountain summits where she

---

* Manuscript page 23 was removed and transferred to the following lecture (10 February), where it becomes page 6; see below, p. 103.

blazes when the sun sets; and the bronze age in which she shines only at night over the heavenly vault where she has withdrawn to.

The *dikaion* is linked therefore to an order of the world. Present in the world, *Dikē*[30] ensures that men's happiness corresponds to the soundness of judgments; absent from it, she sees to it that the town and fields suffer unjust judgments.

Whereas in the categories of Roman juridical thought the "just" refers to the real right of the subject, the Roman judge's just judgment must truly express the true right;

[ ... *]

—Why basically the function of the judgment is not to declare or constitute law, but rather to insert itself as reparation, redistribution, and compensation in the cycle of allocations. Justice corrects rather than allocates. See Aristotle.[31]

—How *true* and *false* are distributed and function in the judgment; their role in relation to the oaths of the litigants, the judge, and the just and unjust.

—Why justice is immediately and in principle political. It is one of the means of establishing order in the city; not so much making each recognize what is due to him naturally, but properly fastening the bonds of the city, seeing to it that the place of each is in harmonious balance with that of the others. Which entails: (a) that it is the political authority that deals with justice, and (b) every man who concerns himself with justice, by that very fact, concerns himself with the city's politics.

Judicial discourse is immediately recognized as [political†] discourse.

—Why, finally, saying what is just (*dikaion*) is at the same time saying—singing or knowing—the order of things. The lawmaker will be at the same time someone who speaks of the order of the world; he watches over it, jointly, through his songs and knowledge as well as through his prescriptions and sovereignty. Conversely, someone who knows the order of the world will be able to say what is best and most just for men and cities.

---

* Manuscript page 25 missing.
† The manuscript repeats: judicial.

The notion of *nomos* becomes central and ambiguous. On the basis of this juridical form of *krinein*, a singular type of true discourse appears which is linked to the *dikaion*, to the *nomos*, to the order of the world and the organization of the city. It is still very far from what is true discourse for us, but, through multiple transformations, ours derives from it.[32]

We belong to this dynasty of *krinein*.

## CONCLUSION

With *krinein*, a whole new type of assertion of the truth is constituted in judicial discourse and practice.

This assertion of truth connects the discourse of justice with political discourse in which sovereignty is exercised, with the discourse of knowledge (*savoir*) in which the order of the world is set forth. This discourse found its highest formulation in Solon and Empedocles, kings of justice, poets of the written law, and masters of truth. This type of assertion disappeared with the Sophists—or rather, its scattered fragments are found again in the Sophists, as if it was circulating in the wild state in a game in which it does not settle or halt anywhere. Assertion of the law opposing nature; assertion that there is no truth and that all discourse is true; assertion of a universal knowledge and that knowledge is nothing; assertion that one teaches justice and that one can win any case. The drunkenness of the fragmented old Greek truth.

From that *krinein* of which Hesiod sung and which he opposed to the *dikazein* of the gift eating kings, from that *krinein* institutionalized by the Gortyn law to the merchants of discourse and crushing arguments, the route in any case was long. It passed roughly through three stages:

—The establishment of a written law fixing, to a certain extent, the *nomos* which governs the just and judicial practice. This is the first great defeat of the aristocratic and warrior justice dispensed on the basis of decisive moments. The judicial utterance which wins out is no longer that in which the imprecation has greatest weight, it is what conforms to the *nomos*. This is the epoch of Charondas,[33] Zaleucus, and Draco. [It is] *eunomia*.[34]

—The establishment of a political-judicial power with the form of the city state and which is exercised, in principle at least, in the same way with regard to all citizens, even though these are unequal by wealth and birth. This is the epoch of Solon.[35] It is *isonomia.*[36]

—Finally, the seizure of power, in some cities at least, by the people, through, despite, or following tyranny.[37]

But what we now need to recount is the political history that can account for the appearance of *krinein*—of that deployment of a just and true discourse across judicial institutions and practices. And which can account for its transformations.

1. The judge declares the truth in archaic Greece: we frequently encounter the liaison *dikaios kai alēthēs*: see Euripides, *The Suppliant Women*, 855; Plato, *Laws*, IX, 859a; Démosthène, *Harangues*, II, ed. and trans. M. Croiset (Paris: Les Belles Lettres, 1925) pp. 110-112; Sophocles, *Oedipus the King*, 1158 (according to R. Hirzel, *Themis, Dike und Verwandtes. Ein Beitrag zur Geschichte der Rechtsidee bei den Griechen*, Leipzig, 1907, pp. 108-115; reprinted Hildesheim: G. Olms, 1966).

2. G. Dumézil, *Servius et la Fortune* (Paris: Gallimard, 1943) pp. 243-244.

3. On the ordeal, see G. Glotz, *L'Ordalie dans la Grèce primitive* (Paris: 1904), G. Glotz, *Études sociales et juridiques sur l'Antiquité grecque* (Paris: Hachette, 1906) pp. 81-84, p. 94; G. Sautel, "Les preuves dans le droit grec archaïque" pp. 125-126.

4. The guilty woman put herself in the hands of the marine divinities by throwing herself from a high rock. (Leap from the Leucadian rock.)

5. Foucault is referring here to the "theatrical realization of madness" tried out in the seventeenth century (see Z. Lusitanus, *Praxis medica*, 1637), described in *Histoire de la folie à l'âge classique*, pp. 400-405; *History of Madness*, pp. 329-334. "It was normal to accept the truth of the patient's delirium as if by challenge." The moral treatment of madness, often commented on by Foucault, corresponds rigorously to the inverse procedure of this theatricalization of delirium. [The French edition does not give a text or page reference for the quotation in this note, which does not appear in the section of *Histoire de la folie* the note cites. Moreover, it is not clear what the difficulty of autopsy due to the relations between truth and torture have to do with "theatrical realization of madness"; G.B.]

6. Hésiode, *Les Travaux et les Jours*, ed. and trans. P. Mazon (Paris: Les Belles Lettres, 1928), 35-39, p. 87; English translation by Dorothea Wender, Hesiod, *Works and Days*, in *Hesiod and Theognis* (Harmondsworth: Penguin, 1973) p. 60.

7. Hesiod is addressing his brother, who has despoiled him of part of his heritage. Ibid., Fr. p. 87; Eng. p. 60: "Come, let us settle our dispute at once,/And let our judge be Zeus, whose laws are just./...but you/Grabbed at the larger part and praised to heaven/The lords who love to try a case like that,/Eaters of bribes."

8. Epigraphic document made up of several inscriptions: the main one must date from 450; but in fact the legislation of Gortyn (Crete) must have remained almost in its archaic state: fragmentary inscriptions from the seventh and sixth centuries. See F. Bücheler and E. Zitelmann, *Das Recht von Gortyn* (Frankfurt/Main: J.D. Sauerländer, 1885)

9. L. Gernet, "Le temps dans les formes archaïques du droit," *Journal de psychologie normale et pathologique*, LIII (3), 1956, pp. 379-406.

10. The concealing and un-concealing character of truth, its ambiguous essence refers of course to Heidegger's *Alētheia*, and especially to his *Vom Wesen der Wahrheit* (Frankfurt/Main: V. Klosterman, 1943); French translation by A. De Waelhens and W. Biemel, *De l'essence de la vérité* (Paris: J. Vrin and Louvain: Neuwelaerts, 1948); English translation by John Sallis, "On the Essence of Truth" in Martin Heidegger, *Basic Writings*, ed. David Farrell Krell (London: Routledge Classics, 2010). But Foucault here takes up rather the description of the antithetical couple "*Alētheia/Lēthē*" developed by Detienne (who is also never cited in these lectures) in *Les Maîtres de vérité dans le Grèce archaïque*; *The Masters of Truth in Archaic Greece* in order to circumvent it [Heidegger's *Alētheia*] on the basis of a reconstruction of judicial practices. (See "Course context" below, pp. 266-278).

11. See L. Gernet, "Sur la notion de jugement en droit grec," *Archives d'histoire du droit oriental (AHDO)*, I, 1937, pp. 115-116.

12. R. Dareste, B. Haussoullier, and Th. Reinach, eds., *Recueil des inscriptions juridiques grecques* (Paris: E. Leroux, 1st series, fasc. 3, 1894) p. 352 et seq. Cited in Gernet, "Sur la notion de jugement en droit grec."

13. K. Latte, cited in Gernet, "Sur la notion de jugement en droit grec."

14. Amphictyons: name given to delegates from Greek cities brought together in political and religious confederation, the assemblies of which where held in the Spring at Delphi (and in Autumn at Anthela, near Thermopylae). The amphictyons had a military force at their disposal for punishing perjurers. See J. Gaudemet, *Les Institutions de l'Antiquité*, pp. 176-177.

15. G. Glotz, *Études sociales et juridiques sur l'Antiquité grecque*, p. 145 (quotation copied by Foucault in his documentation).

16. Hesiod, *Works and Days*: "Men will do injury/To better men by speaking crooked words/And adding lying oaths" (p. 64); "The god of Oaths/Runs faster than a crooked verdict" (p. 65).
17. These criticisms of the decisive judgment are cited by G. Sautel, "Les preuves dans le droit grec archaïque," p. 131. [The French gives the Aeschylus reference as verse 432, however in the English translation by Robert Fagles, *The Eumenides*, in Aeschylus, *The Oresteia* (Harmondsworth: Penguin, 1979) p. 250, the quotation is at verse 445: "Injustice, I mean, should never triumph thanks to oaths"; G.B.]
18. *Agōn* or *neikos*: struggle or discord.
19. *Dikaion*: the "just"; see Hesiod, *Works and Days*, 225; the decisive sentence according to E. Wolf, *Griechisches Rechtsdenken*, four volumes (Frankfurt/Main: Klostermann Verlag, 1950-1956).
20. *Dikaion kai alēthēs*: what is just and true; an equivalence of these words is found in the tragic authors (Hirzel, *Themis, Dike und Verwandtes*).
21. Herodotus, *Histories*, vol. I, Book 1, 97, trans. A. D. Godley (Cambridge, Mass., and London: Harvard University Press/William Heinemann Ltd., "Loeb Classical Library," 1981) pp. 126-129: "The number of those who came [to plead before Deioces] grew ever greater, for they heard that each case ended as accorded with the truth (*tas dikas apobainein kata to eon*)" cited with other examples by R. Hirzel, *Themis, Dike und Verwandtes*.
22. See H. Frisch, *Might and Right in Antiquity*. "*Dike*" I: *From Homer to the Persian Wars*, trans. C.C. Martindale (Copenhagen: Gyldendal Boghandel, 1949).
23. Aristote, *Politique*, II, 1274b 15-16: "There are the laws (*nomoi*) of Draco, established according to the existing constitution (*politeia*)"; English translation by B. Jowett, Aristotle, *Politics*, in *The Complete Works of Aristotle*, Vol. Two, p. 2022: "Draco has left laws, but he adapted them to a constitution which already existed." These *nomoi* (laws) or *thesmoi* (customs) are the object of historical controversy. See F. Ruzé, *Délibération et Pouvoir dans la Cité grecque de Nestor à Socrate* (Paris: Publications de la Sorbonne, 1997) pp. 342-345.
24. L. Gernet, "Sur la notion de jugement en droit grec," pp. 126-129.
25. Ibid., pp. 111-144.
26. L. Gernet, *Droit et Sociéte dans la Grèce ancienne* (Paris: Sirey [Publications de l'Institut de droit romain de l'Université de Paris, t.XIII], 1955, 1964²).
27. E. Wolf, *Griechisches Rechtsdenken*, pp. 85-94, cites in fact five uses: Book Nineteen, 55; Twenty-three, 539; Eighteen, 497; Sixteen, 542; Sixteen, 388.
28. H. Frisch, *Might and Right in Antiquity*, pp. 98-99, identifies all the uses of *dikē* in Hesiod.
29. Aratos, *Les Phénomènes*, an astronomical poem extremely popular throughout the Greek world. See M. Detienne, *Crise agraire et attitude religieuse chez Hésiod*, pp. 30-31.
30. E. Wolf, *Griechisches Rechtsdenken*, pp. 34-45.
31. See L. Gernet, *Droit et Société dans la Grèce ancienne*.
32. How not recall here Heidegger's comment on Nietzsche: "The primordial Greek conception of being solidifies into what up to the present is the most ordinary and taken for granted ... There is no point in examining here in detail this doctrine and its historical derivatives, which coincide with the principal stages of Western metaphysics"; M. Heidegger, *Nietzsche*, trans. P. Klossowski (Paris: Gallimard, 1971) vol. I, p. 420; English translation by David Farrell Krell, *Nietzsche. Volume III: The Will to Power as Knowledge and as Metaphysics* (New York: Harper & Collins, 1987) p. 58: "... the primordial Greek conception of beings congeals into something well known and taken for granted in the course of Western history to date ... We need not follow in detail this two-world doctrine and its historical transformations, which coincide with the main stages of Western metaphysics."
33. The first legislators, called by the Greeks tyrants, or "*patrons*," without any pejorative sense before the fifth century: Charondas was at Catana around 600, Zaleucus at Locris in Magna Graecia around 663, and Draco at Athens around 621. See H. Frisch, *Might and Right in Antiquity*, pp. 116-118, and M.I. Finley, *The Ancient Greeks: Introduction to their Life and Thought* (London: Chatto and Windus, 1963).
34. *Eunomia*: harmony, good administration. See Xenophon, *Oeconomicus*, trans. E.C. Marchant, in *Xenophon, IV* (Cambridge, Mass.: Harvard University Press, 1979) IX. 14, pp. 444-445; Herodotus, *Histories*, I, 65, pp. 76-77.
35. Solon, archon at Athens, 594-591. For Aristotle, democracy begins with Solon.

36. *Isonomia*: equality before the law, in fact: the law, real sovereign of the Athenian city, the Greeks often designate the democratic regime by this term. See G. Vlastos, "Isonomia" in *American Journal of Philology* (Baltimore), LXXIV, 1953, pp. 337-366.

According to E. Will, another of Foucault's sources, *isonomia* is not equality before the law but equal distribution (from *nemein*, to distribute); see E. Will, *Le Monde grec et l'Orient* (Paris: PUF, 1972), vol. I, p. 73. Foucault also consulted P. Lévêque and P. Vidal-Naquet, *Clisthène l'Athénien* (Paris: Les Belles Lettres, [Annales littéraires de l'Université de Besançon] 1964).

37. J.R. Dunkle, "The Greek tyrant and Roman political invective of the Late Republic," *Transactions and Proceedings of the American Philological Association* (Cleveland), XCVIII, 1967, pp. 151-171.

seven

# 10 FEBRUARY 1971

*Distribution of the word of truth according to* dikazein *and*
krinein. ∽ *Appearance of a Hesiodic* dikaion *as demand for
a just order.* ∽ *Role of the neighbor in the game of justice and
injustice.* ∽ *From ordeal truth to truth-knowledge (*savoir*).* ∽
*Contribution of Assyrian and Hittite forms of knowledge. Their
transformation in Greece.*

THE TEXTS FROM HESIOD and the later Gortyn legislation have
revealed a contrast between two types of juridical action, *krinein* and
*dikazein*:

— [a] formal contrast: in one case, the two parties swear on oath;
in the other case, the judge too utters the ritual formula of the
oath and imprecation;

— [b] contrast in the way the sentence is arrived at: in one case
through the mechanism of oaths; in the other by a decision of the
judge who is not bound by the oaths of the parties.

From one judicial practice to the other, the entire distribution of the
word of truth changes.

a—In *dikazein*, it is uttered by the litigants. Far from the necessarily contradictory character of these two assertions of truth creating a problem
and invalidating both of them, it is their conflict that, in the form of the
symbolic struggle, of the *agōn*, carries the day; the weightiest imprecation

necessarily triumphs. The sentence is not arrived at above the opposing discourses, it is brought about in and through the game of their
opposition. The judge does not weigh the value of proofs measured with
complete neutrality by a third and indifferent opinion, but the weight
of uttered assertions, in the game of their real clash.

b—In *krinein*, on the other hand, the word of truth is shifted from
the litigant to the judge. If we are to believe the ritual formula of the
Amphictyons,[1] it is for the judge to tell the truth and, if he does not
do so, to expose himself to the vengeance of the gods. He takes on the
ordeal form of the truth—test and torture—on his own account. As a
result, the parties' oaths tend to play no more than a declarative role:
the two litigants declare that they are instituting proceedings, that they
leave it up to the judge; that they declare in this way what their argument is, and then, the role of the judge's sentence will be to say which is
true, or more true, or better. The real opposition of two discourses is no
longer to be resolved by its own dynamic; a third instance is to choose
between them and say which is more valid. The truth is what is said of
one or the other from a point which is not that of either of them.

But a problem arises: when the judge exposes himself by swearing on
oath, what criterion does he use for the case in which his sentence is not
good? In the name of what does he make the division? To what rule is
this third discourse subject in order to arrive at its decision?

## A—THE APPEARANCE OF *DIKAION*

On what must the judge's word be modeled in *krinein*?

It is not the set of existing laws, as is proved by provisions which can
be found in the Gortyn law, or which we can infer from it. *Krinein* comes
into play where law is lacking, tradition is silent, and the role assigned
to the litigant can no longer be properly fulfilled.

It may be that this is in cases of inter-family disputes (where the tradition was not well established) (Gernet's hypothesis);[2] it may also be that
*krinein* comes into play when it is a matter of assessing an injury, a good, or
a share. In short, it is legitimate to suppose that the use of *krinein* is linked
to the development of a society in which there are increasingly extensive
economic relationships which extend beyond the family framework.

In any case, what guides the judge's sentences in *krinein*, what he is bound to by his oath, is not the law, *thesmos*,[3] but something else.

It is what is designated by the term *dikaion*.

The notion and the word do not exist in Homer. *Dikē* appears in the *Iliad* and the *Odyssey* (five times in the *Iliad*, more often in the *Odyssey*),[4] but with the meaning of:

—verdict or sentence (*Il.*, XVIII, 505; *Od.*, XI, 570);
—exercise of justice (*Il.*, XVI, 542);
—legal or lawful procedure, an action initiated, a complaint formulated according to the rules (*Il.*, XXII, 542);
—right and prerogative of each (*Il.*, XIX, 180);
—lawfulness of actions and sentences (*Il.*, XVI, 388).

So, in sum, *Dikē* is what is at stake in the procedure, the procedure itself and its compliance with the rules; the sentence, and what results from it. *Dikē* is not what governs judicial action, but rather its deployment, its game, and what is at stake in this game. What governs *dikē* is *thesmos*, i.e., custom—law and rule.

## B—HESIOD'S *DIKAION*

In Hesiod, on the other hand, the term *dikaion* appears linked to *Dikē* as its correlative.[5] This correlation *dikē-dikaion* appears quite clearly in the passage in *Works and Days* devoted to the happiness and misfortune of the City: a whole series of misfortunes will ensue if kings do not deliver justice according to the principle of *dikaion*. What are these misfortunes and how are they distributed?

a—As regards the actual nature of the misfortunes, they are the same as those that strike perjurers according to the old Homeric and traditional formulae of imprecation: the death of individuals, the sterility of women, cattle, and crops; war and disasters:

"Men die, women cease to give birth, and households wither, on the counsel of Olympian Zeus. Sometimes the son of Kronos will destroy a city wall, a vast army, or wreck their fleet in the middle of the sea" (*Works and Days*, 243-247).[6]

b—On the other hand, the distribution of these traditional misfortunes changes. In the sacramental formula it is the perjurer himself who pays, or his descendants and race. The vengeance of Zeus, guarantee of oaths, follows the same lines as human retributions. Blood, *genos*, race define the limits, the privileged points of application, the lines of communication of punishments. In Hesiod, the whole town is the victim of the injustice of its kings; family kinship does not indicate in advance the possible victims; the State or the City envelops them all without distinction.

"Often an entire town suffers for the fault of just one who reigns and plots the crime" (*Works and Days*, 240-241).[7]

"The people must pay for the madness of its kings, who, with grim intentions, pervert their rulings with crooked expressions" (*Works and Days*, 262-263).[8]

c—But the theology of this punishment is also partially modified. In Homer, when there was perjury, Zeus, his sovereignty having been scorned, took revenge directly, even if he happened to delay the day of settlement.

In Hesiod, when kings do not judge well, *Dikē* serves as an intermediary; it is *Dikē* who is offended, who leaves Earth and, taking refuge on Zeus's lap, requests his vengeance.[9] First of all, bad judgments provoke the absence of *Dikē*; and then, secondarily, the insult to *Dikē* provokes the anger of Zeus.

The discourse and practice of justice no longer deal directly with Zeus, who sends decrees, guarantees oaths, and punishes perjurers; they come into contact with him through the intermediary of *Dikē*. A strange goddess: the correlative of human practices, since their bad judgments drive her away, but because she is absent, bad judgments multiply.

d—But even more than this different theological causality, a whole new system of correlations is set up. The new system has a number of characteristics:

—A whole set of economic conducts, like dishonest purchases, fraud on goods, are assimilated to perjury, false oaths, crooked sentences, and impiety. It is as if Hesiod was calling for the same sacred guarantees around transactions as around judicial oaths; it is as if he was seeking to give this behavior the same juridical-religious structure as disputes and litigations.

"Wealth must not be robbed ... One may gain an immense fortune through violence ... one may conquer it with one's tongue, as often happens, when gain deceives man's mind and shamelessness gets the better of honor. But the gods then are quick to annihilate the guilty, and to ruin his house and his wealth soon after. The crime is the same for whoever mistreats a suppliant, a guest ... " (*Works and Days*, 320-327).[10]

—The system involves a new partner, who plays an ambiguous role in this game of justice and reward, injustice and punishment. This new element is the neighbor, *geitōn*. On the one hand, the neighbor is like a form of abundance, a good harvest: a gift of the gods, a reward offered for piety and observance of the rules.

"A bad neighbor is a calamity, just as a good neighbor is a real treasure. His lot is good who finds a good neighbor" (*Works and Days*, 346-347).[11]

But, on the other hand, the neighbor is a source of retribution: he rewards and enriches, he spreads misfortune:

"Your cow will not die, if you do not have a bad neighbor ... what you take from someone, without his consent, heeding only shamelessness ... turns his heart to ice against you" (*Works and Days*, 349-360).[12]

—If the neighbor is in this ambiguous position, it is insofar as he is an indispensable element in the system of exchange. Exchange which, as in Homeric society, has the form of gift and counter-gift; but here, imbalance (giving more than one has received) is no longer a matter of prestige, but of calculation and measure:

"Measure exactly what you borrow from your neighbor and give back to him the same in equal measure, and even more if you can, so that you will be sure of his help in time of need" (*Works and Days*, 349-352).[13]

Justice takes shape in the measured system of services, debts, and their repayment, instead of exposure to the both imminent and indefinite vengeance of Zeus.

—Finally, this just and measurable order of debt is linked to another, also measurable order, which is that of the seasons, weather, harvests, stars, and days. The relation between the order of neighborliness and debts, on the one hand, and the order of work and days, on the other, is established through the contrast between begging and subsistence.

—If you do not give to your neighbor, you will get nothing from him when in need: you will not have what you need to sow at the right moment, hence poverty.

—If you do not sow, if you do not labor at the right time, you will be reduced, not to the system of measured debt, but to that of demand without compensation, that is to say, of begging.

Work... "if you do not wish to go one day, with your wife and children, with troubled heart, begging from neighbor to neighbor, without any of them caring. Twice, maybe three times you will succeed; but, if you bother them more, you will get nothing" (*Works and Days*, 399-403).[14]

The order of things, the time of work, favorable seasons, and good days are the kind of elements on which just conduct must base itself; just as this natural order, in turn, will spontaneously reward just conduct (see the last verses of *Works and Days*):

"Happy and fortunate is he who, knowing what concerns the days, does his work without offending the Immortals, following heavenly advice and avoiding all wrong" (926-828).[15]

Let's not forget that the relation between Zeus's decree, the regular order of moments, just retribution, and the game of borrowing and debt repaid without conflict is formulated in the *Theogony*:[16]

"[Zeus] married the shining Equity (*Thēmin*) who was mother of the Hours (*Horas*)—Discipline (*Eunomiēn*), Justice (*Dikēn*), and blooming Peace (*Eirēnēn*), who watch over the fields [*erga*[17] the text says] of mortal men ... " (901-903).

Finally, the just, on which *krinein* rests and which must serve as immanent rule to this practice of justice, is therefore completely different from what governs the old justice of the decisive oath: the latter knew only the formal rule (*thēmis*); now, *krinein* must rest on a justice which is:

α—linked to the very order of the world (and not just to the anger of the Gods);

β—linked to the time of cycles and restitutions (time of the promised return, return of the debt and return of the seasons, passage to the same point and no longer to the more or less delayed imminence of divine vengeance);

γ—linked to the promise, to the expiry date, the moment when the debt must be repaid;

δ—linked finally to measure: measure of temporal cycles, of the quantity and value of things.

In the system of challenge-truth, time was the time of the lightning event, the thunderbolt event, which strikes without one being able to avoid it, but at a moment which cannot be predicted: there is no danger of Zeus's vengeance ever failing, but one does not know when it will take place. Moreover, payments, rewards, and retaliations always take the form of imbalance: when Agamemnon makes peace with Achilles, he offers him much more than he had taken from him.

In the system of judgment, restitutions are made in the form of balance and measure, and the events take place, must take place, at moments that are well-defined in advance and can be exactly measured. These two systems of measure are not impervious to each other since, as Hesiod says, if one gives back a bit more than the measure, it is so that one will be able to ask again in due course.

These four elements of the measure and of "a little more," of the expiry date and of "again," structure *dikaion* which constitutes the immanent rule of *krinein*.

We can see that underlying the appearance of *dikaion* is a whole new set of economic relationships which call for it and make it possible: peasant debt (with what this implies regarding the separation of *genos* and collective property, the formation of a small individual property, overpopulation also, and the absence of money and standard of measure).

*Works and Days*, poem of this peasant debt which the return of the seasons and fixed times pays off or renews, and which measures, in the absence of money, make uncertain. The calendar and the measure: the cycle of time and the monetary symbol is what is required by peasant debt; and it is on this that *krinein* must be structured.

## C—THE CORRELATION *DIKAION-ALĒTHĒS*[18]

The decisive oath is replaced (or at least begins to be replaced) by the judgment-measure. At the same time, the truth-challenge, truth by ordeal is replaced by truth-knowledge. (The truth which strikes down or protects. The truth which one knows.)

1. In fact, for judgment to be just, for *krinein* to be part of the order of *dikaion* and be governed by it, it is necessary:

—On the one hand, that it take into account, that it is based on the exact return of time, the exact measure of things. It's not just a matter of remembering the rules, of keeping *Thēmis* in one's memory. One has to remember seasons and times; one has to have measured the goods. One has to have made this measurement and one has to remember it.

Memory of a different type: in the justice of the oath-decision, it was a matter of keeping the rules, customs, and decrees of Zeus in one's memory. And they had to be remembered at the right time in order to apply them on the right occasion. So: this is an exegetical memory.

In *krinein*, a new memory is needed, a memory which has to keep the measure over time so that the return of time restores the same measures. This is an accounting memory which does not have to remember the occasion, but has to preserve the identical. Writing.

—On the other hand, for the sentence to be just it has to manifest the truth, to say both what must be (how reparations are to be made) and what is (identical elements, dates which recur, the return of time).

Here again there is an important transformation: in the decisive oath, a single formulation asserted the truth, carried the day, exposed the formulator and marked him out him to the gods' vengeance. In the judgment-measure, we do still have a tight formula which says both what is and what must be, but we can see that the elements are not the same:

—the judgment measure no longer indicates the protagonist, it discloses things;
—the judgment-measure imposes a decision, it is a sovereign utterance.

Disclosure of the truth and exercise of sovereignty are interdependent and jointly replace the indication of the agonist and the risk he voluntarily accepts.

So we discover three fundamental characteristics of *krinein*:

—memory of the identical and of its measure,
—disclosure of the truth
—exercise of sovereignty.

We are already in the space in which the Sophists and Plato struggle with each other.

2. But another characteristic is to be noted: this is that *dikaion kai alēthēs*, which serves as rule for the sentence, extends far beyond its location in judicial practice. If the decision of justice is just because it remembers the measure and time, then any other speech that remembers them will also be just speech. And in a more general way, any action and any person who remembers the measure and time will be just.

Two consequences of this:

—It is no longer only the king of justice, but every man who has to be just. He will be just insofar as he will have paid attention, pricked up his ears, and kept what is just in his memory. Justice is not only what is said, it is what is listened to; and the just man is not only the one who utters the good sentence, he is the man, every man who has listened to justice.

"For you, Perses, think about this advice; listen then to justice (*dikēs epakoue*), leave violence behind for ever" (*Works and Days*, 274-275).[19]

The punctual debtor, the laborer who does each thing in its time, the person who knows what to do and what not to do at the right time, is someone who, without even having to hold the staff of sovereignty, is a just man. He should even be the model and norm for whoever has to dispense justice.

"That man is complete who, after reflection, always sees (*noēsē*) for himself what will be best later and for always" (*Works and Days*, 293-294).[20]

"Observe the measure: appropriateness is the supreme quality in everything" (*Works and Days*, 694).[21]

—But if, on the one hand, any man may be just when he knows how to listen to the true word of measure and order, conversely, the true cycle of things, their real proportions, the return of the calendar, is justice itself in the distribution of things.[22] According to Hesiod, Zeus sees to it that the wealth of harvests exactly rewards men's work. And he even allows them to make up for their forgetfulness. If one has sown too late, one may nevertheless have a good harvest, for Zeus has so wished it ...

And we still find this theme of the just world for a long time after in the "philosophical" poetry or prose of the sixth and seventh centuries.

Anaximander: Things render justice to each other.
     Heraclitus: If the sun were to stray from its path, the Erinyes would pursue it and chastise it.

*Dikaion*, as it takes shape in the practice of justice, extends far beyond it: it becomes the rule of daily life; it becomes organization of the world. It prescribes what is to be done every day and traces the course of things. We have to have listened to it in order to act rightly; but it is what we see when we look at things.

We have a relation to it in the form of knowledge. Justice is no longer ordered so much by reference to an asserted and risky truth; rather it is linked to a truth we know. Being just is no longer merely applying the rules and risking the truth. It is not forgetting to know the truth; it is not forgetting the truth we know.

This is why Hesiod himself can also deliver a discourse of justice. Certainly, he does not deliver a sentence, but he gives advice. Advice to kings of justice, advice to a peasant like Perses. He can tell of the justness of justice; he can pronounce sentences on sentences, opinions on decisions. He can judge the judges. *Krinein*, suddenly, no doubt at the very moment of its birth, acquires a breadth in which sententious poetry, statement of nature, and political demand are not yet distinguished from each other.

It is a discourse which has two sides throughout its development: that of justice and that of the truth. Right at the start of the poem, Hesiod says to Zeus: "May justice rule your decrees! For myself, I shall tell Perses some truths" (*Works and Days*, 9-10).[23]

3. But a problem arises. What is this truth in the form of knowledge that *krinein* needs, on what is it based? Following Hesiod, but also his successors, it is the truth of days and dates; of favorable times; of the movements and conjunctions of the stars; of climates, winds, and seasons: that is to say, it is a whole body of cosmological knowledge. It is also the truth of the genesis of the gods and the world,[24] of their order of succession and precedence, of their organization as system of the world. Theogony. Knowledge of the calendar and of the origin; knowledge of cycles and of the beginning.[25]

Now these two types of knowledge have a well-known historical and geographical location: they were formed and developed in the great empires of the Euphrates and the Near East, in the Hittites, the Assyrians, in Babylon.[26] And their formation there is linked directly with the form of political power.

In fact: (a) the structure of the State and the administrative system of these regimes involved keeping rigorously to an official calendar which indicated the good and bad days for decisions, works, battles, and sowing; (b) they also involved the measure of quantities and a system of equivalences for raising taxes and, at least, services and fees;[27] finally (c) royal power, as both political and magical-religious structure was, on a set date, and in accordance with an identical Indo-European ritual, regularly reestablished by ceremonies which included the recital of the genealogy, of the exploits of ancestors and the king himself. A sort of new beginning on the basis of the beginning. This was the revivifying epic of royal power.

The three great types of knowledge developed by the Assyrians—observational and magical knowledge of days and stars; technical knowledge of quantities and measures; mythical-religious knowledge of origins—were linked to the exercise of power in a society in which the State apparatus was relatively developed.

Now it is to these types of knowledge that *dikaion*, on which *krinein* in turn is based, appeals. We know the meaning of this appeal:

(1) demand for a political power (or for an *analogon* of political power) over and above the power exercised by traditional chiefs;

(2) assimilation by individuals of all the powers linked to this knowledge;

(3) reference, beyond the Dorian invasion, to earlier structures which remained external.[28]

But we should note straightaway that in the seventh to sixth centuries there really is a return and reappearance of older mythical forms; if writing, obliterated at the time of the Dorian invasion, regains strength, if a whole network of cosmological and magical correspondences are transplanted from the East, this knowledge immediately takes a new form. It is no longer socially located in those who hold political power, exercise it by delegation, or serve as its instrument.

In Greece it will no longer be the knowledge of the functionaries, scribes,[29] accountants, and astrologers of power; it will be the knowledge every man needs in order to be just and to demand justice for all. Knowledge moves from the exercise of power to the control of justice.

And at the same time this means that it is no longer linked to the secret (or at least tends to be separated from the form of the secret) and following a necessary line it tends, no less than justice, to be placed in the public arena.

Finally, we should note that these three major directions of oriental knowledge are, up to a certain point, what will organize Greek and Western knowledge.

(1) knowledge of the origin, of genesis and succession: cosmological, philosophical, and historical knowledge;

(2) knowledge of quantities, of accounts and measures: mathematical knowledge, physical knowledge;

(3) knowledge of the event, occasion, moment: technical knowledge of agronomy, medicine; magical knowledge.[30]

NB: The first two ultimately organized Western science: origin and measurement; succession and quantity; the order of time and numerical order.*

On the other hand, knowledge of the moment has been gradually marginalized: Stoic logic, magical knowledge; the medical tradition which leads to clinical medicine, which replaces the knowledge of the moment, of the medical opportunity, with the spatialization of pathogenic seats.

[It is in] military, political, and revolutionary strategy that knowledge of the event, moment, and opportunity is developed.

It could be that psychoanalysis has...†

---

* On a preparatory sheet without reference, M.F. notes:
"It is from the fifth century that the world of geometers and astronomers split off from the world of the city. The physicist of the fifth century is a pan-Hellenic figure who, as we see in the example of Anaxagoras, precedes the Sophist down this path, coming up against traditional religions as well as civic beliefs... A universe of geometry thus appeared, that of a qualitatively undifferentiated space that no longer has anything in common with civic space." (The source could be G. Vlastos, idea already mentioned by Nietzsche.)

† The usual continuation and conclusion of the development of each session is missing. The notes of Hélène Politis clarify the sense of the reference to psychoanalysis (see Lacan on the interval (*delai*) and the moment in the development of logical structures).

1. See above, p. 90, and p. 98 note 14.
2. L. Gernet, *Recherches sur le développement de la pensée juridique et morale en Grèce* (Paris: E. Leroux, 1917), p. 449; quoted by G. Sautel, "Les preuves dans le droit grec archaïque," pp. 147-160.
3. *Thesmos* is not originally the written law or *nomos*, but a custom established either by a college of magistrates, or by a single legislator (Draco is a thesmothete, Solon a nomothete). But Solon employs the two terms as synonyms. *Thesmos* disappears in the fifth century. See P. Vinogradov, *Outlines of Historical Jurisprudence* (London: Humphrey Milford, 1920) Vol. I, p. 73 and p. 75; J. Gaudemet, *Les Institutions de l'Antiquité*, pp. 85-94.
4. H. Frisch, *Might and Right in Antiquity*, pp. 46-47; also E. Wolf, *Griechisches Rechtsdenken*, pp. 85-94.
5. See H. Frisch, *Might and Right in Antiquity*, pp. 98-99.
6. Fr., Hésiode, *Les Travaux et les Jours*, p. 95; Eng., Hesiod, *Works and Days*, p. 66: "...the people die./Their wives are barren, and their villages/Dwindle, according to the plan of Zeus./At other times the son of Kronos will/Destroy their army, or will snatch away/Their city wall, or all their ships at sea."
7. Ibid., Fr. p. 95 (Foucault has "reigns" for the French translator's "strays"); Eng. p. 66: "But there are some who till the fields of pride/And work at evil deeds; ... /And often, all the city suffers for/Their wicked schemes ... "
8. Ibid., Fr. p. 96; Eng. p. 67: "Until the city suffers for its lords/Who recklessly, with mischief in their minds, Pervert their judgements crookedly."
9. Ibid., 256-262, Fr. pp. 95-96; Eng. pp. 66-67.
10. Ibid., Fr. p. 98; Eng. pp. 68-69: Money should not be seized ... / ...If a man gets wealth/By force of hands or through his lying tongue,/As often happens, when greed clouds his mind/ And shame is pushed aside by shamelessness,/Then the gods blot him out and blast his house/ And soon his wealth deserts him. Also he/who harms a guest or suppliant ... "
11. Ibid., Fr. p. 99; Eng. p. 69: "It is a curse/To have a worthless neighbour; equally,/A good one is a blessing; he who is/So blest possesses something of great worth."
12. Ibid., Fr. p. 99; Eng. pp. 69-70: "No cow of yours will stray away if you/Have watchful neighbours ... / ...but if/A man forgets his shame and takes something,/ ...his [the victim's] heart grows stiff and cold."
13. Ibid., Fr. p. 99; Eng. p. 69: "...Measure carefully/When you must borrow from your neighbour, then,/Pay back the same, or more, if possible,/And you will have a friend in time of need."
14. Ibid., Fr. p. 101; Eng. p. 71: "...go to work! ... / ...don't let it be/That you should take your children and your wife/And beg, with downcast spirit, for your food/From neighbours who refuse to care. You may/Succeed two times or three. But after that,/You'll bother them in vain, and all your words/Will come to nothing ... "
15. Ibid., Fr. p. 116; Eng. p. 86: "He is truly blest/And rich who knows these things and does his work,/Guiltless before the gods, and scrupulous,/Observing omens and avoiding wrong."
16. Hésiode, *Théogonie*, ed. and trans. P. Mazon (Paris: Les Belles Lettres, 1928) p. 64; English translation by Dorothea Wender, Hesiod, *Theogony* in *Hesiod and Theognis* (Harmondsworth: Penguin Books, 1973) p. 52: "And shining Themis was his second wife./She bore the Horae: Order, blooming Peace,/And Justice, who attend the works of men,/ ... " See E. Wolf, *Griechisches Rechtsdenken*.
17. Foucault emphasizes Mazon's translation of *erga*. Vernant indicates about fifty occurrences of the term in *Works and Days* with the meaning, essentially, of "agricultural labor": see M. Detienne and J.-P. Vernant, *La Cuisine du Sacrifice* (Paris: Gallimard, 1979). Ch. H. Kahn, in *Anaximander and the Origins of Greek Cosmology* (New York: Columbia University Press, 1960) pp. 191-193, recalls that the Hours are the seasons that will become the astronomical Hours, sisters of the *Moïrae*, the Fates of the human species.
18. A sheet entitled "On justice and truth" gives three references: R. Hirzel, *Themis, Dike und Verwandtes*, pp. 108-109; V. Ehrenberg, *Die Rechtsidee im frühen Griechentum* (Leipzig: S. Hirzel, 1921) p. 59; and G. Glotz, *L'Ordalie dans la Grèce primitive*.
19. Hésiode, *Travaux*, p. 96; Hesiod, *Works and Days*, p. 67: "But you, O Perses, think about these things;/Follow the just, avoiding violence." Perses is Hesiod's brother, in favor of whom

the "kings" of Thespiae, no doubt venal "gift eaters," had unequally shared out the paternal inheritance. The dispute runs throughout the *Works and Days* (see above, p. 98 note 7) along with Hesiod's anger.

20. Ibid., Fr. p. 97; Eng. p. 68: "That man is best who reasons for himself,/Considering the future."
21. Ibid., Fr. p. 111; Eng. 81: "Preserve a sense of right proportion, for/Fitness is all-important, in all things"
22. See J.-P. Vernant, "Travail et nature dans la Grèce ancienee," *Journal de psychologie normale et pathologique*, LII (1), 1955, pp. 18-38; English translation, "Work and Nature in Ancient Greece" in J.-P. Vernant, *Myth and Thought Among the Greeks* (London: Routledge & Kegan Paul, 1983) pp. 248-270.
23. Hésiode, *Travaux*, p. 86; Hesiod, *Works and Days*, p. 59: "Hear, Zeus, and set our fallen laws upright/And may my song to Perses tell the truth." The French Belles Lettres edition points out that analogous words are found in the Prelude of the *Theogony* (28): Hesiod sings only the truth.
24. Comparing with Detienne's analysis: "In the *Works and Days*, we thus find a double instantiation of *Alētheia*. First, there is the *Alētheia* pronounced by the poet in the name of the Muses... Second, we find the *Alētheia* possessed by the farmer of Ascra himself. In the latter case, 'truth' is explicitly defined as a 'nonforgetfulness' of the poet's precepts." M. Detienne, *The Masters of Truth in Archaic Greece*, p. 50.
25. W. Jaeger, *The Theology of the Early Greek Philosophers* (Oxford: Clarendon Press, 1947).
26. G. Vlastos, "Equality and justice in early Greek cosmology," *Classical Philology*, XLII, 1947, July; B.L. Van der Waerden, *Science Awakening*, trans. A. Dresden (New York: Oxford University Press, 1954); O. Neugebauer, *The Exact Science in Antiquity* (Copenhagen, Munksgaard/ London: Oxford University Press, 1951).
27. Marshall Clagett, *Greek Science in Antiquity* (New York: Collier Books, 1955, 2nd ed. 1963).
28. See Nietzsche's idea according to which the political chorus called for a coryphaeus, to wit the tyrant, who prepares the advent of democracy. For Nietzsche, the sixth century was the great revelation of the oriental hour that took possession of the Greek people.
29. See Marshall Clagett, *Greek Science in Antiquity*.
30. Ch. H. Kahn, *Anaximander and the Origins of Greek Cosmology*, pp. 208-209; J.-P. Vernant, "Geometry and Spherical Astronomy in the First Greek Cosmology" in *Myth and Thought Among the Greeks*, pp. 176-189 (see below, p. 147 note 9).

# eight

## 17 February 1971

> *Hesiodic* dikaion *(continuation).* ∿ *Tyranny and money: two borrowings from the East.* ∿ *The Greek transformation: displacement of the truth from ordeal to knowledge; movement of knowledge from the domain of power to that of justice.* ∿ *Recurrence of two oneiric figures: Saint Anthony and Faust.* ∿ *Agrarian crisis and political transformations in the seventh and sixth centuries.* ∿ *Hoplites and peasants. Craft industry.* ∿ *Homeric truth-challenge and Eastern knowledge-power transformed into truth-knowledge.*

GOING BACK OVER TWO points:

1. The nature of this *dikaion* that Hesiod speaks about and asserts against the injustice of the gift eating kings:

> a—It is the justice of exact returns: giving back exactly what one has received and on the appointed day.
> b—It is the justice of the common measure: one must measure what one loans or borrows in order to receive or give back an exact equality (with a very slight difference: giving back a little more so as to be able to borrow again).
> c—It is the justice of consent and mutual agreement: it is not the justice of the rule which is applied; it is that of the voluntary understanding one comes to with one's neighbor and which implies that both use the same measures and follow the same calendar.

d—Finally, it is justice which accords with the order of the world and which the gods have prescribed: it is justice which observes timeliness, propitious moments, daily prescriptions of the auspicious and the inauspicious.

Such justice is very different from the justice at work in the Homeric type of dispute:

—It is not linked to the exercise of a certain sovereignty and to the moment of its ritual exercise; it is a justice of every day which is implemented by every man when he works and exchanges.

—It does not consist in remembering immemorial rules which have to resolve a conflict and reestablish equality; it consists in remembering quantities, moments, and gestures which have to preserve equality.

—It does not involve a truth-challenge which one side throws down and the other picks up; it assumes a truth, in the form of observation and measurement; in the form of the opportunity grasped and equality observed.[1]

—Finally, it assumes an equivalence between the justice of Zeus and the truth of men, for if human justice consists in following the vein of the truth of things—the exact order of the stars, days, and seasons—this order is nothing other than the decree of Zeus and his sovereign law.

Hesiod began *Works and Days* by [invoking] Zeus: "May justice rule your decrees! For myself, I shall tell Perses some truths" (so that he be just). The truth of the world as visible form between these two justices (*Works and Days*, 9-10).[2]

In comparison with the justice exercised with sovereign power by traditional chiefs, the kings of justice, by the powerful of crooked judgments, Hesiodic justice, going from the decree of Zeus to the order of the world, and from this to peasant vigilance and exactness, to the interplay of good understanding and debts repaid, calls for a whole transfer of sovereignty. Calls for it, but does not record it, for at the time of *Works and Days* justice is institutionalized only in the hands of the kings of justice. The justice Hesiod calls for in his song is a justice organized around a new

knowledge (that of the calendar and natural chronologies), a new practice of measurement (of exchange, of restitution, something like money),
and a new distribution of sovereignty. The search for a new type of political authority, for a monetary measure, and for a knowledge of things and
time manifest themselves interdependently in Hesiod's texts.

2. Now the Greeks find the model for this knowledge, monetary measure, and political form in the East: in the Empires and States of the
Euphrates, of Lydia, of the Mediterranean coast of Asia.[3] (Borrowings
and resurgences).

But the important thing is what, in a disorganized manner and with
some essential modifications, becomes of these borrowings from the
seventh to the sixth century.

As regards political form, the Greeks borrow from Asia only the general forms of an absolute power imposed on the aristocracy of birth and
on the polycephalous power of the *genē*. But this form of politics will
be transitory and precarious in the Greeks; it will have a role in the
destruction of the aristocracy, in the foundation of the City-State, but
having played this role, "tyranny" will disappear.[4]

With regard to money, Greece will borrow its technique from Lydia;
but the monetary standard in the Asian Empires is above all an instrument in the hands of the State enabling taxes and fees to be established
(commercial use being secondary). Greece will no doubt make use of
money for the first purpose (in the epoch of tyranny), but then, very
quickly, above all for commercial purposes and in its relations with the
colonies. In short, the knowledge Greece borrows from the East was
originally linked to the State apparatus.

The establishment of a precise calendar was necessary for tax collec-
tion, the development of irrigation works, fixing the times of sowing
and harvest, and so for determining when war could be waged. (At the
center of this, the problem of intercalation: the lunar calendar determined the months, but, since the twelve lunar months did not completely fill the solar year, there was a constant gap which was made up
for gradually, and then in one go, with the intercalation of a thirteenth
month.)

At the level of an extended empire, these calculations and the decisions which followed from them could only be centralized. Cosmo- or

theogonic knowledge was also linked to political power. Every four years, royal sovereignty had to be reinforced by magical–religious ceremonies: by reciting the king's genealogy, the exploits of the ancestors or god he reincarnates, by recounting the foundation of the world and the monarchy, one restored power to the king. The song is true inasmuch as it gives vigor to political sovereignty.

Linked to political power and the State apparatus in these two ways, knowledge is quite naturally located in the hands of functionaries: knowledge is a State service and political instrument. Hence its necessarily secret character. It does not have to circulate or be widespread. It is linked directly to the possession of power.

And this immediately secret character of knowledge manifests itself in a certain distribution of the written and the oral. The complex, difficult to handle pictographic writing of Assyrian tablets, which serves only to note results, tables, accounts, the processes being passed on orally and doubtless in an esoteric way among the brotherhoods of scribes.

Now this is where the Greek transformation[5] comes in to play. Knowledge will be separated from the State apparatus and from the direct exercise of power; it will be detached from political sovereignty in its immediate application to become the correlative of the just, of the *dikaion* as natural, divine, and human order.

The knowledge that was the secret of effective power will become the order of the manifest, measured world, effectuated daily and for all men in its truth. And the truth that was memory of ancestral rule, challenge, and accepted risk, will take the form of knowledge revealing and conforming to the order of things.

There were two correlative transformations therefore: one revealing the truth as knowledge of things, time, and order, and the other shifting knowledge from the domain of power to the region of justice.

This is undoubtedly one of the important phenomena in the formation of Greek civilization. On the one hand, judicial practice, linked to political and priestly functions, and thereby reserved for a small number of individuals, traditional chiefs, becomes linked to the truth. It ceases to be exclusively a matter of decision and the activation of traditional rules, preserved in memory, recalled at the right moment by sages, experts, and exegetes, and applied in the proper way by kings of justice. Justice now tends to be organized entirely around the truth.

In its foundation, in its first word, justice will have to be law, *nomos*,[6] the law of men, which will truly be their insuperable law only if it is in conformity with the order of the world.

The decision of justice will have to be right (*juste*), the sentence will have to express *dikaion* and *alēthēs*, the just and the true, that which is fitted to the order of the world and things, and which restores this very order when it has been disturbed.

Henceforth, justice hangs on the truth and is controlled by it. And the truth itself is the exact order, the correct distribution, the cycle, and the rigorous return.

But on the other hand, and just as important, the knowledge which was linked to power, the knowledge which, in the Asiatic States, was the instrument, and up to a point the condition of its exercise, will now be linked to *dikaion*. Its primary role will be to ensure relations of justice, to help restore order, to put things back in their place and time. Knowledge will not be produced [in order] to triumph, master, and govern, so much as to enable and even constrain repayment of what is due. To be in the truth will be more to be in the just than to be in power.

Of course, this is only a sort of gradient. The justice-truth linkage and knowledge-power break will never be definitively established; they will constantly be called into question. But broadly speaking we can say that the standpoint of truth-challenge or [that] of knowledge-power (the former in Greece, the latter in the archaic East) will be rejected by the West. And the two figures of the just, one of whom is foreign to the truth, and the other able only to exercise unlimited arbitrary power, both belong to the persistent and always repressed dreams of the West.

These two oneiric, desired figures, present but always as extremes, are those of Saint Anthony and, opposite, Faust.[7] Saint Anthony, the just without truth, the innocent, absolute justice of the heart in the mire of non-knowledge, and who, by that very fact is prey to all the disorders of the world in the form of temptation. And the other, Faust, the man who, having arrived at the summit of knowledge, sees it multiplied in the infinite power which is added to it. This power is Mephisto; he seems to subject himself scrupulously to Faust's great knowledge,[8] he makes himself out to be its servant. Mephisto is then like the faithful power of knowledge. But the Western fable has it that the thread of desire and innocence breaks the alliance between this power and this knowledge.

## A—THE AGRARIAN CRISIS IN THE SEVENTH AND SIXTH CENTURIES

The successive waves of the Dorian invasion left the land divided up into unequal but inalienable portions. In principle they could be neither sold nor seized.[9] At the most they could revert by escheat or be abandoned. Now this inequality became, and no doubt quite quickly, more pronounced and gave rise to violent conflicts:

1. Impoverishment of the poorest through demographic pressure. Hence: bringing barren land into cultivation; clearing wooded areas, short term irrigation without overall planning, since there was no State organization, entailing a reduction of the average productivity of cultivated land. And difficulties of uniting together, the need to borrow.
2. With regard to the richest, they too, of course, had the same problems of the dividing up of properties at times of succession. This is shown by the measures taken in various places to prevent it: Philolaus, a Bacchiade,[10] émigré at Thebes, introduced laws on "procreation," or at any rate on succession. In Corinth itself, another Bacchiade (Pheidon) took measures to preserve the number of properties and the number of citizens.[11]

But [the richest*] responded in another way: by passing gradually from cattle rearing (no doubt the privileged form of agriculture among [them†]) to the cultivation of olive trees and the production of oil, a transportable commodity.

The change of the Greek dietary regimen (from a meat diet, in the Homeric epoch, to a vegetable diet) bears witness to this impoverishment and transformation.[12]

Now this situation was only accentuated by the common solution adopted by rich and poor to remedy it: the movement of individuals and colonization.

Later, in order to justify alliances, territorial or financial demands, taxes and tributes, colonization was presented as the collective work

---

\* Manuscript: they.
† Manuscript: the rich.

of the cities themselves. M. Nilsson[13] supposes that colonists from different regions joined together in a port (like Corinth or Miletus) and arranged with a ship owner to go to settle either on land for cultivating wheat or possibly in a commercial staging post. In any case, being essentially agricultural, the effect of the colony was to stimulate the exchange of oil from the home country and wheat from these new lands. Hence a new impoverishment of the poorest.

Two consequences of this:

1. Despite the demographic relief resulting from colonization, the situation of the poor worsens. Of course, lots cannot be sold or seized. But due to the personal character of the undertaking in pre-law Greece, due also to the both symbolic and substantial relationship between landowner and property in cases of insolvency, either the land was compromised (a sixth of its revenues taken by the creditor) or the debtor was reduced into slavery.[14]

2. We can see then what [the poor*] require as means of defense against this constant deterioration:

a—The establishment of a system for calculating time which would enable them to know when was the best time to harvest and sow. And when to pay their debt at the suitable expiry date.

In fact, the religious calendar which broke up the year was a lunar calendar which did not coincide with the solar calendar and the system of solstices and seasons. Hence the search for an astral calendar and a table of meteorological probabilities, such as we find in *Works and Days*.

b—The establishment of a system of measurement enabling one to assess the harvest, maintain a certain rate of exchange, and calculate what is owing. A new system, all the more necessary for the peasants since hitherto measurement was according to units like the heads of livestock, or gold or bronze objects, which were possessed by the rich.

c—The establishment of a new form of power protecting the property of the poor and preventing the violence of the rich (and all

---

* Manuscript: what they.

the assaults they may make on the inalienable property or life of the free man ).

Simultaneously and interdependently, the poorest classes look for a form of knowledge, a system of measurement, and a form of sovereignty. Now the historical problem is how, in the state of deterioration in which it found itself, the poor class of peasants was able to obtain the constitution of this knowledge, the establishment of this system of measurement, and the formation of a new type of sovereignty. At this point, the peasantry no longer has allies, there is no middle class of merchants being formed. There are only two classes.

## B—THE ARMY

What enabled the small peasantry to resist and to win in part are two factors partially linked to each other.

1. The first is one of the developments of iron age civilization.

The Dorians brought with them the technology of iron. But for a long time the techniques were of rather minor significance. Now colonization opened up new metallurgic resources. And above all new techniques for working ore. Hence a considerable fall in the cost of iron objects. And the possibility of a both robust and economic armament. Appearance of a new type of army composed of foot soldiers holding a shield on the left arm, and a javelin or sword in the right hand. Which entails a different strategy: that of the closed front of warriors well aligned alongside each other and in considerable numbers. In contrast with the single combats of chariot drivers.

The new strategy no doubt upset the force relations not only between cities, but within these political units themselves.

a—Between cities: at the beginning of the seventh century the force relations between groups, which can hardly be called cities, are modified in terms of the hoplite strategy. The war between Chalcis and Eretria,[15] which divided Greece, was still conducted in the traditional way. It may be because they did not adopt the new strategy that the Bacchiadae of Corinth were defeated in the war against Corcyra. One thing is a bit more certain: in 669 Argos crushes Sparta using hoplites, and does so led by a tyrant.

b—Within the cities themselves: the force relations change. The people (*laos*; *dēmos*) become indispensable to the defense of the group: the isolated warrior with his chariot, surrounded by only his servants, is disqualified as the basic military unit. But it is still necessary that "the people" be wealthy enough to buy weapons, maintain them, and replace them. There is an economic threshold below which the peasant can no longer be a soldier himself. (No longer can, no longer wants: the Bacchiadae perhaps experienced this.)

Furthermore, this new strategy entails a relationship of understanding and close harmony between soldiers—with the shield on his left, the hoplite protects his comrade on the left and is protected by his comrade on the right. They have to march forward abreast, to coordinate their movement, to change from javelin to sword together, flight leaves them unprotected. Hoplite strategy entailed the reciprocity of service and help, the synchronization of movements, and the spontaneous regulation of the whole in order to arrive at the final harmony. Now, it is this common order, accepted by each and spontaneously realized by all, or at any rate, obtained as quickly as possible by reciprocal adjustment, that ensures the city's strength.

2. Whereas the strength of the Babylonian State was embodied in a royal sovereignty which had to be regularly reconstituted through magical-religious ceremonies; and whereas its strength was ensured by a knowledge of the order of the world and of origins, located in the scribes and court poets, the strength of the nascent city is embodied in the order spontaneously accepted and realized by men in the warrior formation. And so it is not a knowledge which guarantees the maintenance of the group, but something that is both individual courage and acceptance of order: *aretē*.[16]

## C—EMERGENCE OF CRAFT INDUSTRY

Arms lead to the development of craft industry. But it is above all for commercial reasons that craft industry develops in Greece in the seventh and sixth centuries. Actually it seems that it was to ensure exchange with Asia Minor and the colonies of Sicily and Italy that the towns of Greece and Ionia set about manufacturing objects for exchange rather than immediate use.

It is possible that these artisans were recruited among the poor peasants who had been driven from their land and had come to town to find a way to reach the colonies. They would not have had the means to become artisans if there had not been wealthy people to advance them raw materials, tools, and means of subsistence; an advance which they repaid in exportable objects corresponding to a well-defined type prescribed by the backer.[17] A completely different relation of production is formed then, reliant on an entrepreneur's advance to his workforce and no longer on debt, tenant farming, and slavery.

Now this is where a split will occur in the aristocracy.[18] Merchant landowners have agricultural products to export (and to exchange for others). Difficulties of commercialization in a Mediterranean world in which there is scarcely anything to put into circulation apart from oil, wheat, and wine.

On the other hand, the prosperous agricultural colonies of Italy and the Black Sea accept the products of craft industry more readily (both because they can be varied according to demand and because urban civilization is not yet very developed). Hence enrichment of merchant manufacturers at the cost of landowner merchants.

If there is a conflict of interest between these two groups of aristocrats, there is not yet such a conflict between peasants and artisans. In the first place this is because they are often the same people: it is the same peasants who, in winter or in their free moments, supplement their resources through this work; and then later it is because the artisans, when grouped together in town, become buyers of market garden produce, while the peasants, if wealthy enough, can buy from the artisans.

Hence, a class alliance between a fraction of the aristocracy and the artisans-peasants against the landowning and merchant aristocracy.

It may be that, at a given moment, slavery was an instrument and a stake of the struggle, some landowners having wanted to transform their rural slaves into workers-artisans in order to compete with the manufacturers. In any case, measures for or against slavery were among the important elements of political struggle at this time. Up to the fifth century, artisans and peasants were able to keep slavery on the margins of the Greek economy.

With craft industry a type of knowledge appears in Greece and Ionia whose distribution—if not content—is very different from that found in the Asiatic States; in the latter, knowledge was linked to the exercise of a political function or to a particular role in the State. The extraction and working of metal, the manufacture of precious objects, was reserved to groups of slaves under the direction and responsibility of State functionaries who had to preserve its secret and monopoly.

The Greek craftsman has access himself to the techniques of transformation; he is familiar with the techniques because he has been taught them or because he discovered some of them; and knowing them, he passes them on to others. He possesses a knowledge of substances and times, of qualities and occasions, of opportunities and changes. He can make with his hands what formerly the gods made with theirs: and universally the gods have done nothing else but manufacture the world using craft methods.

## D—THE POLITICAL TRANSFORMATIONS OF THE SEVENTH AND SIXTH CENTURIES

The big political upheavals of the seventh and sixth centuries are brought about through an alliance between a fraction of the aristocracy and the still mixed group of artisans-peasants. Our knowledge about these upheavals is very uneven:

> —for some we know only the end result (the precocious democracy of Chios);
> —for others we have only a mythical version, like the reform of Lycurgus in Sparta;
> —and for [still] others, we have some historical scraps (like the tyranny of Cypselus and of Periander at Corinth);[19]
> —on [those] from later, we have more continuous documentation (Athens).

In any case, with regard to these transformations we can consider several fundamental features as more or less certain:

a—That [they] were carried out through a struggle that brought two groups into confrontation: *hoi polloi* and *hoi ploutoi*, translated by the Greeks as the poor and the rich.

All the evidence tallies: in the seventh and sixth centuries, whenever political power was seized by a tyrant, he relied on the most humble, the poor, on what was beginning to be called the *dēmos*. Thus, Theagenes of Megara, who is supposed to have incited the people to slaughter the flocks of the rich.[20] Thus, Cypselus at Corinth. And if, with regard to Peisistratus, one speaks of three parties, it is probable that their difference is geographical, and the one supporting Peisistratus could well be [that] of the artisans (Laurium silver mines).

We should note that if this opposition was, for the Greeks, the source of the great transformations in the seventh and sixth centuries, it continued for a long time after.

Plato: Every city contains at least two cities, each the enemy of the other; that of the poor and that of the rich (*Republic*, 422e).[21]

Aristotle: In the city the two most distinct classes are the rich and the poor: they are parts of the city most opposed to each other (*Politics*, IV, 1291b).[22]

b—It was the armed strength of the hoplites that permitted the more or less violent eviction of the aristocrats and the appearance of a new form of power.

Following a victorious war, the head of the army is often brought to power by those who had been his soldiers. [E.g.] Orthagoras, first tyrant of Sicyon (Aristotle, *Politics*, V, 12, 1315b et seq.).

Several of the tyrants were polemarchs before exercising power (Orthagoras; Cypselus at Corinth). We are not absolutely sure whether the function of polemarch was still a military one at that time. In any case, the famous guard which surrounded the tyrants indicates the military character of the power they exercised and the support it found in the population.

Pheidon had been tyrant at Argos for five or six years when, in 669, he crushed Sparta at Hysiae by using his hoplites against a still aristocratic type of army.[23]

c—The transformations were carried out—obviously to a variable extent—in favor of the peasants and artisans:

α—In favor of the peasants; there was practically always modification of the regime of land ownership:

—either there was violent reclamation of cattle-rearing land;
—or there was land confiscation, with measures of exile;
—or there was cancellation of debts (as with Solon);
—or there was redistribution or new division of land in a more of less egalitarian form (a reform traditionally attributed to Lycurgus).

It is probable that it always involved a set of measures in which, according to the case, land redistribution or cancellation of debts was dominant. In the case of Cypselus at Corinth, there was above all land redistribution (the circulation of coinage enabling the cancellation of debts); in the case of Solon, on the other hand, there was remission of debts, liberation, but not redistribution of land (and even when the farmers reclaimed their land, they did not have the right to uproot the olive trees).

β—The first great measure in favor of the artisans was the limitation of slavery, which constituted competition for the workers (Periander prohibited the import of slaves). [Equally:]

—development of urban civilization: creation of big aqueducts (like that of Megara and Theagenes); development of Corinth (at the time of Periander); Samos (the works of Polycrates);[24]
—establishment of what cannot yet be called an industry, but craft exports: homogenization of production, mass production of Corinthian potteries.

Encouragement of craft industry: Solon, who was not the most radical reformer, far from it, prescribed that no one could ask for the help of his children if he had not taught them a skill (*technē* never meaning agricultural skill).[25] He gave citizenship to all the artisans who came to settle in Athens with their families.

In any case, Corinth in the sixth century and Athens in the fifth owed their political power to the development of craft industry.

Generally speaking, we can say that the political transformations which took place in Greece in the seventh and sixth centuries represented a partial, and always provisional victory of the peasants and artisans; a section of the aristocracy being bound by interest either to the artisans (which was the case of Cypselus or Peisistratus), or to the peasants (like Solon).

This alliance explains the political forms taken by these transformations: that is to say, either tyranny (which, despite the legend of Cypselus, seems never really to have been exercised by men of the people), or the intervention of a reformer or group of reformers installing the reign of the written law.

However lively the opposition, as was later recounted, we should not forget that the tyrants often governed within the legal framework, sometimes no doubt in order to preserve it (Peisistratus);[26] that often too tyranny, having come to its end, led to the organization of a written law and sometimes served as intermediary [to democracy] (Solon, Peisistratus, Cleisthenes).

## CONCLUSION

Through these transformations we see a redistribution of the relations between the discourse of justice and the discourse of knowledge; of the relations between the just, measurement, order, and truth.

The truth-challenge, which was inherited from Greek traditions, and the model of knowledge-power, which was passed on by the East, through Ionia, will now be fitted together and transformed [into] a truth-knowledge linked in its roots to justice, distribution, and order, and supported by a morality of *aretē* and a technique of pedagogy.[27]

All this is to be examined more closely on three points:

—the institution of money, which is not just a measure of exchange, but which was established mainly as an instrument of distribution, division, and social correction;

—the institution of the *nomos*, of written law, which is not just political constitution but the very discourse of the social order;

—finally, the institution of a justice with a religious model.

1. See M. Detienne, *Crise agraire et attitude religieuse chez Hésiode*; Hesiod, *Works and Days*, 765-768.
2. Hésiode, *Les Travaux et les Jours*, p. 86; Hesiod, *Works and Days*, p. 59: "Hear, Zeus, and set our fallen laws upright/And may my song to Perses tell the truth." (See above, p. 111).
3. H. Michell, *The Economics of Ancient Greece* (Cambridge: W. Heffer, 1963²; original ed., New York: Macmillan, 1940).
4. P.N. Ure, *The Origin of Tyranny* (Cambridge: Cambridge University Press, 1922).
5. Concept introduced into historiography by B.L. Van der Waerden, in *Science Awakening*, trans. Arnold Dresden (Groningen: P. Noordhoff, no date) and taken up by J.-P. Vernant.
6. The oldest mention of *nomos* is in Hesiod, *Works and Days*, 276, p. 67: "The son of Kronos made this law for men." See H. Frisch, *Might and Right in Antiquity*, pp. 98-99.
7. Faust and Saint Anthony were brought together already in Flaubert's *The Temptation of Saint Anthony*. See M. Foucault, "Postface à Flaubert" (1964) in *Dits et Écrits*, 1994 ed., no. 20, vol. I, pp. 293-325; "Quarto" ed., vol. I, pp. 321-353; English translation by Donald F. Brouchard and Sherry Simon, "Afterword to *The Temptation of Saint Anthony*" in *Essential Works of Foucault 1954-1984*. Vol. Two: *Aesthetics, Method, and Epistemology*, ed. James Faubion (New York: The New Press, 1998); M. Foucault, "La bibliothèque fantastique" (1970) in *Dits et Écrits*, 1994 ed., vol. II, no. 75, pp. 27-29; "Quarto" ed., vol. I, p. 895.
8. "Faustus, the Fortunate (*Chanceux*) doctor, whose luck is to re-live his life, famously incarnates the German humanists of the Reformation, nourished on the Platonic notion of reminiscence ... [This symbol] is coupled with the theological conflict between the free and servile-will, between damnation and election" recalls Pierre Klossowski in his *Un si funeste désir* (Paris: Gallimard, 1963) p. 12.

   Foucault was familiar with the *Histoire de la Légende de Faust* (1888) by Ernest Faligan, who describes Faust in this way: "He loved too much of what should not be loved and pursued it night and day ... " (M.F. Archive). This mythical figure reappears in 1982 in *L'Herméneutique du sujet*, pp. 296-297 and p. 300 notes 39-41; *Hermeneutics of the Subject*, pp. 309-310 and pp. 313-314, notes 39-41); and in *Le Courage de la vérité. Le gouvernement de soi et des autres II. Cours au Collège de France*, ed. Frédéric Gros (Paris: Gallimard-Seuil, 2009) p. 196; English translation by Graham Burchell, *The Courage of Truth. The Government of Self and Others II. Lectures at the Collège de France 1983-1984* (London: Palgrave Macmillan, 2011) p. 211. The figure of Faust recurs, of course, in Nietzsche.
9. E. Will, "La Grèce archaïque" in *Deuxième Conférence internationale d'histoire économique/Second International Conference on Economic History*, Aix-en-Provence, 1962 (Paris: Mouton, 1965) vol. I, pp. 41-76.
10. A clan that seized power in Corinth between the eighth and seventh centuries. Proclaimed descendants of the king Bacchis, the Bacchiadae were overturned by Cypselus, founder of the tyranny. See E. Will, *Korinthiaka. Recherches sur l'histoire et la civilisation de Corinthe des origines aux guerres médique* (Paris: De Boccard, 1955) p. 317.
11. Aristotle, *Politics*, Book II, 6, 1265b, trans. B. Jowett, in *The Complete Works of Aristotle*, Vol. Two, p. 2008.
12. E. Will, "La Grèce archaïque," p. 62.
13. M. P. Nilsson, *The Age of the Early Greek Tyrants* (Belfast: Mayne, Boyde and son, 1936); A. French, "The economic background to Solon's reforms," *Classical Quarterly*, N.S. VI (1-2), 1956, pp. 11-25.
14. E. Will, "La Grèce archaïque," pp. 63-73.
15. Cities of Euboea, whose control was fought over by the hereditary groups which succeeded the kings. This struggle divided Greece into two large coalitions. The last pre-hoplite battle. See A.P. Andrewes, *The Greek Tyrants* (London: Hutchinson's University Library, 1956) pp. 12-14 and pp. 39-42.
16. *Aretē*: virtue, honor, or excellence, to be understood as moral and intellectual value. See J. Tricot in Aristote, *La Politique*, ed. and trans. J. Tricot (Paris: J. Vrin, 1970) p. 385: *aristos*, excellent man. The aristocratic poets, Theognis and Pindar, opposed the idea that *aretē* (virtue) can be taught. See H.I. Marrou, *Histoire de l'éducation dans l'antiquité* (Paris: Seuil, 1948); English translation by George Lamb, *A History of Education in Antiquity* (Madison:

University of Wisconsin Press: 1982) pp. 40-41. See also W. Jaeger, *Paideia: die Formung des griechischen Menschen* (Berlin-Leipzig: Walter de Gruyter, 1936); French translation by A. and S. Devyver, *Paideia. La formation de l'homme grec* (Paris: Gallimard, 1964); English translation by Gilbert Highet, *Paideia: The Ideals of Greek Culture*, three volumes (Oxford: Basil Blackwell, 1945-1961). (NB: J. Tricot translates *paideia*, not by "education," but by "high culture".)

17. M.P. Nilsson, *The Age of Early Greek Tyrants*.

18. See E. Will, "La Grèce archaïque"; A. French, "The economic background to Solon's reforms."

19. See P.N. Ure, *The Origin of Tyranny*, pp. 257-264; Aristotle, *Politics*, Book V, who reports all the narratives about the tyrants.

20. A. French, "The economic background to Solon's reforms."

21. Plato, *Republic*, Book IV, 422e, trans. Paul Shorey, *The Collected Dialogues of Plato*, p. 664: "There are two at least at enmity with one another, the city of the rich and the city of the poor."

22. Aristotle, *Politics*, pp. 2049-2050: "... the rich and the poor are especially regarded as parts of a state. Again, because the rich are generally few in number, while the poor are many, they appear to be antagonistic ... " See C. Mossé, *La Fin de la démocratie athénienne* (Paris: PUF, 1962) p. 234 et seq.

23. A.P. Andrews, *The Greek Tyrants*, pp. 39-42. The battle of Hysiae was probably the first great hoplite victory. Pheidon is thought to be the first great tyrant not to have a personal guard, doubtless because he was supported by the hoplite population.

24. M.P. Nilsson, *The Age of Early Greek Tyrants*; P.N. Ure, *The Origin of Tyranny*.

25. E. Will, "La Grèce archaïque," pp. 74-94.

26. M.I. Finley, *The Ancient Greeks*.

27. According to the notes of the auditor Hélène Politis, in his oral presentation, Foucault gave more emphasis to the role of *aretē* and *paideia* in the reorganization of Greek knowledge than can be made out from the manuscript.

## nine

## 24 FEBRUARY 1971

*The institution of money.\* Money or different kinds of money?* ∽
*The three functions of Greek currency: metathesis of power, simu-*
*lacrum, social regulation.* ∽ *Money as establishment of* diakaion
kai alēthēs.

## 1—THE INSTITUTION OF MONEY

In Hesiod we saw the vague search for a measure: a measure the sense
and function of which are still hardly specified since it is a matter
of the measure of time, of the calendar of agricultural rituals, of the
quantitative and qualitative appraisal of products, and, furthermore,
of determining not only the when and the how much, but also the
"neither too much nor too little."[1] Measure as calculation and measure
as norm.

Now these measures are established in the seventh and sixth centuries, in the epoch of tyranny; and often by the tyrants themselves.

Herodotus (VI, 127) recounts that Pheidon, tyrant of Argos, invented
a system of measurement for the Peloponnesians.[2] In any case, it was
under his reign that Aegina was joined to Argos and Aeginetan money
appeared.[3]

Cypselus introduced the use of money at Corinth;[4] and it was at this
time that the Euboea drachma was defined (65 grains of silver).

---

\* Manuscript lecture title.

This major activity of measurement is least unknown with regard to Solon:

—redefinition of individual properties;
—assessment of the incomes of each;
—allocation of a part of political power to each in proportion to their wealth;
—circulation of monetary standard.[5]

Tyrant or legislator,[6] the person holding power is the city quantity surveyor: the measurer of lands, things, wealth, rights, powers, and men.[7] Let us just recall, at the same time or very shortly after:

—the work of town planning accomplished (or projected) by Hippodamus of Miletus[8] and the introduction of the grid plan;
—the work of cartography undertaken at this time (and the map of the world constructed by Anaximander);[9]
—Pythagorean research on geometrical and musical proportions.[10]

We should not forget that before being inscribed in Western consciousness as the principle of quantification, harmony, and classical non-excess, Greek measurement was an immense social and polymorphous practice of assessment, quantification, establishing equivalences, and the search for appropriate proportions and distributions.[11]

We can see how introducing measure is linked to a whole problem of peasant indebtedness, the transfer of agricultural properties, the settlement of debts, equivalence between foodstuff or manufactured objects, urbanization, and the establishment of a State form.

The institution of money appears at the heart of this practice of measurement.

A—*Interpretations*

The traditional interpretation attributes the birth of the use of money to the development of a market economy:

—groups of peasants established around the Mediterranean gradually took off from the subsistence economy;

—the appearance and growth of terrestrial and especially maritime commerce (with what this entails in the way of distances, delays, and the unforeseen) made the use of a recognized monetary standard necessary: a metal fragment weighed and authenticated by a stamp—private to start with and then State controlled.

Commercial, international, market origin of money. Mercantilist interpretation of money restricting it from the start to functions of representation and exposing it to that "fetishism" which consists in taking the sign for the thing itself, through a sort of primary and radical philosophical error.[12]

In fact, this interpretation may account for some early uses of money, in Lydia or Phoenicia.[13] But money was not adopted and used in Greece on the basis of this model. This is indicated by certain facts:

a—If we see money institutionalized in most of the big trading cities, some cities, where trade was not non-existent, did not adopt it; and it seems that for a long time many important transactions between individuals took place in the form of barter.

b—On the other hand, the first assessments of equivalence that we see in Homer are not made so much in terms of objects of exchange, but of sacrificial objects. They are tripods, oxen.[14]

More precisely, these objects do not appear in any number whatever (as would be the case if their function was simply calculation); they figure in quantities (9, 12, 100) which are ritual numbers brought into play in sacrifices.

So we may suspect that the calculations of equivalence, even when their purpose is a market type of exchange, no longer took as their model and foundation the assessment of an identical value, but the recognition of religious substitutability. The form of money does not emerge in the abstract sky of the commodity and its representation, but in the game of the sacrifice and its simulacra.

c—To this should be added that the first major uses of money appear to be internal to the city: taxation no doubt, the distribution of money by tyrants, the assessment of wealth, the classification of citizens and the hierarchy of their political rights according to their wealth.

It seems therefore that the use of money was, in an essential respect, other than commercial. But what then is this monetary practice, some dimensions of which refer to religious rituals and others to social regulations?

## B—An example

The institution of money is better known at Corinth than elsewhere.[15] A legend recounts that Cypselus, the son of an artisan and of a descendant of the Bacchiadae, made the following vow to Zeus: If I take power in Corinth, I will give you its territory. Once in power, he taxed the landowners at the rate of a tenth of their wealth, and at the end of ten years the equivalent of the whole Corinthian wealth would have been accumulated in the temple of Zeus.

In fact, it seems that the schema was more or less the following: Cypselus, having been polemarch and having carried off victories thanks to the hoplite army of peasants, drove out the old aristocracy of the Bacchiadae. And he proceeded to redistribute, not all the land, by any means, but some of it. (No text says so exactly, but Solon, a bit later than Cypselus, alludes to a demagogic tyrant who shared out the soil.)

Now this partial redistribution of land did not resolve the problem of existing debts, and especially of those which were going to arise anew. Hence the levy of ten percent, not on properties, but on the highest incomes, a levy which then makes possible direct distributions to the poor, the financing of major works, advances to artisans—and thus the settlement of debts to the rich.

But this complex system (redistribution of the land, taxation of incomes, distribution to the poor, repayment of creditors) would not have been possible in kind. What was needed was the circulation of a constant substitute in the distributions and returns. And it is very likely that Lydian (and Argive, or rather Aeginetan) money served as a model at this time.

But the important thing is that if the material and form of this substitute do have this oriental origin, the system's general arrangement has a religious origin. In fact the system of collective contribution, levy of a tenth, and redistribution to the participants, is the schema of the sacrificial rite (one provides the victim; the god, the temple, the priests levy a tenth, then redistribution takes place: redistribution that imparts a new strength and power to those who benefit from it, deriving from the sacrifice itself).

The game—sacrifice, division, levy, redistribution—is a religious form of individual and group invigoration which has been transposed into a social practice involving the resolution of a class conflict.

We should still add this: Corinth had no silver mines. Will supposes[16] that the first injection of metal into this system was made by the melting down of precious objects belonging to dispossessed rich families; objects which were both taxed wealth and liturgical objects. The transfer of these objects to the community could only take place with the support and intervention of an external religious authority more powerful than family religious practice. This explains the intervention of Zeus demanding possession of Corinthian wealth in his own name. Sacrifice of liturgical objects to the State worship of Zeus. And it is afterwards that this use of metal is linked up with the quest for mining resources: colonization of the Adriatic coast and Southern Italy where silver ore was found. And, by using this currency, commercial development coinciding with the reign of the descendants of Cypselus and above all of Periander.

The policy of Cypselus can therefore be read as a system with several levels:

—Economic reading: the at least partial redistribution of land, the maintenance of debts, the introduction of a monetary circulation strictly controlled by a heavy taxation, the shift of the main economic activity from agriculture to commerce and from the land to the sea, the development of colonization in the search for metallic raw materials.

—Religious reading: a ritual sacrifice in which the participants give up to the god the share that falls to him; the invigoration of the social body through the redistribution of the wealth sacrificed and sacralized in this way; the reduplication and displacement which supplies and sacrifices to the city's god, Zeus, the objects already supplied and sacrificed to the divinities of the *genos* and already made sacred by them.

As we can see: the conjunction, intertwining, and superimposition of the two operations form a single grid. And that is where money starts to

exist, to circulate, to function in a common space of interplay defined by
these two transformations. There is money when the same object is both
sacrifice and tax, income of the poorest and ritual redistribution, the temple's or fire's share and constraint or plunder by power, magical invigoration of the social body and daily activity of potters at their wheel.

I am aware in choosing this example that it is an example.

Maybe there was not a single birth of money in general. Maybe what
appeared on the edges of the Mediterranean from the eighth to the sixth
century were different kinds of money:

—a Lydian money linked to the State apparatus;
—a Phoenician money linked to commercial practices;
—a Greek money linked to class conflict and class alliances characterized by peasant debt, the appearance of craft industry, the
formation of a semi-popular army, a split in the interests in the
wealthy class (agricultural commerce *versus* craft commerce).

So maybe it is not money, in its abstract generality, which marks its
appearance at Corinth in the reforms of the tyrant Cypselus. Monetary
generality is no doubt only the result of a later homogenization, linked
to a new historical process (the development of a large scale market
economy).

In any case, this historical analysis shows us that the mercantile
essence of money is by no means its historical root. The beginning of
money is not a solemn origin already inscribed in market and metaphysical nature.

Money was not instituted "in the exchange of products," the most we
can say is that it "developed" in it (Marx, *Capital*, [I, 2, iv]).[17]

## C—Three functions of Greek money[18]

Power preserved and displaced: the *metathesis of power*.

a—Money is linked to the exercise of power, but not in a simple way
([it is not] because one possesses money that one acquires and exercises power). Rather, it is because some took power that money was
institutionalized.[19]

b—But it is not a matter of the wealthy property owners seizing
power (they already have it) or new property owners, but rather of the

seizure of power by an alliance between a certain type of property owner and the majority of poor peasants and artisans.

The appearance of money is linked to the constitution of a new type of power whose raison d'être is to intervene in the regime of property, in the interplay of debts and settlements. Hence the fact that it always appears at the same time as an "extraordinary" form of political power: tyrant, legislator.

c—What function does money have in this seizure or redistribution of power?

If the tyrant Cypselus introduces the monetary institution, this is because:

—he refused to practice the systematic and entire division of land;

—he did not cancel debts but maintained the interplay of debts and cycles of indebtedness;

—he attracted impoverished peasants to craft industry or wage labor.

Money will have a somewhat analogous role later when Solon undertakes his great reform at Athens. Despite the different particulars: Solon cancels debts, but preserves property. To reduce tensions he develops craft industry (calling on foreign manpower) and exports (banning the uprooting of olive trees).

In both cases, money has a well-defined political role:

—to limit social demands, which have grown continually since Hesiod and which the formation of hoplite armies make more dangerous;

—to preserve, thereby, both the property regime and possession of power by the wealthy property owning class;

—to shift [possession of power*] from an agricultural aristocracy to a more commercial and manufacturing aristocracy;

—to strengthen it, finally, by putting in the governors' hands the double instrument of taxation and wage-earners, accompanied by the power to strike coins.

---

* Manuscript: to shift it.

What is inscribed in the monetary stamp—in those figures of the horse at Corinth, the tortoise at Aegina, and soon the owl at Athens—is not, in its general semiological nature, the sign; it is a struggle for and around political power; it is a shift, preservation, and reinforcement of power.

Certainly, we should not neglect the appearance of this stamp, in its function, but rather than compare the monetary stamp to the linguistic sign, as has been done traditionally since Turgot,[20] it would be better to compare it with the symbols and rites of power.

## 2—MONEY-SIMULACRUM

Let's say, very schematically:

a—The symbol of power in archaic Greece was the scepter, the staff of command,[21] which circulated in the Assembly when anyone had to speak, put forward his views, take part in a decision, or swear an oath and expose himself to the risk of punishment as a perjurer.

Now this power, manifested in this way (power both divided up and circulating between group chiefs), was the power conferred on them by their lands, their goods, the extent of their crops, the size of their household, and the accumulation of tripods and rich fabrics at the heart of their home. The scepter demonstrated power symbolically in a society in which politics and economics were interdependent.

b—In a market society like that studied by the classical economists, money is the sign for an absent commodity; and the visible circulation of money, while showing commercial circuits and market equivalences, hides the true political relations. Through the monetary sign, wealth looks like it circulates, is distributed, and shared according to both nature and skill, necessity and chance; but in fact power is held on to.

The economic and the political are linked, but out of synch with each other; their dependence is hidden and the monetary sign is the instrument of, at the same time, their dependence, their dislocation, and the occultation of this dislocated dependence.

In seventh and sixth century Greek society money is no longer entirely a magical-political symbol like the scepter, but it is far from being already the occulting representation of classical economics. It is the instrument of a power which is being shifted (while preserving itself), and which, through an interplay of new regulations, ensures the preservation of class domination.

At this point, money is no longer a symbol which effectuates and is not yet a representative sign. It should be understood as a fixed series of superimposed substitutions [ ... *]:

   —it effectuates a religious substitution: it makes possible a levy and a redistribution;
   —it effectuates an economic substitution: fortune, investment;
   —it effectuates a political substitution: from one social group to another;
   —it effectuates another substitution: it substitutes a slight shift of power for the social upheaval sought after.

From the myth recounted to the political operation, there is a whole series of substitutions. These substitutions are superimposed on and replace each other. This is the simulacrum: real operations, indefinite series—creating fixation (not representation).

Whereas the sign "represents," the simulacrum replaces one substitution for another. It is its reality as simulacrum that has enabled money to remain for a long time not only an economic instrument but a thing issuing from and returning to power, by a sort of inner intensity or force: a religiously protected object it would be impious, sacrilegious to adulterate.

It has been possible to pick out a number of pieces of evidence for this surcharged character of the monetary object:[22]

   —counterfeiting money treated as sacrilege in Greece; major religious centers [functioned] as banks for deposits and loans;
   —sharing out revenue from the Laurion mines between citizens at Athens (Themistocles was opposed to it);
   —redistribution to the *dēmos* of the tributes paid by the allies of Athens in recognition of its sovereignty, a redistribution which took place by means of indemnities paid to citizens when they exercised their political or judicial functions;

---

* The manuscript adds: which replace each other.

—or distribution of money by Roman emperors to demonstrate and maintain their sovereignty;

—or, in the Christian epoch, gifts of money to sovereigns and redistributions of money;

—the interplay of income and charity in Christian ethics.

The functioning of money is not accounted for by a theory of the signifier, but rather by analysis of the simulacrum. Money was simulacrum before becoming sign.

And maybe we can go further. It is as simulacrum that it is sign: getting it to function as sign in a market economy is an avatar of its real history as simulacrum. Simulacrum of a nature of things, of a value exclusive to it, of a real equivalence. What Marx called "fetishism." To summarize all this, let's say that money is linked to power as simulacrum.[23]

## 3—MONEY-MEASURE

Money appears therefore in a figure whose [outline (*dessin*)*] has the form of the religious ritual and whose essential points are:

—the gift and the gathering,
—sacrifice and dividing up,
—redistribution,
—strength restored to the participants.

In its Greek origin, money is closer to ritual and restorative consumption than to the exchange of two commodities.

a—Money is therefore above all an instrument of regulation between the different elements making up the city:[24] through the distribution of money [in the] form of presents or gifts, one avoids the poor becoming too poor; through the tax levied on the rich, one avoids them being too rich.

Money is indeed *metron*—an instrument of measure—but in the sense that it prevents excess, *pleonexia*, having too much.

But it also prevents excessive poverty, unlimited indebtedness; it enables the poorest to redeem their debts and escape the slavery threatening them. If it is *metron*, it is not because it proposes a yardstick for measuring

---

* Manuscript: *dessein* (intention, purpose, plan...)

the respective value of different things; it is because it lays down a limit to wealth and poverty. It is not measure as definition of a common quantity, but as exclusion of opposed excesses (wealth/poverty).

The formula "not too much or too little"[25] is absolutely in line with the monetary institution.

b—It is *metron* also in the sense that it enables the double political violence accompanying excessive wealth and excessive poverty to be avoided. The institution of money enables the poor to pay their debts; it enables them to be offered work by giving them a wage (or to buy provisions distributed to them).

But by the same token, it enables the rich to avoid major political and social upheavals: at the end of the day, and thanks to the sacrifice demanded, it guarantees that they will keep the greater part of their lands and wealth.

The person who institutes money is he who regulates social conflicts; someone like Solon,[26] who stands like a barrier between the parties, and does not give way to either of them; who holds the shield between them which prevents them fighting.

\*c—Thus money
—maintains order, justice;
—allows one to establish the truth of what one owes, of what it is worth. It institutes *dikaion kai alēthēs*. But at the same time it plays a fundamental role in the game of power;
—it involves the State institution: tax, levy, accumulation, fixing value, distribution;
—it made possible the preservation of class power.

It leaves to each the possibility of assessing truthfully, of measuring: it makes justice possible (measure[†] as non-excess).

Non-excess and the truth: profound Greek affiliation. The relation of money to the truth is therefore:

—by avoiding excess,
—by establishing the equilibrium (and non-violence),[27]

---

\* Synthesis on unnumbered page, which, judging by the paper used, was drafted in Montreal at the time of a presentation at McGill University.
† [*la mesure*, which can mean moderation, limit; G.B.]

—by making the order of the city work,
it allows things to be revealed in their truth.

So it is not because it measures things quantitatively that it states
a truth, it is because it excludes excess that it allows them their value
and to display themselves in their truth. Money-measurement: things
are true in the element of the measure (*la mesure*) (of the non-excess).
Practicing measure (*la mesure*) (that is to say, making use of quantifiable
signs) will be to avoid excess, to establish the equilibrium.

[We may note that even later in Greek thought, the State will be
thought to be composed of rich and poor:[28]

*Republic*, IV, 422e: Every city contains at least two cities, each the
enemy of the other, that of the poor and that of the rich:[29]
    Aristotle, *Politics*, IV, 1291b: In the city the two most distinct
classes are the rich and the poor.[30]

For a long time, excess wealth and poverty will be seen as one of the
sources of the city's destruction:

*Republic*, VIII, 550e: Wealth excludes virtue.[31]
    *Republic*, IV, 421d: When the craftsman is too poor, he can no
longer even work because he no longer has any tools.[32]]

d—Finally, as we see, the monetary institution is not linked to the
value of things in their truth, but to *dikaion*, to the justice that must
reign in the city and prevent it from perishing.
    Or rather, if money is related to truth it is because it is an instru-
ment of social regulation, correction, and rectification. It is what enabled both tyrants like Cypselus and legislators like Solon to make the
city live in accordance with an order which is specific to it. Money is
the harmony and real strength of the city. For a long time the Athenian
tetradrachma,[33] bearing the owl, will be the visible strength of the city
circulating throughout the Ionian world.
    The truth of money is inseparable from the order and vigor of the
State; it is like the other face of the *dikē* reigning within it.

Before we can ask different questions about money (no longer about what it can do in the city, but about what it represents in the exchange of commodities), before it can appear as (natural or conventional) sign, before we can ask whether it truly or deceptively represents the value of things, a whole series of changes will be needed:

—obviously it will require the development of a monetary economy on a Mediterranean scale, with problems of equivalence;
—there will also have to be some monetary experiments like the Hippias devaluation;[34]
—the accumulation of individual fortunes (thanks to the monetary economy) will have to bring about a new imbalance.

Then money will leave definitively the double region of *dikaion* and the simulacrum, the region of sacrifice and just distribution, of religious ritual and social pacification, to appear and be handled as sign—as natural or arbitrary sign—which enables one really to measure or which allows only the exchange of what one desires. A problematic of the monetary signifier will become possible (and to tell the truth, necessary) and its truth function will then have to be questioned.

Right in the middle of the fourth century, a passage in Aristotle's *Politics*[35] is still very revealing. It distinguishes:

—a natural chrematistics, which falls in the domain of domestic economy (which consists in acquiring wealth through cultivation); wealth which is necessarily circumscribed. The use of money is not excluded from this economy, but it is useful for something other than itself: it is useful for acquiring what one needs.[36] Money therefore has the double character of being subordinate to something other than itself, of being acquired only in limited quantities;
—a chrematistics in the strict sense, which seeks only the acquisition of money itself and consequently in unlimited quantities. This rests on exchange. It is subject to the criticism that it is not natural. In a sense it is not true, and yet it is nevertheless regarding this chrematistics that the question arises: is not money true wealth, since it enables one to acquire every kind of wealth, since it

allows one to make every kind of exchange? Things then are worth their cash equivalent.

Is money not rather "pure foolishness"?[37] Something entirely conventional, with "nothing natural," since one can devalue it by decree, demonetize the metal, and since, like Midas, one may die of hunger in front of a pile of gold.

The double problematic of money (arbitrary/natural, truth/illusion) is linked to its late function as sign. Previously, its truth was linked, but in a non-apophantic way, to *dikē* and *nomos*—*nomos* which is not yet convention.[38]

1. The formula is attributed to Solon, a policy favorable to the middle classes in contrast with the aristocratic formula "nothing too much" which fixed an upper but not a lower limit, in G. Thomson, "La Philosophie d'Eschyle" (Paris: CERM [no date]).
2. P.N. Ure, *The Origins of Tyranny*, p. 154 and p. 183: "First third of the seventh century, the reign of Pheidon opened the age of tyranny ... it is Plato and Aristotle who later reinterpreted tyranny as the effect of military victories because they had before their eyes the late example of Dionysius of Syracuse." (Foucault's notes kept on a card relating to the development of a servile labor force in Greece. The tyrants encouraged manual work, but the stage of artisanal work began to be overtaken by enterprises under tyranny. According to this card, slavery spreads only with the Median Wars.) In fact, Aristotle, *Politics*, V, 10, 1310b, 25-35, relates that Pheidon transformed his kingship into tyranny.
3. A.P. Andrewes, *The Greek Tyrants*, pp. 78-83.
4. E. Will, "Réflexions et hypothèses sur les origines du monnayage," *Revue numismatique*, 5th series, 17, 1955.
5. E. Will, "La Grèce archaïque," pp. 74-94; C. Hignett, *History of the Athenian Constitution to the End of the Fifth Century B.C.* (Oxdord: Clarendon Press, 1952).
6. M.I. Finley, *The Ancient Greeks*, p. 42: "... the Greek lawgiver laid down the rules by which the community should govern itself." (Foucault's card on the legislator and the tyrant.)
7. Plutarque, *Œuvres morales. Propos de table*, Book VIII, 719a-b: "It is said that Lycurgus banned the study of arithmetic in Sparta for being democratic and popular in its effects, and that he introduced geometry as better adapted to a strict oligarchy and institutional monarchy. In using numbers, arithmetic distributes things equally; in using proportion, geometry distributes things according to merit. Geometry is not a source of confusion of the State therefore, it includes a principle of distribution between the good and the bad, who do not receive their share according to chance or weight but by the difference between vice and virtue" (quotation copied out by M.F. in his preparatory notes); English translation by Edwin L. Minar, Plutarch, *Moralia* (Cambridge, Mass., and London: Harvard University Press, Loeb Classical Library, 1961), Volume IX, Book Eight, pp. 123-125: "You know, of course, that Lycurgus expelled arithmetical proportion from Lacedaemon, because of its democratic and rabble-rousing character. He introduced the geometric proportion, which is appropriate to a moderate oligarchy or a lawful monarchy. The arithmetical distributes an equal amount to each, measuring by number, whereas the geometric distributes to each an amount corresponding to his worth, measuring by proportion. It does not mix everything together, but has within it a clear principle of the distinction of good and bad; people receive their due not as the balance or the lot directs, but always by the distinction of good and bad in them."
8. According to E. Will, *Le Monde grec et l'Orient*, Hippodamus of Miletus (second half of the fifth century) worked on the reorganization of Piraeus, and, according to B. Gille, *Les Mécaniciens grecs* (Paris: Seuil, 1980) pp. 50-51, also on the construction of Thurii and Rhodes.
9. C.H. Kahn, *Anaximander and the Origins of Greek Cosmology*; J.-P. Vernant, "Geometry and Spherical Astronomy in the First Greek Cosmology." Nietzsche and Rohde have commented upon Anaximander, which is recalled by some quotations copied by Foucault in his preparatory notes, taken from W. Jaeger, *The Theology of the Early Greek Philosophers*.
10. See C. Mugler, *Platon et la recherche mathématique de son époque* (Strasbourg-Zurich: Heitz, 1948).
11. See G. Vlastos, "Equality and justice in early Greek cosmology" pp. 164-168.
12. Althusser and his students undertook a fresh scrutiny of the genesis of the money form in Marx and criticized "fetishism" as an anthropological process of the reification of social relations (money): "a category ['thing'] more foreign to Marx cannot be imagined." L. Althusser, *For Marx*, trans. B. Brewster (London and New York: Verso, 2005) p. 197n.
13. H. Michell, *The Economies of Ancient Greece*, pp. 311-314.
14. The first to have developed this thesis was probably B. Laum, in *Heiliges Geld. Eine historische Untersuchung über den sakralen Ursprung des Geldes* (Tübingen: J.C.B. Mohr, 1924), and *Über das Wesen des Münzgeldes* (Staat. Akad. Braunsberg, 1929). E. Will refers to Laum, notably in "De l'aspect éthique des origines grecques de la monnaie," *Revue historique*, CCXII (2), 1954, pp. 211-213:
(1) the ox is object, not means of exchange,

(2) in sacrifices and evaluations we find the same unit (ox) and the same multiples (9, 12, 100).

15. From here, in the main, Foucault follows the studies of Edouard Will, whose *Korinthiaka* is still today a comprehensive survey of references.

16. E. Will, "Réflexions et hypothèses sur les origines du monnayage."

17. Reference to the transformation of the movements C-M-C into M-C-M, the subject of considerable commentary at the time by Althusserians. Foucault recalled elsewhere the diplomatic function of a quotation from Marx.

18. Is it completely unnecessary to recall the three functions of universal money for Marx: those of means of payment, means of purchase, and social material of wealth in general? See K. Marx, *Capital*, Volume 1 (London: Penguin Books/New Left Review, 1976) Book I, Part One, chapter 3, §3.

19. P.N. Ure, *The Origins of Tyranny*: "The tyrannies in Greece were founded on the monetary economy." (Note by M.F.)

20. See Turgot's article "Étymologie" in the *Encyclopédie*, which, according to Foucault, established the first systematic parallel between money and words. See *Les Mots et les Choses*, p. 90; *The Order of Things*, p. 109.

21. Homer, *The Iliad*, Book One, 234-239, 245-246; Book Two, 100 et seq.; Book Sixteen, 501-506.

22. B. Laum, *Heiliges Geld*; E. Will, "De l'aspect éthique des origines grecques de la monnaie," pp. 211-213.

23. From the 1960s, a growing conceptualization of the simulacrum—*versus* sign and symbol—circulates between Klossowski, who links it to the "eternal return," Deleuze, who associates it with "difference and repetition," and Foucault. See P. Klossowski, *Un si funeste désir*; G. Deleuze, *Différence et Répétition*; *Difference and Repetition*; and M. Foucault, "La prose d'Actéon" (1964) in *Dits et Écrits*, vol. I, no. 21, pp. 326-337/"Quarto," ed., vol. I, pp. 354-365; English translation by Robert Hurley, "The Prose of Acteon" in M. Foucault, *Aesthetics, Method, and Epistemology*, pp. 123-136.

24. E. Will, in "Réflexions et hypothèses sur les origines du monnayage," proposes for "regulation" the Greek term *nomisma*, "instrument of assessment of value," from the root NEM, *nemesis, nomos, nomisma, nomizein*. From this Deleuze also derives the theme of the "Nomad" in *Différence et Répétition*, p. 54; *Difference and Repetition*, p. 36 and p. 309 note 6.

25. See above, note 1.

26. Allusion to a poem by Solon, in G. Vlastos, "Solonian justice," *Classical Philology*, 41, 1946, pp. 65-69.

27. Demosthenes will say that every particle of violence creates injustice; see G. Vlastos, ibid.

28. C. Mossé, *La Fin de la démocratie athénienne*, pp. 234-239.

29. See above, p. 127, and p. 132 note 21.

30. See ibid. and note 22.

31. Plato, *Republic*, p. 779: "May not the opposition of wealth and virtue be conceived as if each lay in the scale of a balance inclining opposite ways?"

32. Ibid., p. 663: "...if from poverty he is unable to provide himself with tools and other requirements of his art..."

33. According to the *Robert* dictionary, "the Academy made this word from the feminine. But archeologists always use it in the masculine." [Foucault writes: "*le* tétradrachme," whereas drachma (*la* drachme) is feminine; G.B.]

34. H. Michell, *The Economics of Ancient Greece*, pp. 331-332.

35. Aristotle, *Politics*, I, 3, 1253b and I, 9, 1257a-b.

36. That is to say, the happy life: *alathēn zoēn*; ibid., I, 8, 1256b32.

37. Ibid., I, 9, 1257b; English translation, p. 1995: "mere sham."

38. M. Ostwald, *Nomos and the Beginnings of Athenian Democracy* (Oxford: Clarendon Press, 1969).

# ten

## 3 MARCH 1971

Nomos.* *Institution contemporary with the written law and money* (nomos *and* nomisma). ∽ *Written law and enunciative ritual* (nomos *and* thesmos). ∽ *The four supports of* nomos. *Corinthian money and Athenian* nomos. *Hesiodic* eunomia *and Solonic* eunomia. ∽ *Economics and politics. The City-State: an absolutely new notion. Caesura between economics and politics.* ∽ *Return to the simulacrum, money, law. What is a* nomos *pronounced by no one?*

IN THE STRUGGLE UNDERWAY in the seventh and sixth centuries, money appeared, following the example of Corinth, as a subtle and detailed instrument; while the land was being divided up, it allowed indebtedness to be maintained along with all the inequalities linked to it; it thus enabled political power (scarcely shifted) to be kept in the hands of the wealthy property owners.

Now the other great institution which is contemporary, or more or less contemporary with *nomisma*,[1] is *nomos*, which has often been characterized as written law.

With regard to money, I have tried to show that it was not initially introduced as sign in the practice of exchange, but that first and foremost it played a role in the social distributions in which it figured as simulacrum.

---

* Manuscript title of lecture.

With regard to the law, I will try to show that it was not initially introduced as writing: that writing is not the fundamental difference in law;[2] that written law arrives within an event in which what is at stake is power and the struggle for power.

The opposition between the written and the non-written is late (fifth century). It cannot account for the *nomos* by which many Greek cities are characterized in the classical epoch. The "new law" contrasts with the old in other terms.

## WRITTEN AND UNWRITTEN LAWS

*A*—Thesmos.

*Thesmos* was an unwritten rule. This does not mean that it was purely and simply an oral rule deployed in the element of *logos*, of uttered discourse, or of the voice.

α—That *thesmos* is unwritten means much more precisely that it is preserved in memory and has to be recalled on the occasion, at the moment, when events or circumstances call for it.

E.g.: In Homer, when the Achaian army is to be brought back to Greece, the *rule* requires that a meeting of the Council be called; when there is a dispute, the rule calls for the test of the decisive oath. The good leader is one who can recall the rule at the right moment, who can recognize when the time has come to apply the rule.

β—Another characteristic of *thesmos* is that it has to be uttered, and uttered ritually, for it come into play. It has no existence, or at any rate, actuality, outside of this singular emergence. The memory that keeps it is not a sort of mute, ever alert presence.

For *thesmos* to function,[3] it is not enough for it to be stuck firmly in memory or habit: it has to be stated as being *thesmos*, with all the appropriate gestures and signs of sovereignty. Not silent and continuous reign of *thesmos*: its effectiveness is linked to the ritual event of its enunciation. The power of *thesmos* is exercised in the event.

γ—Third characteristic of *thesmos*: it comes from a strict system of affiliation and possession. In archaic Greek society, memory is not a matter of individual or collective consciousness so much as a form of both property and power: what deserves to be kept in memory has to be jealously preserved, due to its effectiveness, in closed groups which use it as an instrument of power.

Memory functions as treasure and power in the form of the secret.

Hence those institutions of memory constituted by groups passing on these secrets, with strict rules of exclusion, mnemonic procedures, and systems of discourse:

—as in the groups of bards;
—as in the temples, the "guardians of things said."

Legal rules determined that those who kept the discourse were also those with power and wealth. Memory of the rules was part of the wealth of the big families, one of their reserves, a way of exercising power and a way of holding on to it. There were "exegetes" to say whether the time had come to apply a particular rule, or if such a rule really had to be applied in the present moment. But these exegetes were by no means neutral experts interpreting an anonymous law holding sway over everyone in the same way.

The exegetes belonged to, or were linked to a form of family property: for example, there will still be *exēgētaí Eumolpidōn* late on in Athens.[4]

(It is worth noting in passing this archaic form of exegesis: which is not linked to writing, to the investigation of what it means, to its reactualization in the *logos*; [but which] consists in correlating moment, memory, and rule, and doing so as an exercise of power.)

To summarize all this, with regard to *thesmos*, the most important thing is not its oral character, but rather that its effectiveness is always linked to the lightning flash of the event; that its preservation is ensured in the twin form of property and memory as instruments of the exercise of power.

B—Nomos.

[*Nomos*] can no more be identified with the written law than *thesmos* can be reduced to oral tradition.

In fact, as soon as we pay some attention to the texts, we see that *nomos* designates several forms of quite distinct institutions:

α—Of course, the written law, and more precisely the inscribed law, is engraved publicly for all to see on stone tablets or walls which everyone can look at when they want or need to.

In *The Suppliant Women*, 424, in a discussion with a Theban herald, Euripides has Theseus say that at Athens:

—there are written laws;
—thanks to these, it is the people who govern;
—the wealthy and the weak enjoy equal rights.
And this is in contrast with the tyrant.

β—But *nomos* also designates an unwritten law: this is how Herodotus speaks of Scythian *nomoi* to designate a clearly unwritten set of rules.[5] But above all one often speaks of the laws of Sparta, emphasizing (and always as praise) that they were not written but passed on by education, example, advice, and men's habits of honor and pride with regard to each other.

So writing, in contrast with and alongside *paideia*, is only one of the possible forms of *nomos*. Education and writing function conjointly or alternatively to ensure, protect, and maintain *nomos* whose specific nature is not exhausted in either one or the other (in contrast with *thesmos*, which was imposed and which one remembers).

C—Maybe we should go even further: if it is true that *nomos* is written and that writing manifests the inviolability of the law, its sacred character, in democratic cities like Athens the law could be changed after discourse, discussion, deliberation, and voting. (In some cases, penalties were even envisaged for someone who, having proposed a change in the fundamental law, failed to win the case—[this] in contrast with *thesmos*, which is inviolable: in the fourth century, when one wants to speak of an inviolable law one calls it *thesmos*.)

This proves that the law is exposed to discourse, to *logos*, that it can be affected by or arrived at on the basis of *logos*.

*D—Finally, *nomos* has the meaning of nature, of conduct in conformity with nature,[6] or in any case with what is proper: a custom bordering on conformity with nature.

Nature/law surface of contact.
    Pindar[7] praises Xenocrates of Acragas for rearing horses according to *nomos* (habit, nature).

---

* This page [ms 8'] was subject to numerous rewritings.

Pindar: Chiron taught Jason how to use drugs according to the law.

Hippocrates: There are laws which produce endurance and courage where nature would produce cowardice.

(NB: Congruence is brought about in the form of propriety, conformity, fittingness, harmony, alignment.)

The emergence of the truth happens there and thence.

Hence the intersecting and opposite meanings:

Writing ———————— Change through *logos*
Nature ———————— Pedagogy

These four elements will break up as a result of political changes.*

This leads to several remarks:

α—Through these four† points of support of *nomos* (writing, discourse, pedagogy, nature‡), we can see taking shape, from the outside, some of the features of *nomos* in contrast with what characterizes *thesmos*.

Inscribed in stone, present in the midst of everyone without anyone having to formulate it, *nomos* is no longer uttered by anyone in particular, it speaks as if by itself, in its own name, the only name it has, the historico-mythical one of its founder. Coming from the attack or game of *logos*, of public discourse, of discussion, here too, it no longer belongs to anyone; all may publicly appropriate it, submit to it, or modify it. Passed on by pedagogy, imposed by examples lost in the mists of time, here too, it does not belong to anyone. Adapted to nature, it comes under its authority.

In the four cases, there is a break with the system of appropriation which characterized *thesmos*. In the four cases also, *nomos* is detached from the singular exercise of power and particular event to which *thesmos* was linked. *Nomos* is, as it were, always there, inscribed in stone, activated in *logos*, conveyed by the zeal of habits, and legible in nature.§

---

\* End of ms page 8'.

† An initial "three" has been corrected everywhere to "four"; it seems that the fourth—illegible—term is: nature.

‡ All the following references to nature were added in a more recent ink. The lecture delivered at the Collège de France did not include the word "nature."

§ "Legible in nature": the fourth element has been added but the suppressed page, as well as the two following, remain.

We restore a part of the draft according to three elements, which seems to us to clarify this discussion and which should have been uttered at this time:

"These three institutions of writing, pedagogy, and public discussion both manifest and guarantee β—This semantic organization breaks up very quickly:

For example: the Sophists: pedagogy ≠ nature
Socrates: written laws - unwritten laws.

It was as a response to this dissociation that philosophy was instituted. Through the introduction of a fifth element, a couple: Being-Truth as principle of implication [or complication] of these four elements:

—when *logos* speaks the truth it is in accord with the being of nature.
—when words participate in being in some way the truth is taught.

Consequences:

α—From that moment we see the great philosophical questions of the West taking shape.

---

—the disappropriation of juridical-political rule, its liberation (or its detachment) from the memory-secret-treasure form,
—and its establishment as both collective and permanent form.
All three therefore refer to a fundamental redistribution of political power and of the conditions of its exercise.
The problem is what this redistribution was: for it is here and not at all in writing that the root of *nomos* is found.
Purely for information only, this triple institution (writing, pedagogy, discussion) is that on which *nomos* rests. It refers back through *nomos* to a certain form of power whose principle must be grasped.
Now it is through this triple institution that Western knowledge was established, developed, and passed on in its specific form.
The introduction of *nomos* and the shift of power connected with it are therefore decisive for understanding the site of emergence of this knowledge, its mode of functioning. Certainly, knowledge does not purely and simply reflect relations of power, or, with all the more reason, the forces of production, but the site and conditions of its formation cannot be separated from the manner of its formation.
All the discussions which appear from the fifth century in Greece concerning the privilege to be accorded to *logos*, writing, or pedagogy, all those discussions to find out what is fundamental (of writing, speech, or training) are possible only as the result of incomprehension. Incomprehension of the fact that it is always a matter of political power in this variable distribution of writing, speech, and pedagogy.
Thus Plato's texts on the role of writing, *logos*, *paideia* should not be deciphered in terms of a repression of writing, but in terms of a very precise struggle for power."[a]
[a]. We recognize here a quotation from Jacques Derrida, "Freud and the scene of writing" in *Writing and Difference*, trans. Alan Bass (Chicago: University of Chicago Press, 1980) p. 196: "the analysis of a historical repression and suppression of writing since Plato. This repression constitutes the origin of philosophy as *epistēmē*; of truth as unity of *logos* and *phone*." [trans. slightly modified; G.B.]

—On what conditions will *logos* be able to speak the truth?

—To what extent does language participate in being?

β—Truth, from effect, becomes condition.

In sixth century thought, truth was the general effect of that arrangement. From the fifth century it will be the condition. It is because one possesses the truth that one has good laws, that pedagogy agrees with nature, that the laws one [has] written are in accordance with *logos*, and that *logos* is in accordance with nature.

The traversal of the semantic field is possible on the basis of truth and being.

γ—The semantic field cuts itself off as institution, as social break: philosophy, science, the discourse of truth [are]:

—independent of power,

—founders of power,

—critics of power.

But it was in fact organized on the basis of power.

## *ECONOMICS AND POLITICS

Corinth was the least poorly known example for money. Athens undoubtedly offers the least fragmentary historical material for *nomos*.

### 1—Nomos *and* eunomia

The first thing to note is that the institution of *nomos* has always been associated with the establishment of something that very early on is called *eunomia*.[8]

α—At first sight *Nomos* is the law, and *Eunomia* is good legislation. When Solon prides himself on having established *eunomia* at Athens, he means that he has replaced the defective laws of the previous period with a good legislative system.

---

* M.F. suppressed a first paragraph [of ms p. 13] entitled: "Writing and the tyrant."

Earlier, when Hesiod says that *Eunomia* is the sister of *Eirēnē* and *Dikē*,[9] he means that good legislation accompanies peace outside and justice within.

β—Now this meaning of *eunomia* as good legislation cannot be maintained, because in Greek the term *eunomia* appears well before the word *nomos* and well before the institution designated by *nomos* ( *Odyssey*, Book Seventeen, 487).

Moreover, Solon, to whom is attributed, and who attributes to himself the introduction of Athenian *eunomia*, does not employ the term *nomos*. Except perhaps in one text, but we may surmise ( Vlastos)[10] that the term used was, *omou* [together; G.B.].

*Eunomia* is not derived from *nomos*, signifying an improvement, an adjustment added to the, in itself, neutral institution of (good or bad) *nomos*, but rather it is *nomos*, as institution, that is gradually separated out from the principle of *eunomia*. *Eunomia* preceded *nomos*: it was the element in which the latter was formed. One established *nomos* because one was looking for *eunomia*.

γ—*Eunomia* should no doubt be related directly to the root NEM,[11] which is also found in *nomos*, but the old values of which are better preserved in *eunomia*. This root, NEM, designates distribution and dividing up.

(In Homer, opp.: *hūbris*/*eunomia*.)[12]

We find this value clearly in the passage in Hesiod where *Eunomia* appears as the sister of *Eirēnē* and *Dikē*. And where all three are designated as daughters of the *Horae*: hours, seasons, the rhythm of time. From these regular and regularly observed moments derives peace [*Eirēnē*] between neighbors, between debtors and creditors, and between rich and poor; justice [*Dikē*] too, the right share that falls to each; and, as central divinity, the regular distribution of things, of wealth and land [*Eunomia*].

The *eunomia* Hesiod sings of, and whose reign he calls for, is not then a good constitution, a set of just laws recognized by everyone; it is a just sharing out of goods, a good distribution of wealth and its cycle, a regular movement in the interplay of expenditure, returns, and distributions. It is from this demand for *eunomia* that *nomos* will arise as the juridico-political structure of the city, and it does so through an operation whose development we see quite well in the work of Solon.

## 2—*Solon's eunomia*

Solon describes his own work as the establishment of *eunomia* in contrast with the *dusnomia* that held sway before him.[13] What *dusnomia* is can be seen clearly from his second elegy. The poor are sent into slavery due to their debts; they are driven from the share they possess. The *property owners*, on the other hand, are pursued by violence to the heart of their household; evil leaps over the barriers and walls and reaches the hearth, the most sacred place of the family and the property.

*Dusnomia*: double movement of expulsion and invasion, violent disruption of shares.

In Solon *eunomia*, as remedy for this *dusnomia*, takes on a double aspect.

α—Economic aspect:

—Cancellation, if not of debts, at least of the mortgages which weigh on the land; and no doubt the return of some farmers to their freed land. But no general redistribution of land, and preservation of shares with their existing inequality. And even some of the freed lands could not stay for long in the hands of the farmers who had got them back: in fact, legislation prohibited the uprooting of the olive trees;

—encouragement of commerce and craft industry: commerce in favor of owners of olive trees (Plutarch says that no one had the right to buy foreign commodities if they had nothing to give in exchange); craft industry producing ceramics for export.

β—Political aspect:

—distribution of politico-juridical powers according to the economic distribution of wealth;

—distinction between four poll-tax classes (four categories of citizens whose political rights, access to offices, to deliberative and decisional power are determined by their wealth);

—organization of different tribunals before which any citizen can bring an action against any other citizen.

Solon's reform[14] deserves our attention for a number of reasons.

1. In this *eunomia*, this good and regular distribution, which replaced the disordered struggle between rich and poor, it is not wealth which is ultimately distributed, it is juridico-political power.

*\*Positive aspects*
Compared to the archaic principle of the distribution of power, it is, of course, a distribution according to wealth, but with two fundamental differences:

> a—Every citizen has a share, even the poorest; even the poorest are part of the system. Power is not the property of a few. It belongs to all. It comes from no part, but from the totality. It is applied to itself.
> b—In the archaic system wealth and power were shared out by the same distribution.

With Solon, two principles:

> —if one seizes too much power, one is punished by the city;
> —if one seizes too much wealth, one must expect punishment from Zeus.[†]

*Negative aspects*[‡]
The *eunomia* instituted by Solon was a way of substituting a distribution of political power for the distribution of wealth demanded (*isomoiria*):[15] where land was demanded, power was given. Power as substitute for wealth in the operation of *eunomia*.

> NB: In a certain sense, this is the reverse of the operation carried out by Cypselus [at Corinth twenty years earlier]. The latter carried out an important economic redistribution, thanks to which he kept the exercise of power in the hands of the class that already had it (with a slight shift).
> At the heart of this operation was the simulacrum money.
> Solon, on the other hand, shared out power, up to a point, so as not to have to redistribute wealth. *Eunomia* effectuated this [power] sharing, avoiding that [economic] redistribution.

---

\* Page added at the time of a presentation, in French, at the State University of New York, Buffalo, in March 1972. After 1972, Foucault rewrote his lectures in English.
† End of added page.
‡ Subtitle added later, out of concern for symmetry with previous passage.

There is evidence for the fact that these are opposite solutions, and that Solon's is very clearly opposed to that of Cypselus, in one of Solon's elegies[16] in which he points out to the richest Athenians that, as tyrant, he could have shared out the land.

But the important thing for us is that *eunomia* and *nomisma* are two opposing institutions, which function in two different directions, but the general effect of which is the same:

—where the rich have been forced to make an economic sacrifice, money comes to the fore enabling the preservation of power through the intermediary of the tyrant;

—where the rich have been forced to make a political sacrifice, *eunomia* enables them to preserve economic privileges.

Of course the two institutions call on each other: *eunomia* serves to limit economic redistribution where money plays the main role; and money makes it possible to limit the redistribution of power imposed by *eunomia*.

Obedience to the law is ascribed to Cypselus; conversely, Solon makes reforms or carries out transformations of Attic money which inaugurate the development of a monetary economy at Athens.

2. The second characteristic of Solonic *eunomia* is that, while substituting political for economic sharing, it introduced new and complex relations between economics and politics.

The reform carried out by Cypselus did not succeed in doing this: political power simply took the form of tyranny; economically Solon's reform is much cruder; but maybe it had a much greater historical effect.

What are these new relations between economics and politics?

At first sight, an exact correlation between the quantity of wealth and the degree of participation in power: individuals are divided into four poll-tax classes according to their wealth (measured quantitatively: the pentacosiomedimni,[17] or qualitatively: horsemen, cattle owners).

Are we not still very close to the archaic group in which the powerful were always the richest and where the rich were by right powerful? Actually, I do not think so, and for two reasons.

α—First of all there is an important difference: this is that, in Solon's reform, the poorest is not someone with no power: he is someone with the smallest share of power, whose only power is to take

part in the Assembly,[18] to be able to bring any other citizen before the
courts, to appeal to the popular assembly against a sentence. So there
is no one - apart from slaves and foreigners - who does not possess
some power.

And in this way an absolutely new notion appears: the City-State,
the *polis*, as set of citizens insofar as they are possessors of a part of
power and that power as a whole is exercised through them all.

So power is no longer:

—what is held exclusively by a few;
—that to which others are unilaterally subject;
—what is exercised from time to time and instantaneously in
actions, words, commands, or ritualized levies.

Power is what is exercised permanently through all the citizens.
The totality of a social body begins to appear as the site where
power is applied to itself. Power arises from a body on which it is
exercised

β—But there is another difference between the archaic form of power
and Solon's *eunomia*. In the archaic forms, one had power inasmuch as
one was rich; and power is the possibility of acquiring wealth. The person who exercises power well becomes rich through a gift of the gods;
the person who becomes rich by reprehensible means loses power, the
gods condemn him.

The same principle of distribution shares out, in a single gesture,
power and wealth. In Solon, one's share of power is in fact proportionate
to one's wealth, but the share of wealth and the distribution of powers
are not supposed to be subject to the same mechanisms.

What makes one rich or poor remains outside *eunomia*; it is luck,
chance or fate, it is the will of the Gods. On the other hand, what determines that one exercises more power when one is rich than when one is
poor is the principle that we finally encounter: *nomos*.

Solon says this in his texts: if someone wants to misuse these rights
and commit an injustice by abuse of power, then all the town will suffer from it, and immediately: the *nomos*, which distributes power, must
therefore provide for his punishment. On the other hand, if someone
enriches himself excessively and in a way that is not just, well, let the

Gods punish him, either him or his descendants, according to the ancient beliefs, the *nomos* has nothing to do with it.

*Nomos* is the name given to a principle of the distribution of power which serves to preserve (but [while] hiding) the principles of the allocation of wealth.

*Nomos* is the form taken by the caesura of the political and the economic: a caesura that we can see is the fiction of a real break, since the distribution of political powers between the *five*\* poll-tax classes reproduces, relays, and institutionalizes economic inequalities; and since, the role of the institution of a *nomos*, of an inviolable law prescribing the distribution of power, is above all the maintenance of a certain type of economic relationship.

We have characterized the first role of money as that of simulacrum: religious simulacrum in its form, metal substitute and support for levies, destructions, and redistributions which magically invigorate the entire social body, money is the simulacrum of the power shared out among everyone, while it ensures, at the cost of a certain economic sacrifice, the preservation of power in the hands of some. In the Athenian's hands, the tetradrachma,[19] stamped with the owl, made only the simulacrum of a power held elsewhere shine for a moment.

We can now characterize *nomos* by the caesura: an obvious break between the irregular chances of wealth and the immobility of a political structure which regularly and continually shared out power; a break which hides the fact that the political distribution of power maintains and renews the mode of appropriation of wealth.

Behind money, we do not find the abstract and semiological form of the sign, but the luster of a simulacrum which plays between power and wealth.

Behind law, we do not find the gravity of writing, but the caesura which hides the dependence of the political in relation to the economic.

Money and law occupy different places, to be sure, but they ensure a complementary role in the interplay of the political and the economic, of power and wealth. An interplay which no doubt exists in every society, but the economic transformations of which in the seventh and sixth centuries, and the class struggles which followed, stretched the archaic forms to the limit.

---

\* The Solonic reform distinguishes four poll-tax classes; is Foucault assimilating metics who were taxed to a fifth class—or is this a mistake?

## CONCLUSION

In this position of caesura, *nomos* presents a number of characteristics:

It is a discourse which cannot be delivered by anyone in particular. Neither among those who possess wealth (since it certifies, registers, and transcribes wealth in political terms, but does not enter into it); nor among those who hold power (since it is what distributes power).

Therefore it must speak from nowhere, or from a median point, or from a common place

—either it is given by the oracle (Sparta),
—or by the lawgiver,
—or by the Assembly.

It is this voice from nowhere, or from the middle, or of all, depending on the circumstances (that is to say, on the opposing relations of force), which will be institutionalized

—either as writing, as unchangeable and inviolable as the appropriation of wealth that it protects must be;
—or as discourse delivered in public and by all in such a way that each can exercise power, however poor he may be, in complete independence from economic relations;
—or as pedagogy, teaching indifference to wealth and inequalities, teaching rather respect for the law;
—or as nature.*

Writing, debate, pedagogy, and nature,[†] all three [*sic*] depend on this effect of caesura where the *nomos* finds a place for itself. So ask pedagogy, discussion, or writing to bring back to light this occultation of which they are the indirect effect arising from the constitution of a political power with the form of the State. Their ethical indifference to wealth, their relative independence with regard to the exercise of political power, not only does not give them any sovereignty or liberty [ ... ], but they are only the effect of the occultation that founds their existence and ensures their functioning.

In Babylonian societies, the appropriation of power by the sovereign was renewed and reassured by the ritual recital of legendary narratives,

---

* Nature: addition which cannot be dated. See above, p. 153 note[†].
[†] Ditto previous note.

genealogies, and theogonies. How now will this *nomos*, which does not appropriate but distributes power, be reinforced; from where will this *nomos*, which is not pronounced by anyone, draw its authority and vigor? We can begin to see the need for a discourse which will not sing of the sovereign, but of the *nomos* itself, of the principle of distribution, its value and wisdom, the origin on which it is founded, and the order whose reign it establishes not only over men, but over the stars, seas, animals, and plants. Straightaway we can pick out some of the features of this discourse, which, based on the *nomos*, replaces the old song of sovereignty.

—it no longer has to tell of exploits and events preserved in memory;

—it has to recount the permanence of distributions among things and men;

—it no longer has to recall them as secret truths of memory, recalled by the muses, it has to get them to be seen as a different type of truth;

—it does not have to place itself in the sphere of a sovereignty which it has to reconstitute;

—it must speak from that blank zone, that caesura where the relations of the political and the economic go unrecognized.

It is there that the place of a knowing and neutral subject, the form of a revealed truth, and the content of a knowledge no longer magically connected to the repetition of an event, but to the discovery and maintenance of an order, are located.

It is there, in that zone, that the figure appears of someone who, behind a truth, without wealth or power, will reveal the law of things so as to give strength and vigor to a law of men which is at the same time incomprehension.

\* \* \*

[Added shorthand notes on headed notepaper of the State University of New York, Buffalo, and therefore aphoristic support to the conclusion of the discourse:]

*Eunomia*, fundamental term.

*Nomos* is institutional rule.

*Eunomia* may be

—aristocracy,

—democracy.

*Isonomia* will mean precisely democracy.

Now this *eunomia*

—on the one hand, is profoundly distinct from the Assyrian possession of power:

- the king is power, all power: there is no power except for him, whereas here power belongs to no one;
- *eunomia/turannos* opposition.

—on the other hand, *eunomia* has the same effects since it is always a matter of putting things in order: of making nature fertile, men just, punishing the guilty, suppressing wars.

Now, [in] all the Indo-European peoples, power is linked to speech in two ways:

α—it is exercised through speech

—order

—judgments

—prophecy.

β—it is founded on speech: it is speech that proclaims it, founds it, reinforces it.

We see that the discourse of sovereignty cannot be the same in the Assyrians and in the Greeks

—either in its function

—or in its distribution.

γ—in the Assyrians:

the discourse of sovereignty is ensured by the double of royal power

—its religious splitting (the priests)

—its familial double (the brother).

It recounts the exploits of the king and ancestors in their connection with heaven and earth. Genealogy

It is cyclical; it must remain secret.

δ—in Greece:

the discourse of sovereignty must be permanent

—permanence of the written

—permanence of the poem.

It must belong to no one since it is the distribution of everything.

It must be pronounced "from nowhere" or rather from the center, from the middle.

It must not make use of the heroic splitting: repeating the event, making the hero reappear.

It must operate on a different register of duality: that of the order of things, the order of men. The return of one and the other. Speaking the truth, prescribing justice.

The truth-justice couple.

The internalization of the cycle.

*Eunomia* is the form of the political/economic caesura.

The *isonomia* of Cleisthenes, even more.

It is on this basis that the break takes place at Athens. In any case, *eunomia* is the principle of sharing political power. The *nomos* is the rule of this sharing.

*nomos* and *nomisma*

sharing and measurement

But how will the discourse of *nomos* manifest itself and be exercised?

• In the Babylonian civilizations, ritual recitations

• [In] archaic Greece: the event.

Here, permanent recitation, not trace but *es aei*.

[This recitation] is not the property of a few, or the privilege of scribes, but [of] everyone: *logos*.

Not memory, or secret, but distribution to everyone, pedagogy.

Finally, the function of this discourse of the law is to bring to light and reestablish the order of things, an order which is not that of wealth, goods, and luck, but the order of a different order. A permanent order accessible to everyone through the way of the *logos*.

Wealth has its own order or rather its measure: *nomisma*.

Cities have their order or rather their law: *nomos*.

Truth is the order (less wealth, less the economy).

Money: this is measure (*la mesure*) less order

less order, justice.

1. *Nomisma*: money, currency. See Aristotle, *Nicomachean Ethics*, V, 5, 1133ᵃ, p. 1788: "and this is why it has the name 'money' (*nomisma*) - because it exists not by nature but by law (*nomos*)"; B. Laum, *Heiliges Geld*, notes the difference between *nomisma*: "that which has valid currency," means of evaluation, and *chremata*: wealth; he translates *nomos* by "rule of division," sharing out, distribution.

2. Foucault's auditors heard an allusion to the title of a recently published book, Jacque Derrida's *Writing and Difference*.

3. See P. Vinogradov, *Outlines of Historical Jurisprudence*, vol. II, pp. 76-78; H. Frisch, *Might and Right in Antiquity*.

4. The Eumolpidae interpreters attached to the priestly family of Athens, the Eumolpidae who will establish the cult of Eleusis. See P. Vinogradov, *Outlines of Historical Jurisprudence*. The exegetes will end up playing a role as legal counselors.

5. See Herodotus, IV, 105; F. Heinimann, *Nomus and Physis. Herkunft und Bedeutung einer Antithese im griechischen Denken des 5. Jahrhunderts* (Bâle: Friedrich Reinhardt, 1945, 2nd ed. 1965).

6. T.A. Sinclair, *A History of Greek Political Thought* (London: Routledge and Kegan Paul, 1951).

7. Pindar, *5th Olympian Ode* and *4th Pythian Ode*.

8. See V. Ehrenberg, *Aspects of the Ancient World* (Oxford: Blackwell, 1946) pp. 74-86: "Etymologically *eunomia* should not be related to *nomos* but to *nemein*. We find *eunomia* in Homer (*Odyssey*, Book Seventeen, 487), we do not find *nomos* ... It is not the law, it is the legislator's thought ... *eunomia, dusnomia* express a moral attitude on the part of the citizen." [The French editor indicates these phrases as Foucault's "translation" of Ehrenberg, however I have not been able to find corresponding phrases in the original English, which, in the pages referred to, contains the following: "Since ancient times the views of scholars have differed on this point. Is the word derived from *nomos* or from *nemō* (or from *nemesthai*)? ... "

   In a way both explanations are mistaken, for the abstract noun *eunomia* is based on the adjective *eunomos*. Its origin, however, does not seem any more definite than that of the noun. ... it is in the Odyssey (17, 487) that *eunomia* occurs for the first time ... it becomes at least unlikely that Solon thought of *nomos* when he praised *eunomia* ... There is ... no mention of an ideal or natural law. *Eunomia* was for Solon a goal of his personal policy, the sort of thing he had promised to Athens beforehand for the time when he might be given full power. ... *eunomia* and *dysnomia* expressed a moral attitude, or a state of mind, on the part of the citizen"; G.B.]

9. Hesiod, *Theogony*, 900-902.

10. G. Vlastos, "Ἰσονομία Πολιτική, [*Isonomia Politikē*]" in J. Mau and E.G. Schmidt, eds., *Isonomia. Studien zur Gleichheitsvorstellung im griechischen Denken* (Berlin: Akademie-Verlag, 1964).

11. E. Laroche, *Histoire de la racine NEM en grec ancien* (Paris: Klincksieck, 1949). Laroche stresses the ethical notions associated with this root.

12. *Hūbris*: absence of order, unleashing of forces, a theme taken up in *History of Madness*. E. Will says that the term is untranslatable into French. It includes the field of relations between men and between men and the gods. See E. Will, *Le Monde grec et l'Orient*, vol. I, p. 598.

13. Foucault uses a set of quotations taken from: W. Jaeger, "Solon's Eunomia," *SPAW*, Berlin, 1926; G. Vlastos, "Solonian justice"; I.M. Linforth, *Solon the Athenian* (Berkeley: University of California Press, 1919); P. Lévèque and P. Vidal-Naquet, *Clisthène l'Athénien*.

14. E. Will, "La Grèce archaïque," pp. 79-94.

15. *Isomoiria*, to be translated as "equal shares," hence equal rights. See P. Lévèque and P. Vidal-Naquet, *Clisthène l'Athénien*.

16. Solon's second elegy cited in I.M. Linforth, *Solon the Athenian*.

17. Pentacosiomedimni (*pentakosiomedimnoi*): those with an income of 500 medimni of cereal. (First class of citizens: *pentakosioi*.)

   Only membership of the first two classes of voters gave access to power; the archons were elected from within them. These first two classes represented only one fifth of the citizens whose lands produced more than five hundred bushels of wheat.

18. E. Will, *Le Monde grec et l'Orient*, vol. I, pp. 65, writes: "We do not know whether the thetes, the last class, had access to the *ecclesia*, the Assembly of the people which elected the magistrates."

19. See above, p. 148 note 33.

## eleven

# 10 MARCH 1971

*The pure and the impure:\* Homeric ablution as rite of passage.* ∽
*Reversal of the status of defilement in the seventh and sixth centu-*
*ries.* ∽ Nomos, *money, and new religious practices.* ∽ *Prohibition*
*as democratic substitute for expensive sacrifice.* ∽ *Democratization*
*and immortality.* ∽ *Criminality and will to know.*

## ORGANIZATION OF THE JURIDICO-RELIGIOUS CATEGORY OF THE IMPURE

Purification is an archaic rite; but, in the course of an evolution which has to be traced, it will be articulated on two oppositions which were originally foreign to it: criminality/innocence

ignorance/knowledge.

## 1—THE CATEGORY OF THE "PURE" IN HOMER

1. At first sight, rites of purification seem the rule after a murder, a massacre, a battle, a wound. Dust and blood are the impurities one washes off.

—Achilles returns from battle covered in blood; he goes to Odysseus and Diomedes who orders him to be washed (*Iliad*, XXIII, 31-730).[1]

---

\* Manuscript title of lecture.

—When Odysseus and Diomedes return from their expedition in the Trojan ranks, they dive into the sea, then they bathe in a bathtub (*Iliad*, X, 572-576).

2. But this does not prove that the ritual act is intended to remove a stain. The rite of ablution looks just as much towards what will take place as towards what has just taken place.

If the warrior washes himself after battle, it is because he has arrived at the threshold of a new activity, and one with a sacred, religious, or ritual character.

—When Agamemnon wants Achilles to wash, it because he is offering him a meal.

—Diomedes and Odysseus, returning from battle, wash before pouring libations to Athena.[2]

Generally, ablution is called for when one passes from an ordinary or daily activity to a ritual activity:

—Before going to pray to Athena in the upper chambers, Penelope washes and puts on clean clothing.[3]

—After having given up Chryseis, Agamemnon wants to give a hecatomb to Apollo; he makes his troops wash [*Iliad*, I, 285-327].

That it is not a matter of cleansing a sin, erasing the crime, is proven even more clearly by another passage from the *Iliad*: it is the passage concerning the funeral of Patroklos:

—Achilles has the body of Patroklos (who is the victim, not the murderer) washed carefully. He must not enter Hades defiled, *aiskummenos* (*Iliad*, XVIII, 179-180). But Achilles himself refuses to wash before he has performed his required duties towards Patroklos.

Homeric ablution does not wash the murderer or the guilty and does not restore his original purity. Rather, it scans different moments of time and different levels of activity.

Ablution takes place when one enters the domain of ritual; when the moment of sacrifice arrives; when one is descending to Hades; or also when the supplicant, the stranger, is welcomed into the home. Conversely, ablution does not occur when one has to remain in mourning; it cannot take place when one has not finished performing the required duties.

Ablution breaks contacts; it isolates moments, places, conducts; it marks the threshold crossed, the new level on which behavior is inscribed; it prevents dangerous communications or unacceptable continuities: between the massacre and the feast, between outside and the home, between this world and Hades, between the everyday and the sphere belonging to the god, between the living and the dead.

Far from delimiting a site, an already fully constituted core of defilement, in order to isolate it, we should say rather that rites of ablution mark the discontinuities of a complex, heterogeneous socio-religious space and time; and that there is defilement when two heterogeneous regions are voluntarily or involuntarily brought into contact with each other.

3. Now it should be noted that the criminal is not in himself one of these different regions to be isolated from others; in Homer the murderer is not as such the object of a special treatment.

When Telemachos is praying and pouring libations, Theoklymenos, a murderer, appears. Telemachos receives him like any supplicant.[4] Lykophron serves in the household of Ajax without the murder he has committed giving him a special status.[5] Certainly, Theoklymenos had been forced to leave his town: but this was because his victim's relatives and friends were too many and too strong for him.

We have a customary schema: 1. crime—2. defilement—3. ritual erasure—4. innocence regained. Now this schema is not valid for the Homeric period: rather, we have discontinuities ritually maintained by ablution; then, danger of forgetting, violence, undue communication between these separate regions; finally, in that case, defilement; defilement occurring in such a way that: (a) the region affected is defiled by what bursts into it; (b) the object bursting in suddenly appears as defiled in the region into which it should not have entered.

So, immediately double defilement. What will take place is a complete reversal of the schema: defilement becoming the original fact, or at least the immediate consequence of the crime, separation is then its necessary consequence; finally the purifying rite, intended to erase the defilement.

Now this reversal is important for the constitution of a morality of fault; but it is important for the constitution of a certain will to know.

## II—HOW THIS REVERSAL IS BROUGHT ABOUT

It is linked to a whole series of changes in the religious life of the seventh and sixth centuries.[6]

1. Intensification of ritualism in the working class. Certainly, there were many, doubtless very restrictive peasant rites well before the period we are looking at. But it seems that they were considerably intensified and undoubtedly organized from the seventh century.

α—The importance and meticulousness of rites in Hesiod. As well as the Homeric rites, we see a proliferation of prohibitions, like not bathing at the mouth of a river, not cutting one's fingernails at a sacrificial meal, not sitting a twelve months or twelve years old child on a sacred object.[7]

β—But Orphism in particular intensified a whole series of ritual prescriptions by organizing them.[8]

To what does this intensification correspond?

a—This kind of rite passed on from generation to generation, in its form and mode of appropriation even more than in its content, contrasts with the juridico-religious rules possessed as exclusive and secret property by important families. In their function as juridico-religious armature of existence, these rituals, in the form of effective formulae, counterbalance the secrets and decrees of the important families.

b—These prescriptions are known; their observance may not always be easy, but it is at least easy to establish whether or not they have been observed. Everyone can determine themselves if what they have done is good; everyone can be their own judge; everyone can bring a religious kind of judgment to bear on themselves.[9]

c—These rites allow everyone to take responsibility themselves for the success or failure of their harvests; through the rite, one can take in hand one's good luck or misfortune, the good understanding or quarrel one has with the gods. One no longer depends on the piety or impiety of the powerful and the kings for the success of one's undertakings. A well-observed rite allows one to be loved by the gods directly. But the rite has to be within everyone's reach.

d—Now we should note that, precisely, these rituals are completely different from the more familiar and widespread religious action: that is to say, sacrifice.

Not those sacrifices of cows, sheep, or goats, which can appear only in the religious practice of wealthy breeders of livestock; not even offerings, which were no doubt often a disguised tax when it involved bringing produce to a sacred site belonging to a powerful family. But gestures, ablutions, prohibitions more than sacrifices, arbitrary rites which have to be remembered more than objects which have to be offered.

(Prohibition as substitute for extravagant sacrifice, when the latter is not possible economically).[10]*

We see: in a way, the arbitrariness of the rite is required by its social and political function. Certainly, it is not the function (but no doubt an analysis of magical significations) that explains the particular content of the rite. But arbitrariness has, as such, a function; this is why, far from it dying down or being rationalized, it remains for a long time, and is sometimes even intensified and exacerbated. This is because, faced with the rule possessed, hidden, and imposed from outside by the powerful—and [which] brings into play the display of wealth, albeit sacrificed—the ritual sets up a system of regularities accessible to everyone, applicable by everyone to themselves, open to autonomous control, in short, separated from the possession and sacrifice of wealth through the effect of a magical relationship whose form is arbitrary.

---

* [Endnote 10 is not indicated in the text of the French edition; this seems to be the appropriate place for it; G.B.]

2. The other aspect of the religious transformation of the seventh and sixth centuries is the appearance of religious forms which escape the game of appropriation by wealthy families.

In the forefront, the Dionysian cult.[11] A cult whose popular character is well-known:

α—the importance of agrarian rites and agricultural references in the worship of Dionysus;

β—evidence of some legendary elements recounting the invasion of Dionysus, flooding in and coming up against the city gates. Thus Pentheus, king of Thebes, tries to close the city gates against the Dionysian invasion; the Maenads end up tearing him apart (Euripides, *The Bacchae*);

γ—organization in cultic groups, the *thiasoi*, brotherhoods which emerge spontaneously, *or as a result of proselytism, but quite separately from membership of the groups which traditionally possess the religious rule and secret.

Now among all these singular characteristics of the Dionysian cult, what needs to be stressed is: (a) that membership is an individual matter: one may be young or old, man or woman, foreigner or citizen; (b) that the sign of membership is shown individually in the trance; (c) that sacrifice involves the equal participation of all—the god *isodaitēs*;[12] (d) that the secret is not the possession of a family or clergy, but of every participant; (e) that connection to the god is individual (even if the individual is dissolved in it).

We are very far from the interplay of gods and men in Homer:

—struggle
—being dazzled
—substitutions.†

3. At the same time, a shift in the worship of the great gods and the way in which the rituals related to them function; we can already detect an

---

* Inserted unnumbered sheet, with different writing and ink.
† End of inserted sheet.

important difference between the Homeric gods and those whose history Hesiod recounts.

No doubt the Homeric gods shared out the world between themselves and imposed on it the reign of their power and anger. But their function was also to protect, to cherish certain peoples. There are gods who protect the Achaeans and others who protect the Trojans; and among those who protect the Achaeans there are those who protect the Argives, etcetera. But the protection of each group passes regularly through the intermediary of a leader. It is the leader who, by birth or by his offerings (or, on the contrary, his offences), attracts the god's kindness or hatred.

In Hesiod,[13] the gods do not appear bound by these genealogical privileges or singular preferences. Hesiod recounts the successive births of the gods, the distribution of their power, the dynastic hierarchy established between them, the veneration due to each according to the particular domains in which they rule. Hesiod's gods are connected to forces and domains which are certainly not yet thought in the unity of the *kosmos*, but they are no longer enclosed in the system of familial obligations towards their aristocratic descendants.

4. It is difficult to know the precise processes through which this struggle for the appropriation of the ancient forms of worship, or for the domination of certain new religious forms, passed. But it is fairly easy to recognize in this domain at least the result of the major reorganization of political power which took place in the seventh and sixth centuries. The same constitution of a new political power which enabled the establishment of money, and of a *nomos*, made possible the establishment of a new type of religious practice.[14]

a—A characteristic feature of the seizure of power by tyrants or the new distribution of power imposed by legislators was that it was never undertaken in the name of the popular gods—of *the* popular god. There was never any "Dionysian" legislation or power, any more than there was an exhaustive distribution of wealth (let's not forget that Dionysus sometimes bore the name *isodaitēs* [god of sharing out]).

Power was seized in the name of the traditional gods whose worship was in the hands of the aristocracy. For example, in the name of Zeus (at Corinth) or Athena (at the time of the return of Peisistratos from exile). The legislation of Sparta or that of Cyrene was made in the name of Apollo.

b—But nonetheless with two important modifications:

α—They are reintroduced from outside, playing the part of arbitrators between the parties; stripped, apparently at least, of their bonds of affiliation to the powerful families.

Apollo intervened at Sparta to end the evils ravaging the city. Peisistratos organized a procession on his return to Athens. This clearly means that both of them return from outside to bring peace.

Hence the important shift of religious location: the political weight acquired by centers of worship in each city, precisely to the extent that they are external to the city—Delphi and Olympia especially. And it is interesting to note that the effect of this shift is much more one of reduplication. On the one hand, we find places of worship in the cities devoted to Zeus insofar as he belongs to Olympia, or to Apollo of Delphi (the Delphinion), as if the god had to be honored as external to the city's contending parties. On the other hand, the major religious centers still outside the city framework, and prescribing its laws (before prescribing its politics), remain in the hands of aristocratic families which continue to maintain the form of worship there.

The god inside the city is reimported from outside, and, conversely, the family keeper of this cult continues to maintain its practice in this external location.

β—The second important modification in the worship of the major gods is that they appear as gods of the city.

The whole of Corinth is given to Zeus, and Athena, who returns with Peisistratos, is not only a traditional goddess of the major families of the city: she is the goddess of the craftsmen.

Family possession of the cult (with its traditions and secrets), the game of debts, dues, and services which the family keeps up with its ancestral god, is now replaced (partially at least) by a reciprocal belonging of god and city. The festivals are the symbol of this.

But, for all that, the aristocratic families are not dispossessed of their religious privileges. They are appointed officials in charge of the exercise of this or that form of worship, which previously had indeed been theirs, but which henceforth belongs to the city.

Finally, the major works, the construction of temples (Zeus at Corinth, Athena at Athens), and the system of collective offerings and sacrifices, constitute the economic correlative of these forms of worship which now resemble a State religion.

*Summary*

The intensification of both popular and individualist ritual prescriptions, and their takeover by general religious movements (like Orphism), lead to a religious quality of the individual which depends on the rigor and precision of an observance: the pure and the impure.

The vigorous development of the Dionysian cult forced, not without violent struggles, a readjustment of religious structures, and a cohabitation of traditional divinities with these new forms.

Finally, readjusted in this way, the role of religion as justification of the new political power makes possible the integration of these religious qualities of the individual in the legal system of the State.[15] Pure and impure will now be distributed by the State, or at any rate, be based on State regulation.

## III—INDIVIDUAL DEFILEMENT

The birth of a monetary economy, the formation of a new type of political power, the establishment of the religious structures we have just been talking about, all led to a juridical definition of the individual. This juridical definition is what gives form to the new distribution of the pure and the impure.[16]

How is this juridical definition of the individual formulated? Essentially in legislation that is consistently linked to the major political changes of the time.

This legislation concerns:

—inheritance
—funerary rites
—murders.

We can see that in one way or another it concerns death. It was by ensuring its hold on death, by regulating the event and consequences of death, that political power delineated the form of individuality.[17]

1. Let us go quickly over the laws concerning inheritance and burial:
a—They partially dispossess the *genos*, the family in the broad sense, of its collective rights of inheritance. They give the individual the possibility of maintaining the individual character of his fortune, up to a certain point, and of passing it on to his direct heirs and, if necessary, adopted successors. Individuality begins to take shape as form of property (this in connection with commercial development, the necessity not to divide up estates indefinitely). This is not a democratic measure.
b—The very strict regulation of funerary rites is not a sumptuary measure, but something else. What does it involve?

—prohibition of sacrificing the bull [on the tomb of someone who has just died];
—prohibition of a burial mound too high, of a herm at the top;
—limitation of the time and duration of mourning;
—prohibition of singing threnodies or of mourning an old dead man.

We can see that this is not particularly economic. It is a matter of limiting all the magical-religious processes by which one prolongs, revives, and preserves in existence the material and always about to disappear shadow of the dead man or his ancestors. The more food, tears, praises, and rites, and the more they are repeated, the more a life is prolonged. This means that, by virtue of their wealth, only the rich have the right to an afterlife.

Limiting the conduct of mourning is to make way for, to make possible, legally and ritually, the immortality for everyone that Orphic doctrines were spreading in the people in the same period. Solon's funerary jurisdiction disappropriates the privileged immortality of heroes and aristocrats (or at least that form of *post mortem* life that only wealth, economic power could ensure). It gives form to its possible generalization.

(We are used to saying that belief in immortality is an ideology imposed by the dominant class on the poorest to get them to put up with a life which will be rewarded elsewhere. Actually, immortality should be considered as first of all a class conquest: Solon's legislation is the proof of this. It is only afterwards that ideological effects, of the "opium of the people" type, come into play.)

2. The most important component concerns the jurisdiction of murder. It was established at Athens by Draco;[18] it was no doubt modified, but the Athenians always tended to refer it back to Draco.

It comprises:

a—Recognition of murder of the murderer as legitimate; which, of course, only sanctions an existing practice. But the important thing is that this practice is no longer validated by the traditional rules, but by the laws of the city as such; by fixing murder as the sanction for murder it limits the consequences of murder to that single reciprocal death. As a result it rejects the old indefinite disequilibrium of family revenge. A single retaliation and everything is blocked. It excludes the blood price, mutilation.

b—A qualification of the murder, no longer solely at the level of its effect (the death of a man), but at the level of the act itself:

—voluntary homicide
—involuntary homicide
—homicide in legitimate defense.

The murder is no longer simply what has killed a man: it is an act which, while having entailed death, may have a different quality and in itself be more or less criminal.

c—The bringing into play of practices of exclusion. Someone accused of murder comes to be refused access to ceremonies, feasts, and the *agora*.[19]

—The involuntary homicide is exiled. He may return if the victim's family (or, if he has no family, his phratry) agrees.
—But a murderer in exile cannot be killed. Killing him is viewed as the murder of a citizen.

Here again, Draco's laws take up the old rules of hospitality. But with two important changes:

Exile becomes obligatory in some cases (whereas it had been a remedy when the murderer had to contend with an opponent who was too strong). And it is then justified by the fact that the homicide (except in cases of legitimate defense) gives rise to a qualitative impurity in the person who committed it, and that this impurity is dangerous and intolerable for the city.

This impurity is such that it is not transmitted outside the city: it is the city that decrees it; it is in and with regard to the city that it is dangerous; outside the city it is as if it were defused.

d—Finally, the last characteristic of this Draconian legislation: judgment or reconciliation take on the value of purification. But this is no longer the purification that separates and isolates the heterogeneous regions of existence and in relation to which defilement is always possible. It is a matter of a purification which erases a prior defilement identified with the crime itself and makes it possible to bring back together what defilement had forced to separate.

Henceforth, by means of defilement, impurity, segregation, judgment, and purification, the new political power has power over familial revenge and the indefinite reciprocities of murders. In the old Homeric jurisdiction, in the *dikazein* that the Gortyn legislation provided for, power intervened only with regard to the regularity of the procedures. Now power intervenes at the level of a juridical-religious characterization of actions and of those who committed them.

The schema is inverted: defilement becomes the first element (defilement of blood), then [comes] purification.

Previously death gave rise to purification due to the passage. Now death gives rise to defilement. Everything revolves around the little indelible stain.

Let us summarize all this:

The new political power, which is constituted through the work of lawgivers or tyrants and as sanction of the class struggles which took place in the seventh century

—ensures that the rich preserve their wealth by means of the law of inheritance; with the laws on burials, into which entire fortunes could be sunk, it defends the rich against their own wealth-destroying traditions;

—but at the same time, and by this very fact, [this legislation] ensures that all have the possibility and right to an afterlife, or at any rate an equal chance of survival;

—finally, it puts an end to inter-family struggles, here too defending families against their own destruction. But this involves a juridical-moral quality of individuals, [which] is in the hands of political power (through the intermediary of magistrates and tribunals).

Thus we see emerging at the intersection of all these measures:

α—a legal subject who can assert his will beyond his concrete existence;
β—an identity which can survive beyond death;
γ—a singular support of juridical and moral qualities.

Individuality appears in an at least mediate way as an effect of this displacement, this redistribution, this new organization of political power.

It was by taking control of the economic and social effects of death that political power gave rise to, as effect, that form of individuality with which we are still familiar.

\*     \*     \*

*The pure/impure opposition was fitted over the innocent/criminal opposition.

Certainly, this evolution is well known: the transition from Homeric heroes, soiled with blood but not impure, to Aeschylus' Orestes, who only the intervention of great gods can release from his defilement, has often been studied.[20] The purity-innocence connection or impurity-crime [connection] are not traces of archaisms, rather they are relatively recent formations in the juridical-religious system of the Greeks. But the

---

\* Inserted unnumbered sheets.

important thing is to grasp fully that this transformation is the not the effect of a rationalization or individualization but of a set of complex processes among which we find:

—the intensification of rituals as (autonomous) principle of the religious quality of individuals;
—the organization of popular cults in large scale popular forms;
—the transformation or integration of family cults into city religion;
—the juridical-religious status accorded to the individual (in the transmission of goods through inheritance laws, in the right to the afterlife through funerary laws);
—the intervention of the city in reparation procedures following a murder. Measures of legal exclusion (death, exile) replace traditional retaliation (both regular and indefinite).

Exclusion appears as the final and decisive element by which a social space completes its formation and closure on itself (a social space which we have already seen is, before any exchange, the site of monetary circulation and the exercise of *eunomia*, of the good economic-political distribution).

It is also by exclusion that individuality completes its formation and closure on itself as support of a juridical and religious quality which defines the pure and the impure.

It is not because the social space was formed and closed on itself that the criminal was excluded from it; but the possible exclusion of individuals is one of the elements of the formation of the social space.

Likewise, it was not because one first thought or imagined the criminal's impurity that one brought the practice of exclusion into play. The practice of exclusion is constitutive, and not the result, of the pure-impure division in Greek practice, just as the practice of exclusion is constitutive of the reason-insanity division and the delinquent/non-delinquent opposition.[21] And proof that exclusion is constitutive of impurity (and [not] the consequence of a theory, or theology, or morality, or magic of impurity), is that no Greek text says how the transmission of impurity takes place; through what support or what path of transmission, and with what effects.

The impure is what cannot be tolerated: it is what endangers the city;[22] it is what threatens ruin. Belief in impurity (a barely articulated belief, moreover, and without imaginary shape) is the effect of a practice: the practice in which the intervention of political power in the effects of murder takes shape.

Now, what relationship does all this have with the truth? Actually, we are now close to the question. The impure criminal is someone who can no longer come near:

—he can no longer approach the space in which rites are performed,

—he can no longer approach the public square where the life of the city takes place,

—he can no longer approach the city itself.

He is excluded by the *nomos*, but he is excluded from the *nomos*, from the places where and forms in which it is exercised. He is thrust outside the principle of distribution.*

The impure cannot have access to the truth. But if impurity is the individual quality brought about by the crime once committed, and if impurity is the principle of dangerous contact and the focal point from which evil is propagated throughout the space of the *nomos*, then we can see how necessary it is to know if the crime was committed and by whom. In Homer, or at any rate in the archaic epoch, the factual truth of the crime was not the primary and conditioning element of the whole procedure. The most important thing was the correct sequence of challenges and restitutions.

(If a crime has been committed and the family does not take revenge, the anger of the gods falls on the family. But one could turn to the decisive oath: Are you prepared to swear that you have not killed? If you do, then may the gods settle things with you.)

On the other hand, when the crime produces defilement and defilement affects the city, then it is essential to know whether or not a crime really has taken place.

---

* End of unnumbered sheets.

1. *Iliad,* XXIII, 31-73. [Lattimore's translation has only that "the kings of the Achaians" seek, in vain, to persuade Achilles to wash; G.B.] All the examples taken from Homer are cited by Foucault in the same order as in the work by Louis Moulinier, "Le Pur et l'Impur dans la pensée et la sensibilité des Grecs jusqu'à la fin du IV[e]s. av J.-C." (Paris: Sorbonne, 1950, copy of thesis).

2. *Iliad,* X, 550-579.

3. *Odyssey,* IV, 750-769 and XVII, 45-50.

4. *Odyssey,* XV, 256-281: "godlike Theoklymenos" (271).

5. *Iliad,* XV, 429-441.

6. See L. Moulinier, "Le Pur et l'Impur..." p. 44 *sq.*; G. Glotz, *La Solidarité de la famille dans le droit criminel en Grèce* (Paris: A. Fontemoing, 1904) p. 232.

7. M.P. Nilsson, *Greek Popular Religion* (New York: Columbia University Press, 1940) pp. 104-105.

8. L. Moulinier, *Orphée et l'Orphisme à l'époque classique* (Paris: Les Belles Lettres, 1955) pp. 60-61: "Orphism is 'a new spirit infused' in the ancient religions."

9. According to Moulinier, no Orphic cult is attested.

10. A reference to Nietzsche, for whom ritual and asceticism are substitutes for sacrifice.

11. A.-J. Festugière, "Les mystères de Dionysos," *Revue biblique,* XLIV (3), 1935, reprinted in A.-J. Festugière, *Études de religion grecque et hellénistique* (Paris: J. Vrin, 1972), pp. 13-23.

12. *Isodaitēs:* who distributes to all equally; attribute of Bacchus.

13. Hesiod, *Theogony,* which sings of the genealogy of the gods rather than of the law of work imposed on men in *Works and Days.*

14. E. Will, "De l'aspect éthique des origines grecques de la monnaie."

15. M.I. Finley, *The Ancient Greeks:* "Without wishing it the tyrants permitted the constitution of the State" (translation by M.F.). [No page reference is given for this "translation," but see pp. 44-45.]

16. H. Frisch, *Might and Right in Antiquity,* pp. 122-128.

17. We find here the underlying theme of *Naissance de la clinique* (Paris: PUF, 1963); English translation by Alan Sheridan, *The Birth of the Clinic* (London: Tavistock and New York: Pantheon, 1973).

18. H. Frisch, *Might and Right in Antiquity.*

19. Antiphon, "Hérode," §10 in *Discours, suivis des fragments d'Antiphon le sophiste,* II, γ, 8, ed. and trans. L. Gernet (Paris: Les Belles Lettres, 1954 [1923]); English translation by Michael Gagarin, Antiphon, "On the Murder of Herodes" §10 in Michael Gagarin ed., *The Oratory of Classical Greece, Volume 1. Antiphon and Andocides* (Austin: University of Texas Press, 1998), pp. 52-53.

20. Aeschylus, *The Oresteia,* trans. Robert Fagles (Harmondsworth: Penguin Books, 1979). On this evolution, see L. Moulinier, "Le Pur et l'Impur..."

21. Here, Foucault not only recalls the division of *History of Madness* (*Histoire de la folie,* 1961), from which he set off from the first session, but he also announces *Discipline and Punish* (*Surveiller et Punir,* 1975), the material of which begins to be the object of the same year's seminar (1970-1971).

22. Antiphon, *Discours.*

# twelve

# 17 MARCH 1971

*Crime, purity, truth: a new problematic.* ᰥ *The tragedy of Oedipus. Emergence of visual testimony.* ᰥ Nomos *and purity. Purity, knowledge, power.* ᰥ *Sophocles' Oedipus versus Freud's Oedipus.* ᰥ *What hides the place of the sage.* ᰥ *What is a discursive event?* ᰥ *Usefulness of Nietzsche.*

I—THE JURIDICAL-RELIGIOUS SUPERIMPOSITION of crime and purity entails a new relationship to the truth. In fact:

    α—impurity is now a quality of the individual constituted by the crime;

    β—this impurity is the source of dangerous contacts which spread throughout the space of the city;

    γ—it is therefore important know if the crime has been committed and by whom.

Demonstration of the truth becomes a political task. Impurity and its effects bring with them the need to investigate what happened.

    CREON—The King Apollo expressly orders us to free this country from a defilement which it has nourished in its womb, to not let it grow and become incurable.
    OEDIPUS—By what *purification*\*? What misfortune is involved?

---

\* Underlined by M.F.

CREON—By exiling a guilty man or by expiating a murder by a murder, for this blood causes the misfortunes of Thebes.[1]

...

The god today clearly orders punishment of the murderers whoever they may be.[2]

OEDIPUS—Where are they? Where will we discover this difficult trail of an old crime?

CREON—In this land. He has said so. What we seek, we find; what we neglect, escapes us.[3]

In the archaic epoch, the investigation of what happened was not the primary and determining element of the procedure. For two reasons:

1. The most important thing was the correct sequence of challenges and restitutions. The scene of the shield—not: has there been a crime? But: has there been restitution? The judgment is not brought to bear on the fact, but on the procedure.

The decisive oath does not serve to reveal the truth, but to expose the one who swears the oath to a double risk. If he committed the crime and swears that he has not, then he will be punished for this double offence. But the demonstration of what happened is left to the gods, whose vengeance will make it known.

In the Menelaos-Antilochos dispute there is no appeal to the *histōr*.[4] But what care is taken in *Oedipus* to find the witness.

2. This is because when crime produces defilement, this defilement affects the city,[5] and exclusion is required, it now becomes necessary to know:

—if
—by whom
—how.

α—Draco's laws provided for establishing the fact of the crime and, if it was an involuntary crime, for there to be an inquiry. Of course, it is not yet the city that takes responsibility for the demonstration. Testimonies are provided by the parties and witnesses jointly swear an oath.

Truth is still caught up in the form of the struggle. But judgment, deciding on the victory of one of the two parties, bears on what happened, no longer solely on the fulfillment of a procedure, but on the reality of a fact.

β—For a long time signs of purity are still typically found among proofs of the fact. In the pleas [of the] classic [epoch], the accused often say: I am not guilty,

—since I have not been banned from entering the *agora*,[6]
—since I have not been ruined,
—since I have not suffered any misfortune.

This signifies rather that the test is still present, but as sign of truth. Since the effects of impurity and the reality of the fact are linked to each other, the reality of the fact must be established for one to escape the effects of the impurity.

Conversely, the effects of impurity (or their absence) confirm or infirm the reality of the fact.

γ—The whole of the Oedipus tragedy is permeated by the effort of the whole city to transform the enigmatic dispersion of human events (murders, plagues) and divine threats into [certified] facts.

When the *miasma*[7] reigns in the city, it is because there is something to be known. It is because there is an enigma to be resolved. And the Priest says this to Oedipus: he is turned to because he was able to answer the cruel singer.[8]

The effects of impurity immediately set the snares of knowledge. But this is not the knowledge of the rules to be applied; it is not the knowledge that answers the question: what must be done? It is the knowledge that answers the question: who?

To start with, the Priest and Oedipus still spoke in terms of "what must be done," although the answer to the Sphinx indicates clearly that Oedipus is the man who answers the question: *who?* Apollo's oracle corrects the question; or rather, to the question: what must be done? he replies: what must be done is to look for *who*. And not in order to start a complex rite of purification. But certainly in order to exclude: exile or death.

Now Teiresias will not say who this "*who*" is.[9] He knows, of course, and in a sense tells. But he does not name him and he has not seen him. His sentence is missing the name, as sight is missing from his face.

The question "*who?*" is not answered by the seer, but by the person who saw. Or rather, by those who saw:

—the servant who saw the birth of Oedipus and who is precisely the only witness to survive the murder of Laius;
—the Messenger who saw the child Oedipus and who is precisely the one who comes to announce the death of Polybus.

No wisdom is required to answer the question: *who?* Two frightened servants suffice to answer the question put by Apollo. Among all these blind persons, they saw. And the truth that the priests and kings did not know, that the gods and seers partially concealed, was possessed by a slave in a hut who had been witness, *histōr*.

## CONCLUSION

1. As we see: defilement is linked to the truth. The juridical and social practice in which defilement is an element involves *establishing a fact* as an essential component: it is necessary to know if a crime has been committed and by whom.[10] In the archaic period,[11] responsibility for eventually avenging a crime, should one have been committed, was handed over to the gods, and it was the event of this vengeance that both made the crime blatantly clear and compensated for it beyond any human retribution. There were two events, one of which retrospectively lit up the other, and the moment of its erasure: between the two was a pure waiting—indecision, indefinite imminence.

Now the rite of purification requires the truth of the fact to be set out. The passage from the crime to its punishment takes place through the intermediary of a proven reality and a duly certified fact. Truth, instead of residing in the flash produced between two events, the second of which indicates and destroys the first, constitutes the only legitimate passage from the defilement to what has to remove it.

The *event* is transformed into *fact*.

2. And truth thus becomes the primary or in any case primordial condition of purification. In the archaic system, the thunderbolt of divine vengeance brought, in an instant, the flash of the truth; the truth sparkled only in the event. (The rite did not concern the truth, but the transfer from men to the gods.)

Now truth is required by the *rite* and forms part of the rite. Impurity will become pure again, or rather impurity will be separated from purity only through the intermediary of the established truth. Truth finds its place in the rite. The rite makes room for the truth. And truth does indeed have a lustral function. Truth separates. Lustral function of the truth.

The truth is what makes it possible to exclude; to separate what is dangerously mixed; to distribute the inside and outside properly; to trace the boundaries between what is pure and what is impure.

Truth henceforth forms part of the great juridical, religious, and moral rituals required by the city. A city without truth is a threatened city. Threatened by mixtures, impurities, unfulfilled exclusions. The city needs the truth as a principle of division. It needs discourses of truth as it needs those who maintain the divisions.

II—But the juridical-religious structure of purity envelops another type of relation to the truth. We could indicate this in this way:

α—One who is impure threatens all those around him with his impurity. He is a danger for the family, for the city, and for its wealth. Where he is, "the city is drowned by a swell of blood, it perishes in its deep seeds, it perishes in its herds; it perishes in women's abortions" (*Oedipus the King*, 24-27).[12] Wherever *nomos* reigns, that is to say, throughout the space that constitutes the city, the criminal is dangerous. His pollution compromises the order of things and of men.

β—That is why he must be excluded from this *nomos*, from the "social space" that defines the city.

"No one must receive him, or speak to him, or make him take part in prayers and sacrifice to the gods; no one must share with him the lustral water; all must drive him from their homes" (*Oedipus the King*, 236-241).[13]

The impure is coextensive with the *nomos* in its effects, and the region from which it is excluded must also be coextensive with the *nomos*.

γ—But in what is it impure? Of what does this impurity consist? What gesture, then, qualifies it as impure? It is that of having voluntarily or involuntarily ignored the *nomos*.

For the Homeric hero, punishment took place either because he had forgotten the rule (in a moment of blindness), or because he had provoked the gods' jealousy.

Under the reign of *nomos*, the offence consists in ignoring a law that is there, visible to, and known by everyone, made public in the city and decipherable in the order of nature. The impure is someone who has had his eyes closed to the *nomos*. He is impure because he is *anomos*.

δ—But if one is impure for having been blind to the *nomos*, when one is impure, when one is a source of disorder for the *nomos*, one can no longer see it. One becomes blind to its lawfulness.

*Nomos* as principle of distribution, as principle of the just dividing up, is inevitably inaccessible to the impure. Disclosure of the order of things, which enables the *nomos* to be stated and provides its justification, will remain impossible for someone who is impure. Conversely, purity is the condition for access to the law: for seeing the order of things and for being able to utter the *nomos*. This median place, which as we have seen is the fictitious site where the lawgiver like Solon places himself, can only be occupied by someone who is pure.

Purity is the condition required to tell of and see the *nomos* as manifestation of order. The purity/impurity separation is thus connected to the *nomos* in four ways:

> —impurity produces its effects in the space of the *nomos* (which is why exile is purification in itself) (division, separation, non-mixture);
> —impurity must be excluded from the *nomos* and according to the *nomos* itself. It is the law that says it is necessary to exclude;
> —but impurity occurred only because one was already excluded from the *nomos* due to ignorance or blindness. And if one is blind to the *nomos*, it is because one is impure.
> —The relations between impurity and the law are finally sealed through the intermediary of knowledge. To be able to state the law, one must not be impure. But to be pure one must know the law.

A whole ethics of truth, from which we have not yet escaped, is in the process of being brought together, even though we now receive only muffled echoes from this formidable event.

\* \* \*

A number of important figures in Greek thought revolve around this purity-disclosure of order relation.

## 1. THE FIGURE OF THE SAGE

This figure is located at the origin of the distribution of political power. Not where political power is exercised violently and by constraint, but where its law is formulated. The sage's place is in the middle. Sometimes, like Solon, he does not exercise power and merely expresses the law. And if some tyrants are ranked [at this] level, it is to the (mythical) extent to which they let [the law] be brought to bear by itself, have no need of guards, and the *nomos* passes through them without violence.

But at the same time the sage is someone who knows the order of things. He is acquainted with the world because he has travelled, because he has gathered lessons from afar, and because he has observed the heavens and eclipses.

Finally, the sage is someone who is not stained by any crime.

A certain place is defined which is that of the founder (rather than possessor) of political power, of the expert of the order of the world (rather than the keeper of traditional rules), of the man with pure hands (rather than the one who is forever taking up the challenge of vengeance). But we need to recognize that this is a fictitious figure behind whose mask economic and political processes continue to operate.\*

---

\* The partial oral transcript is even more explicit:
"Thus a certain place is defined which is at the same time that of the founder of political power rather than of its possessor, that of the expert of the order of the world rather than that of the keeper of traditional rules, and that of the man with pure hands rather than that of the hero who is forever taking up the challenge of vengeance. It is this that defines the bond on the basis of which the whole of knowledge as practiced by the Greeks will be deployed: juridical knowledge of the law, philosophical knowledge of the world, moral knowledge of virtue... and the figure of the sage is the mask behind which economic processes are preserved, maintained, and transformed into political institutions."

## 2.  ANOTHER FIGURE, THAT OF POPULAR POWER

This power, the negative figure of which appears in Plato, Aristotle, less [in] Aristophanes than in Thucydides, is a power which does not respect the *nomos* but changes it through discourse, discussion, the vote, and a changeable will. Popular power does not know the *nomos*. It is excluded from knowledge (from political knowledge and the knowledge of things).

Although the procedures are now no longer exclusively in the hands of the important families, knowledge of the law, of *nomos*, of the good order of the city, is confined to that fictitious site that only sages can occupy.

But popular power is not merely ignorant. It is inevitably impure since it is *anomos*. Popular power harkens only to its interests and desires. It is violent: it imposes its will on everyone. It is murderous. And in a privileged fashion, it kills the sage, as the one who occupies the place where the laws speak.

Popular power is criminal in essence—criminal in relation to what, since it expresses the will of all? It is criminal in relation to *nomos*, to the law as foundation of the city's existence. Popular power is crime against the very nature of the city.*

The sage as pure keeper of knowledge and *nomos* therefore has to protect the city against itself and prohibit it from governing itself.[14]

Wisdom: fictitious site which functions as real prohibition.

## 3.  BETWEEN THE TWO, THE TYRANT

Figure of the effective holder of power:

—an absolutely negative figure when he comes close to popular power and embodies it;

—a figure who becomes positive insofar as he lets himself be persuaded by the sage.

---

* The lecture adds:
  "In fourth century aristocratic thought, the murder of Socrates is this exclusion of the sage by popular power."

We can see that this interdependence of knowledge and power, and this connection of *nomos* to truth through the intermediary of purity, are very different from what we were saying with regard to purity and the event.

We have seen that impurity put to knowledge the question of fact, more precisely it put the question: who did it? And we saw that it was fundamentally important to purity that the crime be established. (Truth of the fact, which allows exclusion of the impurity, and purity, which allows access to knowledge of the order.)

But we see that it is not in order to know the facts that purity is essential, but in order to know the very order of the world; whoever is impure cannot know the order of things.

Now in this second type of relation (in which it is no longer a question of fact, but of order; in which it is no longer a question of impurity which demands knowledge, but of impurity which prevents knowledge), we find Oedipus again. Oedipus (this is said several times at the start of the text) is the one who put the city right, who set it straight again (*orthos*);[15] these are the terms traditionally employed to designate the work of the lawgiver. Now he did this by solving an enigma: so by his thought, his knowledge, etcetera. But he became impure by being blind to the most fundamental *nomos*—father and mother.[16] And now he no longer knows what to do, for although he does not yet know this, his impurity has put him outside the *nomos*. He no longer knows the order of things and the human order.

The person whose thought kept the city straight no longer knows.

Hence the appeal to all those who may know: from the god to the shepherd. He places himself at a remove from the sources of knowledge. He is no longer in the middle of the city. And every time a piece of news arrives, a fragment of knowledge, he recognizes (and is not mistaken) that a part of his power is being taken from him.

The dispute with Creon is at the center of the tragedy. Purity links knowledge and power. Impurity covers up knowledge and drives out from power.

And finally, Oedipus, joining together these two forms of relation between *purity* and *truth*, is the one who still does not know the truth of the fact at the point when everyone is already capable of knowing it; and he does not know it because he is impure and, being impure, he does not know the order of things and of men. (He suspects a plot, a threat, he wants to kill, to exile Creon, he is *unjust* as he himself will recognize when the truth will have forced his access ...

\*   \*   \*

Maybe the story of Oedipus points to a certain form that Greece gave to truth and its relations with power and impurity.* Maybe Oedipus does not recount the destiny of our instincts or of our desire. But maybe it indicates a certain system of constraint with which the discourse of truth in Western societies has complied since Greece.

The political, juridical, and religious requirement to transform the recurrences, temporal flashes, and disequilibria of the event into established and definitively preserved facts in the *observation* of witnesses; the political, juridical, and religious requirement to found the principle of the distribution of power on the knowledge of an order of things to which wisdom alone gives access (and so the requirement that the *nomos* be founded on a knowledge-virtue which is quite simply respect for the *nomos*)—these are the historical constraints imposed on true discourse, the historical functions confided to true discourse which Oedipus recounts.

Freud, advancing in the direction of the relations between desire and truth, thought that Oedipus was speaking to him about the universal forms of desire;[17] whereas it was telling him about the historical constraints of our system of truth (of the system that Freud was coming up against). (The culturalists' mistake concerning Freud's mistake.)[18]

If we are subject to an Oedipal determination, it is not at the level of our desire, but at the level of our true discourse. It is this determination that subjects the thunderbolt of the event to the yoke of the observed fact; and which subjects the requirement of the distribution [of power] to purified knowledge—purifier of the law.

The system of the signifier as what marks the event in order to insert it into the law of a distribution is indeed an important element of this Oedipal constraint, it is this that has to be overturned.

But maybe this Oedipal determination is not the most fundamental thing to be found in the determination of true discourse as it functions

---

* From here, ms page 18, corrections and rewritings seem to indicate that it is no longer a matter of one and the same lecture, but of different presentations. (See Appendix below, p. 195 et seq.)

in Western societies. Maybe the most important thing would be this: in the great political reorganization and redistribution in the seventh and sixth centuries, a fictitious place was fixed where power is founded on a truth which is only accessible on guarantee of purity.

This *fictitious place* was marked out by projection from a class struggle, a shift of power, an interplay of alliance and transaction which halted the great popular demand for a full and egalitarian distribution of the land. This fictitious place excludes recognition of the both political and factual character of the processes that enabled it to be defined.

This place can only fail to understand its having been produced historically. A discourse will be delivered from this place which will claim to be:

—as regards its content, what it talks about: a discourse revealing the order of the world and things down to the singularity of the fact;

—as regards its function, its role: a just discourse governing, or serving as the model for political relations between men, and allowing the exclusion of all that is anomic;

—as regards the subject who delivers it: a discourse to which one can have access only at the price of innocence and virtue, that is to say, outside the field of power and desire.

Fiction: that is to say *invented* site which will hold a discourse of truth (which will gradually be specified in philosophical, scientific, and political discourse)—*

\* \* \*

---

\* After this dash, the rest of the page is crossed out. We have thought it illuminating to restore it as a note:

"And it is this fictitious place that, in turn or simultaneously, will qualify the following as able to deliver this discourse:

—the sage (as lawgiver, as teller of the Law, revealer and founder of order),

—the theologian (as the interpreter of God's word, as the revealer of God's thought, will, and being),

—the scientist (as discoverer of the world's truth, one who states things themselves or their relations),

—the philosopher (as one who states the form and foundation of all possible truth).

Now, we can see, if this fictitious place qualifies them for telling the truth, this is subject to a double condition of:

—on the one hand, remaining set back in relation to the exercise of power. They can found it, they can say what the good distribution of power is, but on condition of not taking part in it and of remaining outside the actual exercise of a power;

—and, on the other, the imposition of the restrictive conditions of purity, innocence, and non-criminality."

*1. What is involved is the analysis of what could be called discursive events:[19] namely, events concerning the mode of appropriation of (political-judicial) discourse, its functioning, and the forms and contents of knowledge to which it accords the role that it plays in social struggles.

Two comments:

By *event* I do not mean an indivisible unity that could be situated univocally on temporal and spatial coordinates. An event[20] is always a dispersion; a multiplicity. It is what takes place here and there; it is polycephalous.

By discursive event I do not understand an event that occurs in a discourse, in a text. But it is an event which is dispersed between institutions, laws, political victories and defeats, demands, behaviors, revolts, reactions. Multiplicity that we can recognize and describe as discursive event insofar as its effect is to define:

—the place and role of a type of discourse,
—the quality of the person who must deliver it,
—the domain of objects to which it is addressed,
—the type of statements to which it gives rise.

In sum, the discursive event is never textual. We do not find it in a text.

2. To try to see whether the emergence of truth as we find it in Plato or Aristotle could be treated as a discursive event.

—that is to say, outside of any search for the origin: outside of any search that would like [to find], beyond history, the foundation of the possibility of history itself;
—that is to say, on the basis of a series of humble and external processes: peasant debt, subterfuge in the establishment of money, displacement of the rites of purification, small humble origins;

---

* Here begin three unnumbered sheets with a slightly different handwriting. Are they part of the same lecture, replacing the page crossed out, or part of a summary in other circumstances? It is difficult to decide.

—that is to say again, on the basis of a history [other] than that of [the] struggle conducted around political power by opposed social classes.

All in all, to try to show truth as an effect of this struggle at the level of discursive practices. To find again that something altogether different Nietzsche spoke about.

3. Not to look for a link of expression and/or reflection between these struggles and their effect in discourse. Rather, it is a matter of showing:

—how, at a given moment, the class struggle may call upon certain types of discourse (Eastern knowledge); or
—how the class struggle defines the fictitious place of discourse and the (real or ideal) quality of the person who can and must take it up; or
—how a certain type of object can become an object of discourse serving as an instrument in this struggle; or
—how this discourse exercises a function of occultation in relation to the struggle that made it possible.

It is this set of relations that is to be analyzed in terms of conditions of possibility, function, appropriation, and encoding. And not [in terms] of a reflection.*

\*     \*     \*

APPENDIX     PRESERVED FRAGMENT OF THE
TRANSCRIPTION OF THE LECTURE GIVEN

The Oedipus story points to a certain form that Greece gave to the truth and the relations that truth maintains with power, on the one hand,

---

\* This abrupt ending may indicate that some sheets are missing. A preserved fragment of the oral transcription corresponds faithfully to the synthetic notes of the auditor, Hélène Politis. They are given here as an appendix.

and with purity, on the other. Maybe we should say that the Oedipus fable does not recount the destiny of our desire and our institutions; it could well be that the Oedipus fable speaks rather of a certain system of constraints to which, since Greece, the discourse of truth in Western societies conforms. And this system of constraints shown by the Oedipus fable could be characterized very schematically in the following way:

On the one hand, the political, juridical, and religious requirement to transform the event, its recurrences and figurations over time, into established and definitively preserved facts in the *observation* of witnesses. Subjecting the event to the form of the observed fact is the first aspect of Oedipal truth.

On the other hand, the requirement—also political, juridical, and religious—of founding the principle of the distribution of power on the knowledge of an order of things to which only wisdom and purity give access. In other words, the other aspect of this Oedipal system of truth will be to found the *nomos* on a knowledge-virtue which is quite simply in itself respect for the *nomos*. Truth will be given only to someone who respects the *nomos* and he will arrive at the truth of the *nomos* only on condition of being pure.

The transformation of the lightning flash of the event into observed fact, and access to truth given only to someone who respects the *nomos*, are the two great historical constraints that, since Greece, have been imposed on the true discourse of Western societies, and it is the birth, the formation of these historical constraints that *Oedipus* recounts.

So that Freud, in advancing in the direction of the relation between desire and truth, was mistaken; he thought that Oedipus was speaking to him about the universal forms of desire, whereas, in lowered voice, the Oedipus fable was recounting to him the historical constraint weighing on our system of truth, on that system to which Freud himself belonged. When culturalists reproach the Freudian analysis of Oedipus with the fact that Freud gave it infinitely too much universality, when they say that Oedipus is only valid for certain European societies, they are no doubt mistaken, but they only make a mistake about Freud's own mistake.

Freud thought that Oedipus spoke to him about desire, whereas Oedipus, himself, was talking about the truth. It is quite possible that Oedipus may not define the very structure of desire, but what Oedipus recounts is simply the history of our truth and not the destiny of our instincts. We are subject to an Oedipal determination, not at the level of our desire, but at the level of our true discourse. In hearing the true discourse of desire, Freud thought that he was hearing desire speaking, whereas it was the echo of his own true discourse, whereas it was the form to which his true discourse was subject.

Thus we see taking shape the system of constraints and that determination that subjects the thunderbolt of the event to the yoke of the observed fact; this is what subjects the requirement of universal distribution, regularly repeated, to the purified and purifying knowledge of the unchanging law. If we add to this that the system of the signifier is undoubtedly a system which allows the event to be marked so as to insert it into the law of distribution, we can see how the signifier is what enables the lightning flash of the event to be subjected to the yoke of the observed fact, and what also allows reduction of the requirement of distribution to the purified knowledge of the law. The system of the signifier is the major instrumental element in this Oedipal constraint; which is why the order of the signifier has to be overturned.

Thus, I have tried to analyze the relation between truth and the system of purification in historical terms, but the project of analyzing the "Will to know" has not been carried out.

The hypothesis of this analysis was that the Aristotelian model appeared to characterize classical philosophy. This model entails that the Will to know (*savoir*) is nothing other than curiosity, that knowledge (*connaissance*) is always already marked in the form of sensation, and finally that there was an inherent relation between knowledge and life.

The Nietzschean model, on the other hand, claims that the Will to know (*savoir*) refers not to knowledge (*connaissance*) but to something altogether different, that behind the Will to know there is not a sort of preexisting knowledge that is something like sensation, but instinct, struggle, the Will to power. The Nietzschean model, moreover, claims that the Will to know is not originally linked to the Truth: it claims that the Will to know composes illusions, fabricates lies, accumulates errors, and is deployed in a space of fiction where the truth itself is only an effect. It claims, furthermore, that the Will to know is not given in the form of subjectivity and that the subject is only a kind of product of the Will to know, in the double game of the Will to power and to truth. Finally, for Nietzsche, the Will to know does not assume the preexistence of a knowledge already there; truth is not given in advance; it is produced as an event.

The task proposed was to test the utilizability of the Nietzschean model and to put to work the four principles found in Nietzschean analysis:

1—The principle of exteriority: that behind knowledge (*savoir*) there is something altogether different from knowledge;
2—The principle of fiction: truth is only an effect of fiction and error;
3—The principle of dispersion: a subject is not the bearer of truth, but truth itself passes through a multiplicity of events that constitute it;
4—The principle of the event.

I have begun to tackle the analysis on the basis of these principles.

With regard to the principle of exteriority, I have never tried to analyze the text on the basis of the text itself.

As far as possible I have tried to get rid of the principle of exegesis, of commentary; I have never tried to know the non-said which was present or absent in the texture of the text itself.

I have tried to get rid of textuality by situating myself in the dimension of history, that is to say locating discursive events that take place, not within the text or several texts, but through the fact of the function or role given to different discourses within a society.

Going outside the text so as to find the function of discourse within a society is what I call the principle of exteriority. As for the principle of fiction, I have tried to show how the effect of truth could arise from something that not only had nothing to do with the truth, but that, from the point of view of the truth constituted in this way, we can only recognize as untrue, illusory, or fictitious.

I have tried in this way to show how measurement arose from a currency; how this knowledge of the order of things and the order of men, which was the guarantee of the unity of things with men, arose only as a pretext from an economic and political caesura.

The *sumbolon*

| | (1) *Apollo* | *Teiresias* |
|---|---|---|
| divination | It is necessary to punish<br>Lack: the person one must punish | It is Oedipus |
| hearing<br>memory | (2) *Jocasta*<br>It is not you<br>(a) It was a robber at the crossroads<br>(b) And in any case he had to be killed by his son, who was got rid of | *Oedipus*<br>It is me<br>I killed him at the crossroads<br><br>After having fled my parents |
| testimony | (3) *Corinthian*<br>I got him from the person with whom he had been left | *Servant*<br>I got him from his parents Laius and Jocasta |

The *sumbolon* was Oedipus himself. Given by somebody, received by another. To half of the story held by the servants corresponds the other half held by the masters. Only the gods know everything. King Oedipus was caught between the gods who knew everything and the servants who had seen everything. He knew nothing.

This visual testimony was necessary for the prophecy to be effectuated, realized.

But as a result, he loses power. He really was the tyrant extending his power over *gnōmē*, *technē*. He is the ignorant king. So delivered up to the wheel of Fortune.

Not having really put the city right, he can no longer rule it. See Creon's last question: Do you still want to command?*

---

* This passage is returned to in "La vérité et les formes juridiques" (1974), lecture in Rio de Janiero in 1973, in *Dits et Écrits, II*, pp. 538-646; "Quarto" ed., vol. I, pp. 1406-1490; English translation by Robert Hurley, "Truth and Juridical Forms" in *Essential Works of Foucault 1954-1984. Vol. Three. Power*, pp. 1-89.

1. Sophocle, *Œdipe roi*, 96-101, ed. and trans. P. Masqueray (Paris: Les Belles Lettres, 1922) p. 144; English translation by David Grene, Sophocles, *Oedipus the King* in *Sophocles I. Three Tragedies* (Chicago and London: The University of Chicago Press, 1991) pp. 14-15:

    *Creon* ...

    > King Phoebus in plain words commanded us
    > to drive out a pollution from our land,
    > pollution grown ingrained within the land;
    > drive it out, said the God, not cherish it,
    > till it's past cure.

    Oedipus

    > What is the rite
    > of purification? How shall it be done?

    *Creon*

    > By banishing a man, or expiation
    > of blood by blood, since it is murder guilt
    > which holds our city in this destroying storm.

2. The option of exile or death is normal in Attica. On the other hand, the penalty for parricide is invariably death. If Apollo had announced that the guilty man had to be killed, it would have been understood that he is a member of the family of Laius.

3. Sophocle, *Œdipe roi*, 106-111, p. 145; *Oedipus the King*, p. 15:

    *Creon*

    > The God commanded clearly: let some one
    > punish with force this dead man's murderers.

    *Oedipus*

    > Where are they in the world? Where would a trace
    > of this old crime be found? It would be hard
    > to guess where.

    *Creon*

    > The clue is in this land:
    > that which is sought is found;
    > the unheeded thing escapes;
    > so said the God.

4. *Histōr*: arbiter, one who knows. See above, p. 82 note 12.

5. L. Moulinier, "Le Pur et l'Impur," p. 85: "to punish is to purify the entire city of the pollution."

6. Antiphon, "Hérode" §10; Antiphon, "On the Murder of Herodes" §10.

7. E. Will distinguishes *miasma*, a notion of prehistoric origin (but absent in Homer, according to Moulinier), concrete defilement—literally: dirt to which defilement is limited in Homer and Hesiod—from the *agos* (Sophocles, *Oedipus the King*, 1426), defilement and curse at the same time. The murderer is *miaros*, that is to say marked with an invisible stain which establishes a break between the man and what is *hieros*, sacred, what falls within a transcendent order. To approach the sacred one must make oneself *katharos*, pure. See E. Will, *Le Monde grec et l'Orient*, vol. I, pp. 522-525.

8. Sophocles, *Oedipus the King*, 41-43, p. 12:

    > "*Priest* ... we all entreat you,
    > find us some strength for rescue.
    > Perhaps you'll hear a wise word from some God,
    > perhaps you will learn something from a man."

    See 41-45.

9. Ibid., 333, p. 24: "I will tell you nothing."

10. It seems that at the time of this lecture Foucault did not know of the book by B. Knox, *Oedipus at Thebes* (New Haven and London: Yale University Press and Oxford University Press, 1957), which deals with Sophocles' tragedy on the basis of the judicial procedure of investigation as instituted in fifth century Athens, and with reference to the imperialist policy of Athens.

11. Moulinier, in "Le Pur et l'Impur," pp. 60-61, writes: "It is the drama that teaches us that Orestes and Oedipus are polluted ... Pollutions enter the written legends after Homer and Hesiod. Previously we were not told that they were."

12. Sophocle, *Œdipe roi*, p. 142: Thebes is "drowned in a bloody surf: it perishes in the fruitful seeds of the earth, it perishes in the cattle in the fields, in the sterile abortions of women"; Sophocles, *Oedipus the King*, pp. 11-12: Thebes
    "... can scarcely lift its brow
    out of the depths, out of the bloody surf.
    A blight is on the fruitful plants of the earth,
    A blight is on the cattle in the fields,
    a blight is on our women that no children
    are born to them."

13. Ibid., p. 149; ibid., p. 20:
    "... I forbid any to welcome him
    or cry him greeting or make him a sharer
    in sacrifice or offering to the Gods,
    or give him water for his hands to wash.
    I command all to drive him from their homes."

14. See V. Ehrenberg, *Sophocles and Pericles* (Oxford: Basil Blackwell, 1954).

15. *Oedipus the King*, 39, *orthosai*, 46, *anorthoson*, 50, *orthon*, 51, *anorthoson*.

16. L. Moulinier, "Le Pur et l'Impur" p. 199: "There are two causes of the impurity of Oedipus, the murder and the incest, but sexual purity is not a Greek notion."

17. S. Freud, *The Interpretation of Dreams*, trans. James Strachey, in *The Standard Edition of the Complete Psychological Works of Sigmund Freud* (London: Hogarth Press and the Institute of Pscho-analysis, 1958) vol. IV.

18. Probably an allusion to Bronislaw Malinowski, *Sex and Repression in Savage Society* (London: Routledge, 2002 [1927]): "By implicitly accepting that the Oedipus complex exists in all forms of society, psychoanalysts have seriously vitiated their anthropological work." [I have not been able to trace this quotation in the original English edition of the work. The editor's note cites the French translation, by S. Jankélévitch, *La Sexualité et sa répression dans les sociétés primitives* (Paris: Payot, 1932), p. 189; G.B.]

19. Discursive events: this notion, introduced into Foucauldian analysis fairly recently, appeared in "Sur l'archéologie des sciences. Réponse au Cercle d'épistemologie" (1968), *Dits et Écrits*, I, pp. 696-731; "Quarto" ed., vol. I, pp. 724-759; English translation as "On the Archeology of the Sciences: Response to the Epistemological Circle" in Michel Foucault, *Essential Works of Foucault 1954-1984. Volume Two: Aesthetics, Method, and Epistemology*, ed. James Faubion, trans. Robert Hurley and others (New York and London: The New Press/Penguin Books, 1998). Previously Foucault spoke of "discourse as event."

20. The description of the event: "a set of singularities, of singular points characterizing a mathematical curve, a physical state of affairs, a psychological and moral person," is fundamental for Deleuze. See Gilles Deleuze, *The Logic of Sense*, trans. Mark Lester with Charles Stivale (London: Athlone Press, 1990) p. 52.

# thirteen

LECTURE ON NIETZSCHE*

# How to think the history of truth with Nietzsche without relying on truth

> Knowledge (connaissance) does not have an origin, but a history. Truth too has been invented, but later. ∽ Nietzsche's insouciance in breaking up the implication of knowledge (savoir) and truth. ∽ Subject-object, products and not foundation of knowledge. ∽ Mark, sign, word, logic: instruments and not events of knowledge. ∽ A knowledge deployed in the space of transgression. Interplay of mark, word, and will. Knowledge as lie. ∽ Truth as morality. Is it freedom or violence that connects will and truth? ∽ The paradoxes of the will to truth. Illusion, error, lie as categories of distribution of the untrue truth. ∽ Aristotle and Nietzsche: two paradigms of the will to know.

## I—THE "INVENTION" OF KNOWLEDGE

"In some lost corner of this universe whose blaze pours forth innumerable solar systems, there once was a star on which some intelligent animals invented knowledge. This was the moment of the greatest lie and supreme arrogance of universal history" (1873).[1]

---

* Lecture given at McGill University (Montreal) April 1971.

This term *d'Erfindung*,[2] invention, refers to many other texts. Everywhere it is opposed to origin. But it is not a synonym of beginning (*commencement*).[3]
That knowledge is an invention means:

1. that it is not inherent in human nature, that it does not form man's oldest instinct. But above all that its possibility is not defined by its form itself.
The possibility of knowledge is not a formal law; its possibility arises in a space of interplay where something altogether different is involved,[4] that is to say: instincts and not reason, knowledge, or experience; doubt, negation, dissolution, and temporization, and not affirmation, certainty, conquest, and serenity.

"There is no "knowledge instinct"; the intellect is at the service of the various instincts."[5]

Behind knowledge is something altogether different, something foreign, opaque, and irreducible to it. Knowledge does not precede itself; it is without pre-existence, without secret anticipation. Behind knowledge, the wall of non-knowledge. Difference therefore from empiricism, which puts perception, or sensation, or impression, or representation in general behind knowledge;

2. that it is without model, that it does not have an external guarantee in something like a divine intellect. No prototype of knowledge preceded human knowledge. It was not stolen by some Prometheus from a primordial and divine fire. It was not imitated by human intelligence remembering a divine spectacle.
No reminiscence;

3. that [knowledge] is not joined to the structure of the world as a reading, a decipherment, a perception, or a self-evidence. Things are not made to be seen or known. They do not turn towards us an intelligible face which looks at us and waits for our gaze to meet them.
Things do not have:

—a hidden meaning to be deciphered,
—[an] essence that constitutes their intelligible nervure,

[They] are not:

—objects obeying laws.

"The character of the world is rather that of an eternal chaos, not due to an absence of necessity, but due to an absence of order, structure, form, beauty, wisdom ... In no way does it seek to imitate man ... It does not observe any law. Let us keep from saying that law exists in nature ... When will all these shadows of God cease to confuse us? When will we have completely de-deified nature?"[6]

Finally it means:

4. that [knowledge] is the result of a complex operation.

"*Non ridere, non lugere, neque detestari, sed intelligere!* says Spinoza[7] in that simple and sublime way of his. However, what really is this *intelligere*, if not the very form in which we become aware of the three other [passions] at once? A result of these different and contradictory impulses, of these wills to be ironic, to lament, and to despise? Before an act of knowledge was possible, each of these impulses had first to manifest its partial view of the object or event; the conflict between these partial views came about later, and sometimes, from this, an intermediary state, an appeasement, a mutual concession between the three impulses, a sort of equity and pact between them because, thanks to equity and the pact, these three impulses can establish and assert themselves in existence and watch over reason together. We, who become aware only of the last scenes of reconciliation, the last settlement of scores in this lengthy process, think that *intelligere*, 'understanding,' must be something conciliatory, just, good, something essentially opposed to the instincts, whereas it is only a matter of a certain relation between the instincts. ... In all knowledge there may be something heroic, but nothing divine."[8]

We need to clarify a little what this complex operation consists of:

a—It is allied first with malice—mockery, contempt, hatred. It does not involve recognizing oneself in things but keeping one's distance from them, protecting oneself from them (by laughing), differentiating oneself by deprecating them (despising), wanting to repulse or destroy them (*detestari*). Murderous, deprecatory, differentiating - knowledge is neither of the order of *homoiōsis* [becoming like; G.B.], nor of the good.

b—It is a malice turned also towards *the one* who knows. Knowledge is opposed to a "will to appearance, simplification, mask, cloak, in sum to surface—since every surface is a cloak ... [It] *will* take things profoundly, multiple, in their essence ...,"[9] "while he [the man of knowledge] compels his spirit to knowledge, against the inclination of his spirit and frequently even against his heart's desire ... to affirm, love, worship ... "[10]

Which introduces doubt, temporization.

Knowledge is opposed to utility, for it is a game which involves giving way to the for and against.[11] But this game only succeeds in *transposing* the malice. Appearance of intellectual combat, of rivalry.[12] In *Daybreak*, paragraph 429, knowledge appears as renunciation of the happiness "of a sturdy and vigorous illusion." This renunciation now has such charm for us that we could not renounce it.[13]

This malice is what will go behind the surface of things to seek out the secret, to try to extract an essence behind the appearance, a power behind the elusive flickering, a mastery. And to do this one employs all the means of cunning and seduction, of violence and gentleness towards the thing.[14] But it is also what can recognize that there is still only appearance in this secret finally broken open, that there is no ontological foundation. And that man himself, who knows, is still and always appearance.[15]

Knowledge is not the operation that destroys appearance (either by opposing it to being as Plato does, or by unmasking the object = x hidden behind it); nor is it the futile effort that always remains in appearance (in the style of Schopenhauer). It is what indefinitely constitutes the newness of appearance in the breach in appearance. Knowledge is indeed what goes beyond appearance, what maliciously destroys it, puts it to the question, and extracts its secrets. A knowledge that remained at the level of what is given as appearance would not be knowledge at all.

Against the welcoming mildness of a phenomenon, it is necessary to set the murderous relentlessness of knowledge. But in this work this is never rewarded with access to being or the essence, but gives rise to new appearances, sets them against one another and beyond one another. Hence a certain number of consequences:

a—Instinct, interest, play, and struggle are not that from which knowledge tears itself away. This is not the shameful motive, the constraining and quickly forgotten origin. This is its permanent, perpetual, inevitable, necessary support. We will find it again in the sciences. And it will raise the problem of asceticism, of objective knowledge.

b—Knowledge will always be perspective, incomplete; it will never close on itself; it will never be adequate to its object; it will always be separated from a thing in itself, but neither in Husserl's sense in which perspectives intersect in the very essence of the thing that is both the law and plane of all these perspectives, nor in Kant's sense when he says that knowledge is limited—because, for Kant, what prevents us from knowing is both knowledge itself (its form, and therefore nothing external or foreign to it) and the limit of knowledge (what is no longer knowledge).

For Nietzsche, what prevents us from knowing is the very thing that forms the support, root, and dynamism of knowledge, its force and not its form (instinct, malice, greed for knowledge, desire); but what both prevents and constitutes knowledge is something altogether different from knowledge.

"Why does man not see things? He is himself standing in the way; he conceals things."[16]

c—Hence, in sum, the two great breaks: in relation to being and in relation to the good.

*Knowing and knowing the truth*

Knowledge was invented, but truth was invented even later.
[This] is articulated in several questions:

—What kind of knowledge would it be that is not, from the outset, knowledge of the truth, or knowledge addressing itself to the truth, or knowledge wanting the truth? What kind of knowledge would it be that does not suspend the truth or put it out of circulation, but is the place where truth emerges in a secondary, aleatory, non-essential way?

—What is invention of the truth? What turn of events made it possible? This question involves what knowledge of the truth will be: should it be analyzed as an illusion, or as a will, or as a structure? In other words, is the relation between knowledge and the truth a matter of error (i.e., of untruth), will, or law?

—What is knowledge when it has become knowledge of the truth? And what happens to truth when it has arisen and found its place in knowledge? Is truth a phase? Will there be an end to truth? Can we imagine or conceive of a new knowledge that would once again be knowledge without truth? Is there a future truth or a future without truth? Can we recount the history of truth—the fable of truth?

Despite superficial analogies, this should be distinguished from a Comteian or positivist type of history of the sciences. In positivist history, truth is not given from the start. Knowledge seeks the truth for a long time: blind, groping. Truth is given as the result of a history. But the relation finally established between truth and knowledge is assumed from the outset as one that exists by right. Knowledge is made to be knowledge of the truth. There is an original affiliation between truth and knowledge. And this affiliation is such that:

—truth is the object of knowledge,
—knowledge without truth is not true knowledge,
—truth is the truth of knowledge.

Nietzsche's insouciance consists in his having unraveled these implications. And having said: truth is added to knowledge, later—without knowledge being destined to truth, without truth being the essence of knowledge.

Nietzsche is insouciant first in saying: neither man, nor things, nor the world are made for knowledge; knowledge comes after—preceded by no complicity, guaranteed by no power. It arrives, emerging from the altogether different.

He is insouciant again when he says: knowledge is not made for truth. Truth arrives unexpectedly, preceded by the not-true, preceded rather by something that we cannot say is either true or not true, since it is prior to the division specific to truth. The truth emerges from the state of non-acquaintance with the demarcation of the true.

## II—WHAT IS KNOWLEDGE BEFORE TRUTH?

Two answers emerge through two oppositions established by Nietzsche:

a—Nietzsche presents knowledge not linked to truth as pure "wanting to know" which is opposed to the schematizations, the simplifications of a knowledge orientated towards truth.

(1884): "The whole apparatus of knowledge is an apparatus of abstraction and simplification, organized not for knowledge but for *mastery* over things."[17]
(1888): "In the formation of reason, logic, and categories, it is *need* that is decisive: the need not 'to know,' but to sum up, to schematize in order to understand and foresee ..."[18]

Knowledge in order to know:

"To this will to appearance, simplification, mask, cloak, surface ... is opposed that sublime inclination of the one who seeks knowledge, that inclination that will take things profoundly, multiple, in their essence."[19]
"One person is driven ... to a clear view by the veneration that [the] secrets [of things] inspire in him, the other by indiscretion and malice in the interpretation of mysteries."[20]

We see the possibility opening up of a knowledge deployed in the space of the secret, of prohibition, of unveiling, of transgression.
"We are of an audacious morality" (linked to malice, to profanation).[21]

To this profanation by knowledge for the sake of knowledge is opposed the good, useful, generous, accommodating knowledge, the knowledge that does good, that is to say, does something other than know.

b—Nietzsche puts to work another opposition, the converse of the preceding opposition: a primary and corporeal knowledge prior to any truth and governed entirely by need. It is not a question of knowledge here, but of life, struggle, the hunt, food, rivalry.

"All our *organs of knowledge* and our *senses* develop only in the service of our preservation and growth."[22]

Confronting this knowledge, and after it, a secondary and ascetic knowledge is formed. It suppresses the point of view of the body, suspends usefulness, erases partialities and limits, and wants to see everything with an equal eye and without prejudice. Knowledge that wants to be pure.

"To eliminate the will in general, to suppress the passions entirely, supposing it were possible: what then? Would this not be to castrate the intellect?"[23]

Here the opposition is asserted between a real knowledge, immediately connected up to life, to need, and a both historically effective and illusory, paradoxical knowledge. That of the ascetic scholar, of Kant.

"Such a contradiction..., 'life *against* life,' ...[is] quite simply an absurdity. It can only be *apparent*; it must be a sort of provisional expression, an interpretation, a formula, a compromise, a psychological misunderstanding."[24]

So, knowledge before truth is sometimes defined as the violent and wicked knowledge of the secret, the profanation that unveils, and sometimes as the violent and useful knowledge that serves life; the one-sidedness that allows domination and growth.

In other words, this "altogether different" of violence, which acts as framework to knowing and presents itself in knowledge, gives rise to the useless and profaning wickedness of knowing, to the pure transgression of knowledge, [this "altogether different"] gives rise to the partiality of life articulating itself in its own growth.

What then—finally or firstly—is the nature of a knowledge not yet distorted by the truth? Maybe the question itself is wrong, or rather, in putting this question we again find premises that have to be reexamined. Wondering about the original nature of knowledge is to accept that it is a certain type of relation between a subject and an object. A relation that one then wonders whether it [is] one of usefulness or contemplation, of utilitarian domination or religious profanation, whether it is organized according to the pure gaze or to the needs of life? But, does not questioning knowledge radically, questioning it on the basis of what is altogether different from it, leave intact that subject-object relation on the basis of which knowledge is defined, whereas it is knowledge that constitutes that relation?

Nietzsche says: "There is no knowledge in itself,"[25] which does not mean: There is no knowledge of the in-itself, but: In the violence of knowing there is not a constant, essential, and preexisting relation that the activity of knowledge has both to deploy and effectuate. To say that there is no knowledge in itself is to say that the subject-object relation (and all its derivatives like the a priori, objectivity, pure knowledge, constitutive subject) is not the foundation of knowledge but is in reality produced by it.

Let us clarify this:

a—Knowledge rests on a network of relations:

—different in their form: it may involve destruction, appropriation, punishment, domination;
—different in their points of support and the terms between which they establish relations: a body with another body, a group with another group, an individual with a thing, an animal, a god.

The basis of knowledge is therefore this interplay of differences:

"The world is essentially different at every point; it weighs on all the points, all the points resist and in every case the results are perfectly *non congruent*."[26]

The world is essentially a world of relations which are unknowable in themselves: "formless and unformulable world of the chaos of sensations."[27] And how would they be knowable since it [the world] is not of the order of knowledge? At the root of knowledge, there is not consciousness. (Thought in Nietzsche is not the phenomenon to which we have immediate access in the form of consciousness; thought is not knowledge that is at once and by the same token the act which knows and the instance which recognizes itself as knowing. Thought is itself only an effect. Thought is the effect of extra-thought, not as natural result, but as violence and illusion.)

b—Among these relations, a group of them is characterized by the fact that they forcibly join together several differences, that they exert violence so as to impose on them the analogy of a resemblance,[28] of a common utility or affiliation, which marks them with a common stamp.[29] This mark has the double property:

—of allowing a utilization or a domination, or rather of extending the first level utilization or domination. The mark is the multiplier of the relation. It refers therefore to a will to power;
—of allowing recurrence, repetition, the identity of successive differences—the identification of first level differences. The mark is the identifier of the relation. It refers to a reality.

In a sense we can say that this will is the necessary foundation of this reality:

"We may wonder ... whether the activity that "posits things" is not alone real and whether "the action of the external world upon us" is not the consequence of the presence of such voluntary subjects."[30]

But we can say as well that this will is will to power (i.e., more than action and reaction, [rather] infinity of will) only because there are marks which constitute things, which posit their reality.[31]

This is how Nietzsche turned Schopenhauer's theme: will and representation; a representation which is only illusion, and single will which is all reality.

c—From this is constituted:

α—The subject—which is at the same time the point of emergence of the will, the system of deformations and perspectives, the principle of dominations, and what receives in return, in the form of the word, of the personal pronoun, of grammar, the mark of identity and reality of the object.

β—The object—which is the point of application of the mark, the sign, the word, the category, and to which in return we relate the subject's will in the form of the substance, of the intelligible essence, of nature or creation.

This is why Nietzsche stubbornly refuses to place at the heart of knowledge something like the *cogito*, that is to say, pure consciousness,* in which the object is given in the form of the subject and the subject may be the object of itself. All philosophies have founded knowledge on the preestablished relation of subject and object, their sole concern being to bring subject and object closer together (either in the pure form of the *cogito*, or in the minimal form of sensation, or in a pure tautology A = A).

Nietzsche wanted to account for knowledge by putting the maximum distance between subject and object, by making them products which are far removed from each other and which can be confused only by illusion. Far from the subject-object relation being constitutive of knowledge, the existence of a subject and an object is the first and major illusion of knowledge.

But what does Nietzsche introduce in place of the *cogito*? It is the interplay of mark and will, of word and will to power, or again of sign and interpretation.[32]

—The sign is the violence of analogy, what masters and erases difference.

—Interpretation is that which posits and imposes signs, which plays with them, which introduces radical differences (those of the word and meaning) into the original differences of the chaos.

---

* Foucault uses the same abbreviation for *connaissance* and *conscience*.

The sign is interpretation inasmuch as it introduces the lie of things into the chaos. And interpretation is the violence done to the chaos by the reifying game of signs.

"What, in short, is *knowledge*? It 'interprets,' it 'introduces a meaning,' it does not explain (in most cases it is a new interpretation of an old interpretation which has become unintelligible and which is no more than a sign)."[33]

## Conclusion

a—We can see why Nietzsche speaks of knowledge as lie (the moment of the greatest lie regarding the discovery of knowledge). It is a lie in two senses: first of all, because it distorts reality, because it is perspectivist, because it erases difference, and because it introduces the abusive reign of resemblance; and then because it is something altogether different from knowledge (relation of subject to object). Far from being the truth of knowledge, this relation is its untruthful product. The being of knowledge is to lie.

b—We can see why Nietzsche says both that this primordial knowledge is something altogether different from a knowledge (a plurality of relations without subject or object), and that this knowledge is the only knowledge that is addressed to reality, every other form of knowledge being the result of an interpretive violence distorted by perspective, domination, need.

Roughly, knowledge in the form of relations of reality is not really a knowledge and what we say is really a knowledge is lie with regard to every relation of reality.

c—Consequently, at the core of knowledge, even before we have to speak of truth, we find a circle of reality, knowledge, and lie. Which will allow the insertion of truth as morality.

Speaking in the most general way, such an analysis makes it possible:

—to speak of sign and interpretation, of their inseparability, without reference to a phenomenology;
—to speak of signs without reference to any "structuralism";
—to speak of interpretation without reference to an original subject;

—to connect up analyses of systems of signs with the analysis of forms of violence and domination;

—to think knowledge as an historical process before any problematic of the truth, and more fundamentally than in the subject-object relation. Knowledge-*connaissance* freed from the subject-object relation is knowledge-*savoir*.


## III—THE EVENT OF TRUTH

There is a knowledge before truth. This does not mean, in the positivist or genetic sense, that knowledge takes a long time to encounter or discover the truth, that it fixes its norms belatedly; but that truth is an episode, an invention, maybe a diversion of knowledge, that it will be neither its norm nor its essence. Truth is not the truth of knowledge.

"'Truth' is not...something that exists and has to be found, discovered, but something that *must be created* and that provides a name for a certain *processus*, even more, for a will to do violence to the facts, endlessly: introducing truth into the facts, by a *processus in infinitum*, an *active determination*, not the becoming conscious of a reality that is firm and determined in itself. It is one of the names of the 'will to power' ... "[34]

"To maintain that there was a 'truth' that one could *approach* by some procedure!"[35]


*1. The will to truth*

Nietzsche puts the root and raison d'être of truth in the will. An important shift with regard to the philosophical tradition.

a—For the latter, the truth-will relation is characterized by the fact that the will has only to let the truth assert itself. Willing the truth is willing it to appear, to express itself, to be there. It is to make way for it. Now in order to make way for the truth, the will had to erase from itself anything that might not be empty space for the truth. Erase all its individual characteristics, all its desires, and all its violence. A pure will.

A suspended will at the same time, for it must not predetermine any object; castrated, for none of its own determinations must be allowed to remain.

Hence the fact that the will to truth could be thought only in the form of attention: pure subject, free from determination and ready to welcome, without deformation, the presence of the object; or in the form of wisdom: mastery of the body, suspension of desire, blockage of appetites. Descartes and Plato. Self evidence and pedagogy.

In the philosophical tradition, what we find at the heart of the will-truth relation is freedom. Truth is free with regard to the will; it does not receive any of its determinations from the will. The will must be free to be able to give access to the truth.

Freedom is the being of truth; and it is the duty of the will. An ontology (freedom of the truth will be God or nature); an ethics (the will's duty will be prohibition, renunciation, passage to the universal). This fundamental freedom, which connects will and truth to each other, is formulated:

—in Plato's *homoeōsis tō theō*,
—in Kant's intelligible characteristic,
—in the Heideggerian opening.

b—For Nietzsche, the will-truth relation is quite different. Truth exists in the element of the will only on the basis of its singular characteristics and its most precise determinations, and in the form of constraint and domination. The connection of one to the other is not freedom, it is violence.

This result of this shift is—must be—considerable and we are still far from having been able to gauge it entirely. It should make a whole "ideology" of knowledge as the effect of freedom and reward for virtue impossible. It should make it possible to rethink:

—the history of knowledge and science,
—the status that should be given to its universality, and
—the connection between science and certain forms of society or civilization.

But its effects solely at level of philosophical reflection, as it is traditionally practiced, are especially jolts and disruptions. Some paradoxes arise.

## 2. THE PARADOXES OF THE WILL TO TRUTH

If it is true that truth is violence done to things, then this puts it on the same footing as knowledge (*connaissance*). It is a product or an effect of knowledge. It is not its norm, or condition, or foundation, or justification.

Now, if it is true that it is subsequent to knowledge, if it arises from knowledge and as violence, it is violence done to knowledge. It is not true knowledge. It is a deformed, tortured, dominated knowledge. It is a false knowledge. In relation to true knowledge it is a system of *errors*.

But at the same time, if it leaves behind it, as prior to the truth, a whole process of contents of knowledge—contents of knowledge still without truth that must be worked on again so that they become true—then it makes a non-truth loom up behind it. It appears against the background of illusions and as violence done to illusions.

We must go further. If truth is destruction of the illusion of knowing, if this destruction is developed against knowledge and as destruction of knowledge itself, then truth is lie. It is something other than what it claims to be. It is by no means truthful when it expresses itself as reward for knowing.

"The apparent world and the *mendacious* world, that is the antagonism. Until now the latter was called the 'true world,' 'truth,' 'God.' This is what we have to destroy."[36]

These paradoxes show us that:

—Truth is not true if it is knowledge, since all knowledge is an illusion.
—Truth is not true insofar as it is non-knowledge, since it superimposes on knowledge or replaces knowledge with a system of error.
—Truth is not true when it claims to be knowledge, it is lie.

Which allows us:

a—to lay down as principle that truth cannot be the predicate of itself. Truth is not true. All truth is deployed in the non-true; the truth is non-true. There is no ontology of truth. In the predicative judgment: truth *is* true, the verb to be has the ontological meaning: truth exists.

Nietzsche transforms the skeptical assertion "truth does not exist" into a series of paradoxes deriving from the proposition: truth is not true.

b—to distribute the major categories of the non true truth:

—illusion, that is to say, truth insofar as it is a mode of knowledge;
—error, insofar as it is violence done to knowledge (and therefore non-knowledge);
—lie, insofar as this non-knowledge (*Lüge*) claims to dissipate the illusion of all knowledge although it is knowledge.

Starting from here, we can see the Nietzschean task: to think the history of truth without relying on truth. In an element where truth does not exist: this element is appearance.

Appearance, this is the element of the non-true within which the truth dawns. And in doing so it redistributes appearance into the categories of illusion, error, and lie.

Appearance is the indefinite of truth. Illusion, error, and lie are the differences introduced by truth into the game of appearance. But these differences are not only the effects of truth; they are truth itself.

We can also say:

—Truth makes appearance appear as illusion, error, lie.

Or:

—Illusion, error, and lie is the mode of being of truth in the indefinite element of appearance.
—Illusion, or the root of truth.
—Error, or the system of truth.
—Lie, or the operation of truth.

See the texts on truth as error:

"Truth is a sort of error."[37]

"What in the final instance are man's truths? They are irrefutable errors."[38]

On the renunciation of truth:

"The belief that *there is no truth*, the nihilist belief, is a great relaxation of all the limbs for the champion of knowledge who is constantly struggling with ugly truths."[39]

A conviction that no epoch has ever had: we do not have the truth. Previously everybody had the truth, even the skeptics.

On appearance:

"'*Appearance*,' as I understand it, is the true and sole reality of things, that to which all existing predicates are suited ... I do not posit 'appearance' as the opposite of 'reality'; I assert rather that appearance is reality, that it is that which is opposed to what transforms reality into an imaginary 'true world'."[40]

\*   \*   \*

Let us summarize all this.[41]

In Aristotle, the will to know derived from the preexistence of knowledge; it was nothing other the delay of knowledge with regard to itself and that is why it was desire, even less than "desire," it was desire-pleasure. And this was possible only insofar as knowledge (in the most elementary form of sensation) was already related to truth.

In Nietzsche, knowledge is an illusory effect of the fraudulent assertion of truth: the will that brings both of them has this double character: (1) of not being will to know but will to power; (2) of founding a relationship of reciprocal cruelty and destruction between knowledge and truth.

The will is what says in a double and superimposed voice: I want the truth so much that I do not want to know and I want to know up to that point and that limit that I wish there was no longer any truth. The will to power is the breaking point at which both truth and knowledge come apart and destroy each other.

But what is this will to power brought to light in this way? A reality that has been freed from (immutable, eternal, true) being: becoming. And the knowledge that unveils it does not unveil being, but a truth without truth.

There are therefore two "truths without truth":

—the truth that is error, lie, illusion: the truth that is not true;
—the truth freed from this truth-lie: the truthful truth, the truth that is not reciprocable with being.

1. F. Nietzsche, "Introduction théorétique sur la vérité et le mensonge au sens extra-moral" (Summer 1873) in *Le Livre du philosophe*. *Études théorétiques*, bilingual edition, translation, introduction, and notes by A. Kremer-Marietti (Paris: Aubier-Flammarion, 1969) p. 171 (translation amended by Foucault); English translation by Walter Kaufmann, "On Truth and the Lie in an Extra-moral Sense," in *The Portable Nietzsche* (New York: Penguin, 1976) p. 42: "In some remote corner of the universe, bathed in the fires of innumerable solar systems, there once was a planet where clever animals invented knowledge. That was the grandest and most mendacious minute of 'universal history.'" The mention of universal history mocks Hegel's *Weltgeschichte*. And knowledge is a "moment, a lightning flash, an event, not a faculty," is a criticism of Kant. In "La vérité et les formes juridiques"; "Truth and Juridical Forms," p. 6, Foucault recalls that this text was written in the middle of neo-Kantianism.

2. Literally: *das Erkennen erfanden*.

3. Allusion to Husserl's distinction between origin and beginning (*commencement*). See E. Husserl, "Die Frage nach dem Ursprung der Geometrie als intentional-historisches Problem," *Revue internationale de philosophie*, I (2), Brussels; English translation by John P. Leavey in Jacques Derrida, *Edmund Husserl's 'Origin of Geometry': An Introduction* (New York and Sussex: Nicolas Hays and Harvester Press, 1978).

4. This "something altogether different," forged by violence, spitefulness, or usefulness is what Foucault transcribes also into politics in his reprise of this lecture in the 1973 Rio de Janiero lecture, "Truth and Juridical Forms."

5. F. Nietzsche, *La Volonté de puissance*, aphorism 274, ed. and trans. G. Bianquis, two volumes [reference edition] (Paris: nrf/Gallimard, 1947-1948), vol. I, Book II, ch. 3: "Morphologie et évolution de la volonté de puissance," p. 282; English translation not found.

6. Translation modified by Foucault. F. Nietzsche, *Le Gai Savoir*, ed. and trans. P. Klossowski [reference edition] (Paris: Le Club français du livre, 1965), Book III, §109, p. 192: "...the character of the whole of the world is for all eternity that of chaos, not because of the absence of necessity, but of the absence of order, articulation, form, beauty, wisdom..."; English translation by Walter Kaufmann, *The Gay Science* (New York: Vintage Books, 1974) pp. 168-169: "The total character of the world, however, is in all eternity chaos—in the sense not of a lack of necessity but of a lack of order, arrangement, form, beauty, wisdom...it does not by any means strive to imitate man...it does not observe any laws either. Let us beware of saying that there are laws in nature...When will all these shadows of God cease to darken our minds? When will we complete our de-deification of nature?"

7. Benedict de Spinoza de Spinoza, *A Political Treatise*, ch. I, 4, in *A Theological-Political Treaise* and *A Political Treatise*, trans. R.H.M. Elwes (New York: Dover Publications, 1951) p. 288: "not to mock, lament, or execrate, but to understand."

8. *Le Gai Savoir*, §333, "Que signifie connaître" pp. 333-334. Where Foucault writes "instinct," Pierre Klossowski translates "impulse." In the last part of the quotation, where Foucault writes "in all knowledge," Klossowski translates "within our battling interior" (p. 334); *The Gay Science*: "*Non ridere, non lugere, neque destestari, sed intelligere!* says Spinoza as simply and sublimely as is his wont. Yet in the last analysis, what else is this *intelligere* than the form in which we come to feel the other three at once? One result of the different and mutually opposed desires to laugh, lament, and curse? Before knowledge is possible, each of these instincts must first have presented its onesided view of the thing or event; after this comes the fight of these onesided views, and occasionally this results in a mean, one grows calm, one finds all three sides right, and there is a kind of justice and a contract; for by virtue of justice and a contract all these instincts can maintain their existence and assert their rights against each other. Since only the last scenes of reconciliation and the final accounting at the end of this long process rise to our consciousness, we suppose that *intelligere* must be something conciliatory, just, and good—something that stands essentially opposed to the instincts, while it is actually nothing but a *certain behavior of the instincts toward one another*. ...Indeed, there may be occasions of concealed *heroism* in our warring depths, but certainly nothing divine..." See also §113: Fr. p. 201; Eng. p. 173.

9. F. Nietzsche, *Par-delà le bien et le mal. Prélude d'une philosophie de l'avenir*, ed. and trans. H. Albert (Paris: Mercure de France, 1948, ch. VII, §230, p. 236; English translation by R J. Hollingdale, *Beyond Good and Evil. Prelude to a Philosophy of the Future* (Harmondsworth: Penguin Books,

1973) p. 142: "*This* will to appearance, to simplification, to the mask, to the cloak, in short to the superficial—for every surface is a cloak—is *counteracted* by that sublime inclination in the man of knowledge which takes a profound, many-sided and thorough view of things and *will* take such a view."

10. Ibid., §229, Fr. pp. 233-234; Eng. p. 141: "[the man of knowledge,] when he compels his spirit to knowledge which is *counter* to the inclination of his spirit and frequently also to the desires of his heart...to affirm, love, worship."

11. *Le Gai Savoir*, §110, pp. 194-195; *The Gay Science*, p. 169: "*Origin of knowledge*—...it was only very late that truth emerged—as the weakest form of knowledge. It seemed that one was unable to live with it: our organism was prepared for the opposite; all its higher functions, sense perception and every kind of sensation worked with those basic errors which had been incorporated since time immemorial. Indeed, even in the realm of knowledge these propositions became the norms according to which 'true' and 'untrue' were determined—down to the most remote regions of logic." See also §111: "*Origin of the logical*."

12. Ibid., §110, Fr. p. 197; Eng. pp. 170-171.

13. F. Nietzsche, *Aurore. Réflexions sur les préjugés moraux*, ed. and trans. H. Albert [reference edition] (Paris: Mercure de France, 1912, §429, "*The new passion*," pp. 333-334: "But it is our *instinct for knowledge* which is too developed for us to be able still to appreciate happiness without knowledge, or the happiness of a sturdy and vigorous illusion; we suffer only imagining such a state of affairs!...Knowledge is transformed in us into a passion..."; Foucault's translation: "But [it is] this *instinct for knowledge* which is too developed for us to be able still to appreciate happiness without knowledge, or the happiness of a strong and sturdy illusion; we suffer just from the idea of such a state of affairs."; English translation by R.J. Hollingdale, *Daybreak. Thoughts on the prejudices of morality* (Cambridge: Cambridge University Press, 1982) p. 184: "The reason is that our *drive to knowledge* has become too strong for us to be able to want happiness without knowledge or the happiness of a strong, firmly rooted delusion; even to imagine such a state of things is painful to us....Knowledge has in us been transformed into a passion..."

14. Ibid., §432: Fr. p. 339: "Searcher and tempter"; Eng. p. 185: "*Investigators and experimenters*."

15. *Le Gai Savoir*, §54, *The consciousness of appearance*, Fr. p. 115: "in 'knowing' I dance my own dance; 'knowing' is only for drawing out the earthly dance and...in that sense it is one of the impresarios of the celebrations of existence"; Eng. p. 116: "I, too, who 'know,' am dancing my dance; that the knower is a means for prolonging the earthly dance and thus belongs to the masters of ceremony of existence."

16. *Aurore*, §438, Man and things, p. 339; *Daybreak*, p. 187.

17. *La Volonté de puissance*, §195 (1884), Vol. I, Book I, ch. 2, p. 98; *The Will to Power*, Book Three, 4, §503 (1884) p. 274: "The entire apparatus of knowledge is an apparatus for abstraction and simplification—directed not at knowledge but at taking possession of things."

18. Ibid., Fr. §193 (1888), Vol. I, Book I, ch. 2, p. 97; Eng. Book Three, 5, §515, p. 278: "In the formation of reason, logic, the categories, it was *need* that was authoritative; the need, not to 'know,' but to subsume, to schematize, for the purpose of intelligibility and calculation."

19. *Par-delà le bien et le mal*, §230, p. 236: "To *this* will to appearance, simplification, mask, cloak, surface...*is opposed* the sublime inclination of the one who seeks knowledge, that inclination which takes and *will* take things profoundly, multiple, in their essence"; *Beyond Good and Evil*, p. 142: "*This* will to appearance, to simplification, to the mask, to the cloak, in short to the superficial...is *counteracted* by that sublime inclination in the man of knowledge which takes a profound, many-sided and thorough view of things and *will* take such a view."

20. *Aurore*, §432, pp. 334-336. The aphorism concludes: "We investigators, like all conquerors, seafarers, adventurers, are of an audacious morality and have to accept that we are considered, on the whole, wicked"; *Daybreak*, p. 185: "reverence for their secret will take one person forwards, indiscretion and roguishness in revealing their secrets will do the same for another. We investigators are, like all conquerors, discoverers, seafarers, adventurers, of an audacious morality and must reconcile ourselves to being considered on the whole evil."

21. Ibid., Fr. p. 336; Eng. p. 185.

22. *La Volonté de puissance*, § 192 (1887), vol. I, Book I, ch. 2, p. 97; English translation by Kate Sturge in F. Nietzsche, *Writings from the Late Notebooks*, ed. Rüdiger Bittner (Cambridge:

Cambridge University Press, 2003), p. 147: "all our *organs and senses of knowledge* are developed only with a view to conditions of preservation and growth."

23. F. Nietzsche, *La Généalogie de la Morale* (1887), ed. and trans. H. Albert [reference edition] (Paris: Mercure de France, 1913 [1900]), third essay, "What is the meaning of ascetic ideals?" §12, pp. 206-207; English translation by Carole Diethe, *On the Genealogy of Morality*, ed. Keith Ansell-Pearson (Cambridge: Cambridge University Press, 1994) p. 92: "But to eliminate the will completely and turn off all the emotions without exception, assuming we could: well? would that not mean to *castrate* the intellect?"

24. Ibid., §13, Fr. p. 207. Nietzsche continues: "… *the ascetic idea has its source in the prophylactic instinct of a degenerating life* which seeks to cure itself, which strives by every means to preserve itself, which struggles for existence … The ascetic ideal is therefore the complete opposite of what the admirers of this ideal imagine"; Eng. ibid., p. 93: "A self-contradiction such as that which seems to occur in the ascetic, 'life *against* life', is … simply nonsense. It can only be *apparent*; it has to be a sort of provisional expression, an explanation, formula, adjustment, a psychological misunderstanding … *the ascetic ideal springs from the protective and healing instincts of a degenerating life* which uses every means to maintain itself and struggles for its existence … The ascetic ideal … is therefore the precise opposite of what the worshippers of this ideal imagine."

25. Ibid., §12, Fr. p. 206: "So, fellow philosophers, let us henceforth be more wary of that old and dangerous conceptual fable which fixed a 'a pure subject of knowledge without will, without pain, and freed from time,' let us be wary of the tentacles of such contradictory notions as 'pure reason,' 'absolute spirituality,' 'knowledge in itself.'"; Eng. p. 92: "From now on, my philosophical colleagues, let us be more wary of the dangerous old conceptual fairy-tale which has set up a 'pure, will-less, painless, timeless subject of knowledge,' let us be wary of the tentacles of such contradictory concepts as 'pure reason,' 'absolute spirituality,' 'knowledge as such.'" See also *La Volonté de puissance*, §207 (1888), vol. I, Book I, ch. 2, pp. 101-102; English translation, *Writings from the Late Notebooks*, Notebook 14[122], pp. 257-258.

26. *La Volonté de puissance*, §206 (1888), Vol. I, Book I, ch. 2, p. 101; *The Will to Power*, Book Three, §568, p. 306: "its [the world's] being is essentially different from every point; it presses upon every point, every point resists it—and the sum of these in every case is quite incongruent."

27. Ibid., Fr. §202 (1887), Vol. I, Book I, ch. 2, p. 99; Eng. Book Three, §569, p. 307: "the formless unformulable world of the chaos of sensations."

28. Ibid., §286 (1885), Vol. I, Book II, ch. 4, pp. 285-286; English translation not found.

29. Ibid., §289-290 (1885), Vol. I, Book II, ch. 4, pp. 286-287; *Writings from the Late Notebooks*, 1[28], p. 56. [Only the English translation of the second part of this reference, § 290, has been found. The passage cited refers to "signs" rather than "marks" (*marques*); G.B.]

30. Ibid., Fr. §202 (1887), Vol. I, Book II, ch. 3, p. 100; Eng. *The Will to Power*, Book Three, §569, p. 307: "The question is … whether that which 'posits things' is not the sole reality; and whether the 'effect of the external world upon us' is not also only the result of such active subjects."

31. A good perspective is given on this difficult question by Gilles Deleuze in his *Proust et les signes* (Paris: PUF, 1964); English translation by Richard Howard, *Proust and Signs* (London: Allen Lane/Penguin Press, 1973); more exhaustive, from a philosophical point of view, is M. de Beistegui, *Jouissance de Proust. Pour une esthétique de la métaphore* (Paris: Michalon, coll. "Encre marine," 2007).

32. See the previous note.

33. *La Volonté de puissance*, §197 (1885-86), Vol. I, Book I, ch. 2, p. 99; *The Will to Power*, Book Three, §604, p. 327: "'Interpretation,' the introduction of meaning—not 'explanation' (in most cases a new interpretation of an old interpretation that has become incomprehensible, that is now itself only a sign)." [The English translation notes that the words "What, in short, is *knowledge*?" (Eng.: "What alone can knowledge be?") were inserted by Peter Gast; G.B.] See the quotation of René Char chosen by Foucault for the back cover of the final two volumes of the *History of Sexuality*: "The history of man is a long succession of synonyms of the same word. To contradict it is a duty."

34. Ibid., Fr. §291 (1887), vol. I, Book II, ch. 2, p. 287; Eng. Book Three, §552, p. 298: "'Truth' is therefore not something there, that might be found or discovered—but something that must be created and that gives a name to a process, or rather to a will to overcome that has in itself no end—introducing truth, as a *processus in infinitum*, an active determining—not a becoming-

conscious of something that is in itself firm and determined. It is a word for the 'will to power'."
35. Ibid., Fr. §199 (1883-1888), Vol. I, Book II, ch. 2, p. 99; Eng. Book Two, § 451, p. 247: "That there should be a 'truth' which one could somehow approach—!"
36. Ibid., Fr. §210 (1888), Vol. I, Book I, ch. 2, p. 104; Eng. Book Two, §461, p. 254: "The apparent world and the world invented by a lie—this is the antithesis. The latter has hitherto been called the 'real world,' 'truth,' 'God.' This is what we have to abolish."
37. Ibid., §308 (1881-1882), Vol. I, Book II, ch. 4, p. 292; Eng.: Book Three, §493, p. 272: "Truth is the kind of error without which a certain species of life could not live."
38. *Le Gai Savoir*, §265: "Ultimate skepticism," p. 269; *The Gay Science*, p. 219: "*Ultimate skepsis.*— What are man's truths ultimately? Merely his *irrefutable* errors."
39. *La Volonté de puissance*, §330 (1887), Vol. II, Book III, ch. 3, p. 107; *The Will to Power*, Book Three, §598, p. 325: "Belief that there is no truth at all, the nihilistic belief, is a great relaxation for one who, as a warrior of knowledge, is ceaselessly fighting ugly truths."
40. Ibid., §592 (1885), Vol. II, Book III, ch. 5, p. 181; English not found.
41. In the notes taken at the Collège de France by Hélène Politis—manuscript and then typed (with some differences)—we find again all the linkages of the lectures given at McGill University, but in a more vigorous form, with less textual commentary, maybe because the texts of Nietzsche read by Foucault figure there above all as references to the aphorisms.
At the Collège, Foucault ends on a periodisation of the way in which Nietzschean discourse freed itself from truth:—
First period: by way of tragic knowledge. 1875-1878, knowledge linked to a theory denying eternity, reality.
—Second period (never abandoned): the perversion of marks, bringing a diagnostic knowledge into play (from *Untimely Meditations* to *Daybreak* (1881))—positivist side of Nietzsche in this second period.
—Third period: assertion of the *eternal return*.
Assertion that all these differences having been exhausted, each of them will again have to be repeated an infinite number of times. Everything having been completed, nothing will remain as it was. Everything is also real or unreal, as you will, there are differences of intensity which will return indefinitely.
The assertion of the eternal return is this system that excludes the assertion of truth.
The will to the true but not "truth" appears as will to power which is will to indefinite development in itself, which does not belong to the realm of the true or to that of knowledge.
In the lecture published here, written on the basis of a summary of the lecture at the Collège de France, Foucault suppresses this periodisation of Nietzsche's thought, but
1. He reinserts the Heideggerian opening into the history of metaphysics inaugurated by Plato. This is clearly a response to Heidegger's two volumes on Nietzsche, in which Nietzsche is inscribed in the metaphysical tradition that he wanted to subvert. By setting a Nietzschean paradigm against Aristotle's, Foucault opposes Heidegger's interpretation of the history of philosophy.
2. Moreover, Foucault ends this lecture on a violent diatribe against the "ideology of knowledge as the effect of freedom." It is difficult not to hear designated here: "The openness of comportment as the inner condition of the possibility of correctness is grounded in freedom. *The essence of truth is freedom*" from chapter 3 of *The Essence of Truth*,[a] although Foucault recalls that this is the classical conception (certainly, since Descartes).

[a] M. Heidegger, *On the Essence of Truth*, trans. John Sallis, in Martin Heidegger, *Basic Writings*, ed. David Farrell Krell (London and New York: Routledge Classics, 2008) p. 72; French translation by *De l'essence de la vérité*, trans. A. De Waelhens and W. Biemel, *De l'essece de la vérité* (Paris: J. Vrin/Louvain: Neuwelaerts, 1948); original edition: *Vom Wesen der Wahrheit* (Frankfurt/Main: V. Klostermann, 1943).

# COURSE SUMMARY*

THE COURSE THIS YEAR begins a series of analyses which seek to put together, fragment by fragment, a "morphology of the will to know." Sometimes this theme of the will to know will be taken up in specific historical research; sometimes it will be treated for itself and in its theoretical implications.

This year involved situating its place and defining its role in a history of systems of thought; laying down, at least provisionally, an initial model of analysis; and testing its effectiveness on a first batch of examples.

1. Previous research had made it possible to recognize a specific level among all those that enable one to analyze systems of thought: that of discursive practices. This involves a type of systematicity that is neither logical nor linguistic. Discursive practices are characterized by the separating out of a field of objects, the definition of a legitimate perspective for the subject of knowledge, and the fixing of norms for the elaboration of concepts and theories. Each of these thus presupposes an interplay of prescriptions which govern exclusions and choices.

Now these sets of regularities do not coincide with individual works, and even if they are manifested through them, even if they happen to be distinguished, for the first time, in one of them, they extend well beyond individual works and often group together a considerable number of them. But

* Published in the *Annuaire du Collège de France*, 71e année, *Histoire des systèmes de pensée* année *1970-1971*, (*1971*), *pp. 245-249*, and in *Dits et Écrits, 1954-1988*, ed. D. Defert and F. Ewald, with the collaboration of J. Lagrange (Paris: Gallimard, 1994) vol. 2, pp. 240-244; "Quarto" ed., vol. 1, pp. 1108-1112. An earlier translation of this summary by Robert Hurley appears with the tile "The Will to Knowledge" in M. Foucault, *The Essential Works of Michel Foucault, 1954-1984, Vol. 1: Ethics: subjectivity and truth*, ed. Paul Rabinow, trans. Robert Hurley and others (New York: New Press, 1997), pp. 11-16.

no more do they coincide with what we are accustomed to calling sciences or disciplines, although their delimitations may sometimes provisionally be the same; more often than not a discursive practice brings together various disciplines or sciences, or it cuts across a number of them and groups several of their regions into a sometimes invisible unity.

Discursive practices are not purely and simply modes of fabricating discourse. They take shape in technical ensembles, institutions, schemas of behavior, types of transmission and circulation, and in pedagogical forms which both impose them and maintain them.

Finally, they have specific modes of transformation. We cannot reduce these transformations to a precise, individual discovery, and yet we cannot make do with characterizing them as an overall change of mentality, of a collective attitude or state of mind. Transformation of a discursive practice is linked to a whole, often highly complex set of modifications which may take place outside it (in forms of production, in social relations, in political institutions), in it (in techniques for defining objects, in the refinement and adjustment of concepts, in the accumulation of information), or alongside them (in other discursive practices). And transformation is not linked to these modifications in the form of a simple result, but as an effect which has both its own autonomy and a set of precise functions with regard to what determines the transformation.

These principles of exclusion and choice, which have a multiple presence, an effectiveness which takes shape in practices, and whose transformations are relatively autonomous, do not refer back to a (historical or transcendental) subject of knowledge that invented them successively or founded them at an original level; they designate rather an anonymous and polymorphous will to know which is open to regular transformations and caught up in an identifiable play of dependence.

Empirical studies of psychopathology, clinical medicine, natural history, etcetera, made it possible to pick out the level of discursive practices. The general characteristics of these practices and the specific methods for analyzing them had been inventoried under the name of archeology. Research undertaken with regard to the will to know should now be able to give a theoretical justification to this ensemble. For the moment, we can indicate in a very general way the directions in which it will have to advance: distinction between knoweledge-*savoir* and knowledge-*connaissance*; difference between will to know (*savoir*) and will to truth; the position of the subject, and subjects, in relation to that will.

2. Until now, few conceptual tools have been developed for analyzing the will to know. Most of the time we use rather crude notions. "Anthropological" or psychological notions: curiosity, the need to control or appropriate by knowledge (*connaissance*), anguish before the unknown, reactions to the threats of the undifferentiated. Historical generalities, like the spirit of an epoch, its sensibility, types of interest, conception of the world, system of values, essential needs. Philosophical themes like that of a horizon of rationality that becomes explicit over time. Nothing, finally, allows us to think that the still very rudimentary developments of psychoanalysis on the positions of the subject and object in desire and knowledge can be imported as such into the field of historical studies. We no doubt have to accept that the tools which will enable us to analyze the will to know will have to be formed and defined, as we go along, according to the requirements and possibilities revealed by concrete studies.

The history of philosophy offers theoretical models of this will to know whose analysis may make possible a first survey. Of all those who will have to be studied and tested (Plato, Spinoza, Schopenhauer, Aristotle, Nietzsche, etcetera), the last two were picked out first and studied this year, insofar as they constitute two extreme and opposed forms.

The Aristotelian model was analyzed mainly on the basis of texts from the *Metaphysics*, the *Nicomachean Ethics*, and *De Anima*. It is brought into play from the level of sensation. It establishes:

—a link between sensation and pleasure;
—the independence of this link with regard to the vital usefulness that sensation may involve;
—a direct proportion between the intensity of pleasure and the quantity of knowledge delivered by sensation;
—the incompatibility between the truth of pleasure and the error of sensation.

Visual perception, as sensation at a distance of multiple objects given simultaneously, and which are not immediately related to the usefulness of the body, manifests the link between knowledge (*connaissance*), pleasure, and truth in the satisfaction it brings with it. This same relationship is found again, transposed to the other extreme, in the happiness of theoretical contemplation. The desire to know, which the first lines of the *Metaphysics* posit as both universal and natural, is founded on this primary affiliation already manifested in sensation. And it is this desire that ensures the continuous passage from this first type of knowledge to that final type expressed in philosophy. In Aristotle, the desire to know presupposes and transposes the preexisting relationship of knowledge, truth, and pleasure.

In *The Gay Science*, Nietzsche defines a completely different set of relations:

—knowledge is an "invention" behind which there is something altogether different from it: an interplay of instincts, impulses, desires, fear, will to appropriation. Knowledge appears on the stage where these battle with each other;
—it does not come about as the effect of their harmony, of their happy equilibrium, but of their hatred, of their dubious and provisional compromise, of a fragile pact which they are always ready to betray. It is not a permanent faculty but an event, or at least a series of events;
—it is always servile, dependent, interested (not in itself, but in what is liable to interest the instinct or instincts which dominate it);
—and if it passes itself off as knowledge of the truth, this is because it produces the truth through the action of a primary and always renewed falsification that posits the distinction between true and false.

Interest is thus posited radically prior to the knowledge it subordinates as a simple instrument; knowledge, dissociated from pleasure and happiness, is linked to struggle, hatred, and malice exerting themselves against themselves to the point of renouncing themselves through a supplement of struggle, hatred, and malice; its original link to truth is undone since truth is only an effect in it—and effect of a falsification that calls itself opposition of the true and false. This model of a fundamentally interested knowledge, produced as an event of the will and determining the effect of truth through falsification, is undoubtedly at the furthest remove from the postulates of classical metaphysics. It is this model that, used freely, has been put to work in this year's course on a series of examples.

3. This series of examples was taken from archaic Greek history and institutions. They all belong to the domain of justice. It involved following a development which took place from the seventh to the fifth century. This transformation concerns the administration of justice, the conception of the just, and social reactions to crime.

Studied in turn were:

—the practice of the oath in judicial disputes and the evolution from the challenge-oath of litigants exposing themselves to the gods' vengeance to the assertoric oath of the witness who is supposed to assert what is true on the basis of having seen and been present to it;
—the search for a just measure, not only in commercial exchanges but in social relations within the city, through the institution of money;
—the search for a *nomos*, for a just law of distribution ensuring the order of the city by installing a reigning order in the city that is the order of the world;
—the rituals of purification after murders.

The distribution of justice was the stake of significant political struggles throughout the period considered. These ultimately gave rise to a form of justice linked to a knowledge in which truth was posited as visible, ascertainable, measurable, compliant with laws similar to those governing the order of the world, and the discovery of which in one's presence has a purificatory value. This type of assertion of truth was to be decisive in the history of Western knowledge.

\*   \*   \*

The general framework for this year's seminar was the study of penality in nineteenth century France. It focused this year on the first developments of penal psychiatry in the Restoration period. The material used was to a large extent the text of medico-legal expert opinions given by Esquirol's contemporaries and disciples.

# OEDIPAL KNOWLEDGE

# (*Le savoir d'Œdipe*)*

> *In Sophocles' tragedy,* Oedipus the King, *five types of knowledge confront each other and fit together. The mechanism of the sumbolon, or law of halves, governs the confrontation.* ⌒ *The judicial procedure of inquiry, installed in the sixth and fifth centuries, facing traditional divinatory procedure.* ⌒ *Ignorant Oedipus is the bearer of the tyrant's knowledge (*savoir*); Oedipus, blazon of the unconscious or old oriental figure of the expert king (*roi savant*)?* ⌒ *Oedipus the King, or transgressive power-knowledge.*

IN *OEDIPUS THE KING*, recognition, *anagnōrisis*,[1] by which the one who does not know becomes one who knows and by which the one who thought he did not know realizes that he already knew—has two particular characteristics. First of all, that of being "reflexive": the one who seeks is the object of the search;[2] the one who is ignorant is the one it is a question of knowing about; he who unleashed the dogs is himself the prey; the trail on which he set them takes them back to the point where he is waiting for them.

* This development of the lecture of 17 March 1971 was given at the State University of New York, Buffalo, in March 1972, then at Cornell University in October of the same year. Foucault gave at least six versions of his reading of Sophocles' tragedy. (See "Course context" below, pp. 279-280).

But there is something else: this recognition is not only the passage from darkness to light, from ignorance to knowledge; it takes place through the confrontation of different types of knowledge (*savoir*). In *Oedipus*, the battle to know unfolds through a struggle between types of knowledge. And if there is indeed a return to the same point (he who wants to discover is discovered), this is brought about through different types of knowledge. In the dimension of knowledge (*connaissance*)-ignorance there is in fact perfect identity of subject and object, the person who does not know and the person who must be discovered, the person who wants to discover and the person about whom we are ignorant. But the differences between the types of knowledge (*savoir*) put to work are huge, or rather, let us say that they are precisely measured and marked. From knowledge characterized by listening—*akouein*—to knowledge characterized by sight, by what one has seen with one's own eyes; from the knowledge brought back from the distant place of the god to the knowledge one questions right here in the person of present witnesses; from the knowledge of leaders (or their equals, seers) to the knowledge kept by their slaves holed up in their huts; from knowledge in the form of prescription-prediction (this is what you must do, this is what will happen to you, this is what you will discover) to knowledge that has the form of testimony (that is what I saw, that is what I did); from knowledge that deliberately withdraws into enigma and incompleteness (hence the king himself does not succeed in extracting it) to knowledge that was hiding behind fear and that threat manages to flush out. So five[3] different types of knowledge: in their medium, their origin, their bearers, their relation to time, and the source of obscurity that veils them.

From the god's answer (86: *tou theou phēmēn*),[4] to the interrogation of the slave (1121-1122: *phōnei blepōn osan serōtō*; "Answer my questions"),[5] which frame the play, or at least the inquiry conducted by Oedipus, we pass from one type of knowledge to the other. Two questions consequently:

1—How and by what mechanism is the transition carried out?
2—What are these types of knowledge which confront each other, re-place each other, and finally confirm each other and fit together?

The mechanism of the transition is easily described. It takes place through incomplete pieces of information and fragments which complement each other. But what is most characteristic is that it is governed by a sort of "law of halves."

When questioned, the god gives his answer: the murderer of Laius must be driven out. (In truth, if we follow the account given by Creon, King Apollo's answer orders the land to be delivered from a defilement; an order that still fails to say what defilement. He clarifies: a murder. But a murder presupposes a victim and a murderer. Phoebus[6] has indeed specified the victim, but his answer still lacks the other half, the criminal part.) So, it is a matter of finding the part that is missing from Apollo's oracular answer. And there would be no point asking the god himself: he is not one of those one forces to speak; one does not constrain the will of the gods (280-281).

For the moment there is only one course of action. If there is a third way—Oedipus says to the Chorus—do not fail to tell me. But on this point, there is no other way: all the witnesses hide away; even the rumored eye witness was unable to provide any useful information. The only recourse is that sort of half of the god who can be questioned, the divine seer (298: *ton theion mantin*), Teiresias. He is closest to Apollo. A king like him (284: *Avakt avakti*). Seeing the same things (284: *tauth orōnt[a]*). Twinned with him, as is shown by the clash of the two names in line 285 (*phoebō Teiresian*).[7] The night of his eyes complements the god's light; and what the latter insists on hiding, Teiresias, in his darkness, says clearly (286: *saphestata*). Now Teiresias does indeed name the guilty party, but he names him without proof; he names him in the same way in which Apollo spoke. Prescription: "I order you ... to obey the edict you have proclaimed" (350-351);[8] solemn and oracular assertion (362: *Ponea se phēmi*; 366: *Lelēthenai se phēmi*); prediction (417-427: "From both sides the terrible footed curse will one day drive you out ... No one among men will be more harshly crushed than you");[9] Teiresias and Apollo speak in the same way: one proclaims that there is defilement and that the city must be purified; the other says who was responsible for the defilement and proclaims that he must be driven out. The two of them, divinity and seer, have said everything.

And yet, an essential part of the whole is missing: that double of itself that would give it a visible reality, that would give it substance in what happened, that would prevent it from having been said in vain (365: *matēn*). The future of the announced discovery requires that what really happened be brought to light; the proclamation has to be put together with an account of a memory; the prescription requires a corresponding factual observation. This is what the Chorus asserts in the middle of the argument between Oedipus and Teiresias: the latter's accusations are no doubt no more valid than the former's suspicions; the King and the seer are only speaking in anger. It is what the Chorus asserts again after the departure of Teiresias: it can neither blame nor approve; it does not know what to say; it sees neither in the present nor the past (484-486). In the eyes of these mortals, a prophecy without evidence, an oracle without testimony, is no more than an unfounded suspicion. The Chorus waits to see: "I should never approve those who accuse [the King], before having seen (*[prin] idoim[i]*) the prophet's words justified" (504-505).[10] Oedipus no doubt has the divine words against him; but in his favor he has visible things (506: *phanera*), proofs (*basanos*). And no less is needed for the seer's word to become "*orthon epos*."[11]

After the divine, oracular, divinatory part there is the human and visible half which will fit together with it. This in turn is divided into two halves: one devoted to the murder of Laius; the other to the birth of Oedipus; and, once joined, the whole they form will fill the gap left by the prophecy. But each of these two halves is itself subdivided. The murder of Laius is first established by Jocasta's memories; by indirect memories of what she heard and what she was told: a murder at the place where three roads meet. With which the memory of Oedipus will fit exactly (729-730 and 771-834): "I killed an old man at the place where three roads meet." There is a perfect fit between the immediate testimony of the Servant, who has now disappeared, and the present memory of Oedipus, apart, however, from the fact that the witness spoke of several murderers. A slight uncertainty which calls for verification: it is necessary to ask the person who was there (835: *pros tou parontos ekmathēs*). This detail will be enough for the whole of the god's prophecy, for all of the seer's divination—or at least the half concerning the murder of Laius—to be reduced to nothing.

The other half, the birth of Oedipus, is attested by the alignment of two other fragments. The messenger from Corinth arrives to assert that Oedipus is not the son of Polybus, but a child given to him by a shepherd from Cithaeron; and the shepherd from Cithaeron asserts that Oedipus was given to him by Jocasta to be exposed. It is worth noting that here again, in this "birth half," just as a moment ago in the "murder half," there is a slight, scarcely perceptible remainder, a hitch, a very small missing piece. For the murder of Laius it was the number of murderers, one or several—and this is by no means the same thing, Oedipus recalls*—; only the shepherd's disappearance, fleeing Corinth when Oedipus takes power there, is a silent proof; but, even when he is present, the shepherd will not testify that he actually saw Oedipus killing Laius: this is never said. There is a symmetrical gap with the birth of Oedipus: the shepherd knows only one thing, that he got the child from Jocasta's hands, and that public rumor had it that he was her son. But only she could provide irrefutable evidence of this: "But she, within, better than anyone, your wife, will tell us what is the case" (1171-1172).[12] But precisely while the shepherd is uttering these words, Jocasta, who has also fled so as not to see and hear, is killing herself. Now no one will be able to authenticate the birth of Oedipus.

For the moment, let us leave to one side the meaning of these tiny and essential gaps. The mechanism of the two halves which fit together is clear. The divine half, itself made up of an oracular half and a divinatory half; and the human half, made up in turn of a murder half, one fragment of which is held by Jocasta, and the other by Oedipus, and a birth half, one half of which comes from Corinth in the messenger's hands, and the other at Thebes buried in a slave's hut. The four halves of the human testimony (Oedipus, Jocasta, the messenger, the shepherd), form two pairs which fit together, filling exactly the gap left by the prophecy and transforming the double speech of the seer and the god into "*orthon epos.*"

Now this transformation is established by a double displacement. A displacement, first of all, from the top to the bottom of a hierarchy: it is

---

* If, at least, 845 is authentic. (Note by M.F., following Masqueray.)

the gods or their servants who speak first of all, and who lack—at least in Oedipus' eyes—the testimony of men; then come the kings, but who lack the confirmation of their slaves; finally come the slaves themselves, who say precisely what the gods predicted, recount exactly the events they had prescribed. The slaves too, like Teiresias, have seen and say the same things, *ta auta*, as Phoebus. The slave's humble memory corresponds word for word to the "immortal Voice" (157: *ambrote phama*).

But there is also a displacement in the forms of knowledge: Apollo, who sees everything and speaks to his servants, was invoked first of all, or his blind seer, who listens to the god's word and sees in the dark. Listening and looking whose power has nothing in common with human listening and looking, since they see the invisible and understand the puzzle. Corresponding to them in the human half are completely different kinds of looking and listening: regarding the death of Laius, Jocasta says what she has heard, and Oedipus recounts what he has seen with his eyes and done with his hands; in turn, the messenger from Corinth recounts what he has seen and done; the shepherd of Thebes, what he has done and heard. In this half the seeing and hearing intertwine (Jocasta heard what the shepherd saw; Oedipus heard what the messenger saw; the shepherd heard what Jocasta saw and did), just as the light and voice in the god and the seer intertwine (the god of light makes his voice heard by the blind man who sees everything). But *oran* and *akouein* do not have the same meaning in the two cases.

And it is by virtue of this very difference that they are able to fit together and finally form an "*orthon epos.*" Now the form of this alignment and its mechanism are easy to recognize: they are named by Oedipus himself at the beginning of the play: "I would not be able to follow the criminal's track for long if I did not have some clue (*sumbolon*)" (220-221).[13] The halves which come to complement each other are like the fragments of a symbol whose reunited totality has the value of proof and attestation. *Oedipus* is a "symbolic" story, a story of circulating fragments, which pass from hand to hand and the lost half of which one is looking for: from Phoebus to the seer, from Jocasta to Oedipus, from the messenger to the shepherd—so from the gods to the kings and from the kings to the slaves. And when, finally, the last slave leaves his hut with the last fragment of knowledge still needed in his hand, then the "narrative" half has joined the "oracle" half, the "incest" half has joined the "murder" half, the "Theban" half has joined the "Corinthian" half, and the total figure is reconstituted. The tessera has been reformed from its scattered fragments. The *sumbolon* is complete. The entire procedure of the search has followed the dictates of this mechanism of the symbol: examination and authentication of what one has in one's hand, definition of what is missing and was of supreme importance to know; designation of the person who must have the absent and complementary fragment in his possession. This is what Oedipus calls "making an inquiry" (258: *exereunan*).[14]

But Oedipus himself is a *sumbolon*—a figure pulled apart. He has a Corinthian half: son of Polybus, the object of a drunken insult, then of a fearful prophecy, a voluntary exile, murderer of a passer-by, finally welcomed in Thebes, which he has saved from misfortune; but he also has a Theban half: conqueror of the Sphinx, welcomed in the city as a savior, husband of the queen, sovereign. Each of these two halves, joined along their edges by the episode of the Sphinx—which turns the exile into a king, someone doomed to misfortune into someone who has won happiness, a Corinthian into a Theban—is only a visible fragment lacking a hidden part. The Corinthian half of Oedipus, son of Polybus, is itself only the half of a story which was missing the episode of the child taken in on Cithaeron, that of the childless king and queen, and of the adoption disguised as birth. And the other half, Oedipus the adventurer-tyrant, is far from constituting the Theban totality of Oedipus; there is a hidden half of this half: child of Laius and Jocasta, destined to crime from before his birth, and given to a slave to abandon on Cithaeron.

Such, then, is the "double game" of the symbolic mechanism: [piece by] piece, it reconstructs the cause of the plague ravaging Thebes; all that was missing finally finds a place and recomposes the whole; but this missing half reconstruction of the story reveals Oedipus himself as monstrously endowed with "too many" halves, as twinned with unforeseen and impure halves: the son of Polybus is also the son of Laius, the king is also the king's murderer, the murderer is also the child; the husband is also the son; the father is also his children's brother; the person who seeks is also the person sought; the person who banishes must be banished, the person whom the gods condemn condemns himself. Reduplication to which the whole of the end of the play bears insistent witness: "It is natural that among so many afflictions you double

your groans as you bear double evils" (1319-1320); "O marriage, marriage, you gave me life and after giving it to me, you made the same
seed germinate a second time; you showed to all fathers brothers of
their children, children brothers of their father, spouses both wives
and mothers of their husband" (1403-1407).[15] What the mechanism of
the *sumbolon* has revealed through the interplay of missing halves is a
composite figure of excessive, monstrous halves that no man's eyes can
any longer bear to see.

This mechanism of the *sumbolon* makes Oedipus a monstrous double[16] and multiplies intolerable reduplications around him. But there
is more: it makes many of the speeches uttered by Oedipus, or concerning Oedipus, appear double, as saying two things at the same time:[17]
Crying for the city, he groans for himself (64); he condemns the murderer to banishment, even were he to live under his own roof (249-251),
he knows that one cannot force the gods to do what they do not wish
to do (280-281). All these phrases and many others said two things at
the same time: in that each of them was like a *sumbolon*, a piece in two
parts of which Oedipus and the Chorus saw only a fragment, but whose
other fragment had to come back to them later, at the moment of the
last alignment. Then Oedipus in turn understands that his words were
saying two things, which the audience informed about the *sumbolon* had
already fully grasped; the two parts of the "symbol" were separated only
for the characters on stage.

The form of the *sumbolon* is dominant throughout *Oedipus the King*. It
is what governs the relations between the dramatic turn of events of different episodes and recognition; it governs the entrance of the hoped for,
summoned, or unexpected characters; it governs the series of searches,
waits, and discoveries; it governs very often the meaning of phrases—
threats, promises, or curses. But it is by no means (to start with at
least) a rhetorical form: it is a matter of a ritual and juridical form which
makes it possible to establish proof, recognition, to identify individuals,
or authenticate messages. It is an old traditional practice which makes
it possible to seal orders and decrees, to prevent fraud and the lie, to
establish a contract, and to receive orders, decrees, and oracles without
alteration. It is a ritual instrument of the exercise of power.

Now, there is a point that has to be recalled here. The keynote of the
inquiry launched by Oedipus (which he reproaches the Thebans with

not having undertaken themselves, when there was time) is very quickly one of mistrust. If the inquiry took so many detours, if it advanced so slowly and through the juxtaposition of so many different fragments, it is because the seer's words, however precise and accusatory, were not believed: Oedipus suspects a plot and the Chorus thought he spoke in anger. Oedipus turns his back on these sacred words and the Chorus with him; a bit later, Jocasta has scarcely more faith in the gods' messengers (945-953). Do not the gods themselves fall under the charge of this incredulity? No doubt Jocasta is careful to distinguish between the gods and their servants. But after all, did not Oedipus and Jocasta believe that it was possible to escape the inevitable decrees of the gods? And do they not rush to cry victory over the oracles as soon as they can? No matter for the moment. The important thing is that to verify, or ward off the threatening words of the seer, Oedipus employs a procedure that is very distant from oracular listening.

Oedipus launches an inquiry: Who killed? When and in what circumstances was the murder carried out? Who witnessed it? Where is he now? Did you see what you know, or did you hear about it, and from whom? Is the man I am confronting you with, the man you see here, really the man you saw previously? All this is very far from supplication to the gods and his servants' faithful listening. But the stages of the inquiry and the facts it gradually discovers follow one another according to the ritual form and political-religious mechanism of the *sumbolon*.

This mechanism ultimately makes it possible to show that the knowledge extracted by the inquiry exactly matches the knowledge expressed by the seer. More precisely: the slave questioned at the final stage, at the end of the inquiry, opposite Phoebus and at the other end of the hierarchy, the only one to have as much knowledge as the god and his prophet: he too, and he alone, knows everything. No doubt he is summoned only so as to complete the last missing fragment (the Theban side of the origin of Oedipus), but he was in addition the only witness to the murder of Laius; the only one to *know* that the murderer of Laius, Jocasta's husband, was the son of both of them (this is not said explicitly, just as the essential and decisive points are not expressed; but he shows that he knew by his flight when Oedipus takes power, by his silence when he is asked to recognize the king as the child who had been handed to him). So the slave saw everything, like the blind seer whom nothing escapes, like the god who sees everything. From end to end of the great inquiry, from end to end of all these painfully matched fragments of knowledge, the slave and the god face each other, one saying what he sees through the enigmatic mouth of oracles, the other keeping quiet about what he has seen and what no one should have seen. Can we say that the slave's silent gaze and the all-seeing sovereign's word "symbolize" each other?

It is always the form of the *sumbolon* that enables testimony to be matched with the oracle. Does *Oedipus* involve giving a ritual, sacred character to this practice of the inquiry, raising its validity to the level of that of oracles pronounced by the gods? Or is it, under the cover of symbolic ritual, a question of replacing the old practice of oracular consultations with the new judicial practice of the inquiry? Or is it a question of founding these two types of knowledge simultaneously? In any case, we now have to examine the roles, the confrontations of these "knowledge rituals," which are at the same time juridical, political, and religious rituals.

*    *    *

So, in *Oedipus the King* there are two types of knowledge which fit together and finally form an *orthon epos*. Two types of knowledge which know the same thing (the murder and the incest), but one proclaiming it in the form of the oracle, of clairvoyance, of divination; a knowledge that nothing escapes, the seer's blindness equivalent to the god's light. The other is a knowledge extracted in the form of testimony, memory, and confession: he knows only what he has seen and done; beyond this he can say nothing. One knowledge overarches time because it sees the future as well as the past, and the past in the same form as the future (in his great prophecy of 408-428, Teiresias tells Oedipus what he has done, the hatred of which he is presently the object, and the evils soon to overwhelm him); the other knowledge can say only what took place in the past, it is subject to the constraint of the long period of time (1141)[18] and must comply with the law of *mnēmē*, memory (1131).[19]

Oedipus stands between these two types of knowledge. Oedipus forces both to express themselves—"You have forced me to speak against my will," Teiresias tells Oedipus (357); and Oedipus says to the Herdsman: "If you do not answer willingly, you will be forced to answer" (1152)[20]—he forces them to fit together. Now is Oedipus purely and simply the one who knows nothing, ignorance that blindly seeks to know? Oedipus is traditionally the one who was able to answer the riddle of the Sphinx, but could not solve the riddle of himself. The text frequently emphasizes this opposition between a knowledge which saved the city and an ignorance dooming him to misfortune: "Are you not naturally clever at solving riddles?" asks Teiresias ironically (440).[21] Oedipus, the riddle solver, completely ignorant about himself. Know-nothing Oedipus;[22] Ignorant Oedipus, unless we were to want to turn him into the one who, at bottom, knew, who knew his birth and his crime, but refused to know; unconscious Oedipus. Anyway, he contradicts the etymological play on words of his name; he knew neither from whence came his pierced feet nor to where his feet of exile had carried him.

Now in Sophocles' text it seems that Oedipus is not purely and simply the one who does not know; it seems rather that he is himself the bearer of a certain type of knowledge which is distinct both from the oracular knowledge of Teiresias and the slave's memory. Oedipus is also a man of knowledge,[23] of a very particular knowledge with its own characteristics, conditions of exercise, and effects. This knowledge, mid-way between [that] of the god and [that] of the slave, is the "tyrant's" knowledge. The "tyranny" of Oedipus, the form of power he exercises, and the way in which he conquered it, are not marginal with regard to the great inquiry undertaking: they are quite central [in the] relations of power and knowledge.

Whenever Oedipus appears, his power is at the same time brought into play and questioned. It is because he has power that the inhabitants of Thebes resort to him against the plague (33-34); but the calamity threatening Thebes affects him no less than the city itself (64). It is in the interest of his own kingship that Oedipus seeks out the killer of King Laius: the same criminal might well attack him (139-140). It is from the height of his political-religious power as king that Oedipus condemns the murderer of Laius to banishment; but he himself would accept to share such evils if the murderer inhabited his household (249-251). It is as king, bound to the city in the common undertaking of salvation, that Oedipus appeals to Teiresias (312); and it is this royal power that Teiresias threatens with his prophecy (350-353); and when

Teiresias accuses him of being the murderer, he does not hear his innocence being called into question, but his power, and it is his power he
defends (380-404).

In the great confrontation with Creon [532-631], the issue is power,
and power only, not facts, signs, or proofs; not: "Is it true that I have
killed?" but: "Is a plot likely?"; not: "Am I innocent or guilty?" but:
"It's either him or me at the head of this city" (in particular, lines
658-659 and 669-672). Again, it is the sovereign, whose glory may
well be the issue of three generations of slaves, who asserts himself when
the messenger reveals that Oedipus is not the son of Polybus (1063).
It is the king as chief officer of the law[24] who questions and threatens
to torture the slave who holds the final secret; and at the very moment
Oedipus is brought down, the Chorus evokes the typical features of the
sovereign or tyrant: he launched his arrow furthest, he won complete
happiness, he stood like a tower: "He was called my king." Finally, after
the fall, the final word addressed to Oedipus, before he is dragged out of
sight inside the palace, is pronounced by the new king: it is the decree
that drives him from power, the prohibition, henceforth, against giving orders: "No longer seek always to be the master (*kratein*)" (1522).[25]
And this same word is immediately repeated twice: first by Creon in the
following line in a play on words (*akratēsas* [1523] in which are heard
both the summits (*akras*) to which he has risen and the power of which
he has been stripped, *a-kratein*);[26] and then by the Chorus two lines
further on in the last retort of the play: You were a man at the summit
of power (*kratistos*), the object of every citizen's envy (1525-1526).[27]
In which the Chorus only takes up again the words of the first greet-
ing addressed to Oedipus at the start of the play: "*ō kratunōn Oidipous*"
(14).[28*] It is in fact the power of Oedipus that is brought into play in
this great test of knowledge.

What power? There is a whole series of traditional characterizations
in the tragedy which serve to designate those legendary characters, the
heroes, founders, and "kings," the political and religious sovereigns of a
city. Oedipus is greeted as *basileus*, *anax*, the first amongst men; he is said
to have *krateia*, that he holds *arkas* (259); and, in several of its usages at

---

* See also line 40: O *kratiston pasin Oidipou kara*. (Note by M.F.) [*Oedipus the King*, p. 12: "Now
Oedipus, Greatest in all men's eyes."]

least, the word *turannos*, by which Oedipus, but also Polybus and Laius are referred to, no doubt does not have any particular connotation: to replace the "tyrant" Polybus, the Corinthians chose Oedipus as "tyrant" (939-940); and the latter had already replaced Laius, "the tyrant."

Nevertheless, at several points in the tragedy Oedipus's sovereignty is given a particular stamp. He was already familiar with a mixed destiny, misery and glory; from the highest he fell to the lowest; and when he was at the lowest point, he rose back to the summit: "The years which have grown with me have sometimes humbled me, sometimes exalted me" (1083).[29] Certainly, such alternation in fortune is peculiar to the tragic hero, whether or not he is a tyrant. But, for the moment at least, rather than seeing this as the result of the gods' hostility, as their punishment of him, or the result of some unjust fury, it proclaims the very law of his existence; the changeability of fortune is his lot, and far from complaining about it, he vaunts it. He is the son of beneficent fortune, and the years which sometimes bring him favor and sometimes misery are his "fellow kind" (*suggeneis*, 1082):[30] such is his birth, such he is by nature (1080-1084; *Toiosde d'ekphus*).[31] Now such an alternation of fortune, this linking of grandeur and disaster, was characterized by the Chorus shortly before: it is the destiny peculiar to the tyrant and his pride (872-873).[32]

Now there are many specifically tyrannical traits in the life and character of Oedipus. Sophocles' text does not fail to pick them out. Some are positive. He arrived, a stranger in the city, no one knew him, and no one asked him his origin; he won his power alone by raising himself above the citizens (1196: "He shot his arrow further than the others"),[33] only to arouse their jealousy (1526); he was possessed by happiness, he had mastered it (1197; *ekratese*). And in this enterprise, he was alone; he carried it out himself (*autos*). But if he was able to seize power in this way, it is because he had served the city; when it was perishing, he saved it; when its enemies were on the point of destroying it, he delivered it from them; he had been its bastion and tower (1200-1201); he had enabled the city to breathe and sleep (1220-1221). He had put it right, back on its feet (39, 51, 443, 695).

Such exploits are typical of the historical-legendary figures of tyrants or lawgivers who have exercised power for a time, shaken the traditions and quite often changed the archaic structures of Greek society. The expression, "*orthōsai, anorthōsai polin*," which recurs in this connection, is characteristic: it is the expression Solon himself employed to define his work. Oedipus, like the mythological heroes, conquers a power which did not belong to him by overcoming a test; but, like the "constitution makers" of the sixth century, he puts the city back on its feet, he cleans it up, he puts it "straight." And in doing so he establishes a relationship of recognition, debt, and affection with his subjects which has nothing to do with the privilege of birth. The saving exploit has bound the citizens to their master, and unless otherwise constrained by some twist of fate they remain faithful to him: "It was by a good test that he made himself loved by the city. So my mind will never accuse him of a crime" (510-511);[34] "Know that I would seem a madman ... if I were to abandon you, who alone, in the sufferings to which my dear land was succumbing, put it back on the right road" [690-695].[35] The power of Oedipus in Thebes is based no less on the affection of the *plēthos* than on his marriage to Jocasta. And Creon is well aware of this: one needs money and the support of the *plēthos* to acquire power. Here again, on the legendary figure of the hero who, after the test, establishes his power through marriage, Sophocles' *Oedipus* superimposes the historical figure of the tyrant or "reformer" whose rule relies upon the more or less spontaneous affection of the *plēthos*.

But there is more. Oedipus is also endowed with some of the tyrant's traditionally negative traits. He does not identify himself with the city because he was born there and is both its son and citizen (which is precisely what he does not know), but because he has taken it over. It is his city in the sense that he possesses it, and he alone possesses it. Creon reproaches him for having this attitude: "And I too am part of the city; it does not belong only to you (*oukhi soi monō*)" (630).[36] When he fires off orders, it matters little whether or not they are just, it is enough that he has given them ("It is necessary to obey all the same," 628);[37] is not the city his alone (629)?

This is why, a bit further on, when the Chorus draws the tyrant's portrait and gives it his excessive features, it can say that he does not fear "*Dikē*." Some commentators have been surprised that precisely this Chorus should give such a harsh portrait: presumption, injustice, refusal to honor the gods, culpable insolence, unjust gains, sacrilege, profanation of sacred things, refusal to listen to the oracles, neglect of worship. Should we really recognize Oedipus in this portrait of the sovereign who, shortly before, had the people's grateful support, and who, in the city's misfortune, was so prompt in dispatching Creon to the god of Delphi? In fact, too many of these traits traditionally attributed to the tyrant refer to the words or conduct of Oedipus scattered throughout the text for us not to see him in this portrait (and I leave to one side for the moment the problem of listening to oracles). At the point when Oedipus' luck begins to turn again, the Chorus—symbolizing the swift about turn of the *plēthos*—inverts the positive image it had hitherto given of the tyrant and contrasts his rule with that of the laws (*nomoi*) "born in the heavenly Ether and whose father is Olympus" [867-888].[38] Certainly, the Chorus will make another switch when the calamity is over; it will take pity on the one who, for a while, allowed the city to breathe.

But such is precisely the uncertainty peculiar to the tyrant's destiny: loved, then rejected, then pitied; obeyed in each of his strange wishes, which have the force of the city's decrees, then banished and doomed to an execrable fate when his arrogance is confronted with the laws formulated by the Olympians.

The tyrant's perilous situation: he is not entirely of the city, a citizen amongst the other citizens, even if the latter owe their salvation to him; and although the gods may have helped him, at least in order to overcome the test (38), he does not establish the rule of their decrees in the city. There is a triad which recurs at several points in the text of *Oedipus the King*: the gods, the sovereign, and the land (*gē* or *khōra*); a triad uttered by Oedipus himself, and defining the tyrant's position. When the enemy divinity was ravaging the land, Oedipus placed himself like a tower between the "oracular virgin" and the dying city; moreover, he did not do so without help from the gods, which allowed the city to be saved. So he is at the same time city wall against the gods and the gods' envoy in the city.

But conversely, and this is the tragedy's reversal, he himself is the plague the gods have visited on the city; the city has turned away from the divine laws and oracles because of him, and the city will have to drive him out in order for the gods to reestablish their order within it. When Oedipus solemnly declares that the murderer, who pollutes the city and draws down on it the gods' anger, must be driven out, and that this must be done "for me, for the god, for this land" (253), by putting himself forward in this way he indicates, despite himself and unknowingly, the tyrant's dangerous position between the god and the land. And if the power of Oedipus is ultimately destroyed, it is in fact because these two types of knowledge are directly fitted together, the first coming from the gods—that is the knowledge of the seer—and the second from the land, from that *khōra* in which the slave who was born in the royal household has taken refuge, so as not to see (756-764).[39]

In this unique and fragile position, the power of Oedipus is linked to a type of knowledge (*savoir*). If he seized power at Thebes, or rather if he was given power, it was because he won the "knowledge (*connaissance*) test." At several points Oedipus and the Chorus remind each other that the bond between them is based on knowledge; and on a double knowledge moreover: that of Oedipus, who demonstrated his superiority by solving the riddle, and [that of] the city, which was able to ascertain beyond doubt that Oedipus knew; it is because he was recognized "*sophos*," and on evidence (*basano*), that he was loved by the city (510, *adupolis*). This knowledge demonstrated in the test enables Oedipus to govern; and whenever he appears, exercising his power, it is in the form of the one who knows: I know, I have seen. In this way Oedipus manifests interdependently his knowledge and his power [58, 65, 67]. *Oida* is the word through which he asserts himself, and which precisely is inscribed in his name.[40] It is this power-knowledge that is exposed, risked, endangered by the plague of Thebes: if the king does not know what is to be done, if he does not know who is responsible for the defilement, if he does not know to whom the purifying rite must be applied, then he will be lost along with the city. But, precisely, once again he will solve the riddle, he will discover what no one knew, and he will lose his power. But we are running ahead.

What is this knowledge linked to the conquest and exercise of power? To characterize it, Oedipus himself uses the term *gnōmē*: he had dominated the Sphinx, with its secret and its cruelty, by *gnōmē* (398, *gnōmē kurēsas*). In another passage, evoking the power with which he is invested, and which he thinks is threatened by Creon and Teiresias, he exclaims: "*O ploute kai turanni kai tekhnē tekhnēs*" (380).[41] Power appears here flanked by its two major attributes [*tekhnē* and *gnōmē*][42]*—which are at once its instruments, conditions, and manifestations: the abundance of goods and the resources of art, supreme skill, superior knowhow: *tekhnē tekhnēs*. What do these two words, *tekhnē* and *gnōmē* refer to here?

They are contrasted very clearly with a mode of knowledge involving learning something from someone. Oedipus boasts about it: he alone, by himself (*autos*) was able to solve the Sphinx's riddle. Nobody had taught him anything. And the Priest, right at the start of the play, proclaims it openly: "You delivered the city of Cadmus ... without any knowledge from us or anyone, without being taught by us" (35-38).[43] In order to know, Oedipus does not need to listen to what he says, or to learn (*ekmathein*). But this principle is not only valid for what the people of the country—of the *khōra*—may know, it also concerns what the birds and all the traditional means of divination could teach him. Oedipus says this to Teiresias: When the Dog was ravaging the city, neither the gods nor the birds came to your aid to teach you what had to be done. And he continues: "It was not up to the first comer to explain the riddle, it needed divination (*manteias*)" (393-394).[44] A clearly ironic phrase: for it was precisely the privilege of the "first comer," of the one who "was passing by" (*toupiontos*) to solve the riddle; the passer-by—whom Teiresias now wants to get to believe that he is ignorant of everything (*mēden eidōs* [397])—needed to employ, not divination, which interprets the flight of birds, but *gnōmē* (390-398). The knowledge of Oedipus, the same knowledge by which he conquered power, is a knowledge that does not learn anything from anyone; it resorts neither to divine signs nor to human rumor. It did not need to draw its knowledge from elsewhere (*ekmathein*; *ekdidakhthein*, 38). It could no doubt be said that the knowledge of King Oedipus does not belong to the dimension of *akouein*, of a listening which is at the same time

---

* [The Greek terms inserted here by the French editor—*tekhnē* (art, skill) and *gnōmē* (knowledge)—do not correspond to the "two major attributes" given in the Sophocles text quoted by Foucault and repeated immediately after as flanking power: power or sovereignty is flanked on one side by wealth or the abundance of goods, and on the other by the resources of art or skill (*tekhnē*); G.B.]

submission. The *gnōmē* of which Oedipus boasts, and which has taken him to power, is contrasted with the listening-obedience of which the seer gives proof with regard to the gods, and the people with regard to the orders it receives. We should note that Jocasta—who shares the power, crime, and ignorance of Oedipus—also shows the same refusal of listening-submission. She says so very clearly, even seeming to go further than Oedipus: "No mortal knows anything about the art of divination" (709).[45] And did they not both demonstrate this refusal, each in their own way, but symmetrically, when they learned of the prophecy concerning them? Certainly, they heard it, understood it, believed it; but they did not listen to it; they thought they could escape it. They respected the word of the gods enough not to be indifferent to it and defy it without misgivings; but they both thought that it had not read the future and that no divination could say what was going to happen in advance and without error. It is not that Oedipus and Jocasta do not believe in the gods or refuse to respect them. But they think that the gods manifest their will themselves, and clearly. Jocasta says so in lines 724-725: "What the god judges it necessary to make known, he easily shows to us himself" (*radios autos phanei*).[46] And Oedipus, for his part, does not think that one can force the silence of the gods; they say only what they want to say.

Two procedures of knowledge are also rejected by the royal couple: one which consists in seeking to know through obscure signs what the gods wish to hide (no bird screeching, 965-966, no signs, no means of forcing the silence of the gods); and the other which seeks to see in advance the share of fate fixed by the gods (no predictions, no "*pronoia*," 978). All those decrees-predictions (*thespismata*, 971) which ambiguously fix the future should count for nothing (*aksi'oudenos*, 972).[47]

One of the words which recurs most frequently in the discourse of Oedipus, in correlation with his exercise of power and exaltation of his knowledge, is *euriskein*. Oedipus is the man who finds. Of course, he found the answer to give to the Sphinx, thus saving the city. In the new disaster, the city again appeals to his ability to find: "find some rescue" (*alkēn tin'eurein*) the Priest pleads at the start of the play (42);[48] he tells the troubled people the solution he has found (69 et seq.); he reproaches the Thebans for not having undertaken to discover (*eksere-unan*, 258) the murderer of Laius in time; but he is now determined to discover himself what will make it possible to know and to save the city (120, 304); at one point in his search he even thinks he has "discovered" a plot hatched by Creon (531-546). Furthermore, Teiresias tells him, not without a threatening irony: "are you not skilled at finding these things" (440, *taut aristos euriskein ephus*).[49] In saying this, Teiresias describes Oedipus as the opposite of what he, Teiresias, himself is; did not Teiresias say of himself shortly before that he "nurtures the all-powerful truth in [himself]" (356)?[50] And the Chorus greeted him as the only mortal in whom truth is innate (*talēthes eupethuken*, 299).[51] One, the seer, is like the place for the growth of a truth sown in him by the gods; the other, the king, has the ability to find.

Now finding—*euriskein*—has three, interconnected characteristics. First, one finds alone, by oneself. Oedipus insists somewhat on the fact that he was alone when he found the answer to give to the Sphinx. But at several points in his regal behavior, he stresses that he wants to inquire, find, and decide himself. From the first lines, he says so: "I did not want to learn from others serving as messengers, I came myself" (*autos ... elēlutha*, 7).[52] To find a solution he closes himself in his thoughts, reflects at length (67), and immediately acts on what he finds (68). The other characteristic of discovery is that, when one cannot do it alone, one relies on what one sees and hears oneself, or on what witnesses saw and heard. If the murder of Laius troubles Oedipus so much, it is because he was not there; he has heard it spoken about, he did not witness it or see it with his own eyes (*eiseidon*, 105); being foreign to the affair, he cannot himself (*autos*) find the guilty party (219-222); now what one needs is somebody who witnessed the misfortune (116-119); at least one needs somebody who saw the person who saw (*ton d'idont[a ... ] ora*, 293). And when he is on the track, he insists on seeing himself the person who was present: "I wish to see him" (*eisidein*, 1052) he says, referring to the shepherd who was present at the death of Laius; hope, the Chorus tells him, until "*pros tou parontos ekmathēs*" (835).[53]

Thus, from presence to presence, one goes back, as if on the trail, from present ignorance to past knowledge (*connaissance*). The "discovery" of what the king himself did not witness personally comes about through the search for marks, traces: it is not the cries of birds that have to be interpreted, but the visible elements linking the past to the present (*sēmēnas*, 957; *sēmeia*; 1059; *basano*, 509), the slender, single detail which may sometimes reveal a great deal (120), everything that makes it possible to follow the criminal's tracks (221), in short, taking things up again *eks uparkhēs* ([at their start] 132). Imprudently, Jocasta reproaches Oedipus for "not explaining the present by the past," but relying on what the last person tells him (916 et seq.). In fact Oedipus does so only too much: it is precisely by listening to the last person to speak—the slave—that he manages to find in the terrible past the reasons for the present calamity.

We can see that the *tekhnē* of Oedipus is not tuned to knowledge (*connaissance*) of the gods' hidden decrees which fix the destiny of men in advance, but to the discovery of what happened and is happening. It does not listen to the words of the gods which bind man once and for all; it lends attention to those irregularities, detours, and highs and lows which constitute Fortune [*Tukhē*]. The knowledge (*savoir*) of Oedipus is on the side of *Tukhē*. This proximity of *tekhnē-Tukhē* in Oedipal knowledge has a double effect: on the one hand, it allows one to give credence only to what has happened, not to look, "either to the right or the left," for what side the prophet's birds are flying (857-858), to consider all prediction,* all *pronoia* (978) idle, and not to see a realized prediction but a blow of *Tukhē* in the events that occur, like the death of Polybus (949). The *tekhnē* of Oedipus allows him to consider divine oracles, "*theon manteumata*" (946),[54] as nothing. But on the other hand, to consider them as nothing is to be able to escape them; it is always possible to substitute a different destiny for the *moira* [fate; G.B.] that prophets seem to reserve for man (713). This is what Jocasta asserts (707 et seq.); it is what she wanted to demonstrate through action by exposing Oedipus. It is what Oedipus asserts and wanted to do (964 et seq.) by fleeing Corinth. And it is no doubt Jocasta who expresses best the tyrant's relation [to] his knowledge and destiny,† when she says that what controls (*kratei*) man are the things of fate (*ta tēs tukhēs*); and that what is best, strongest (*kratiston*), is to live as one has the power to do (*opōs dunaito tis* [979]). Interplay between the force of *Tukhē* and the power of man: such is the lot of the one who considers the signs of

---

* [The French text has *précision*, but the sense of the sentence, and the textual reference, would suggest that this should be *prévision*; G.B.]
† Manuscript: relation of the tyrant, of his knowledge and of his destiny (*du tyran, de son savoir, et de son destin*).

divination and the terror they convey to be nothing (977-983). Oedipus will be able proudly to proclaim himself child of *Tukhē* (1080). And in this too, he is closely akin to the historical-legendary figure of the traditional tyrant.

So, we have two contrasting series, each characterizing a type of knowledge and a type of power. On one side, the series of divination, which overarches time, is deployed in the dimension of *pronoia*, and, through the intermediary of messengers, listens out for the prophetic decrees to which one has to submit: this knowledge is linked to the power of the religious figure-sovereign. On the other hand, there is the series of *gnōmē*: this is deployed between past and present, and, relying on the testimony of those who saw, who witnessed, who "were there," it enables one to "discover" and find the remedy oneself; it is the tyrant's knowledge. The tyrant and the seer, both hailed as *Anax*,* confront each other with the arms of their respective knowledge. Oedipus is not the one who does not know: he is the man who has chosen another type of knowledge against the oracular, prophetic, divinatory mode of knowledge which has constantly pursued and condemned him.

But, however much this other knowledge may be distinguished as knowledge of the tyrant who wants to see for himself, it is nonetheless highly ritualized. In fact, in *Oedipus the King*, oracular knowledge and the knowledge of inquiry are presented as the effects of two well-ordered procedures. The former is the procedure of religious consultation and develops in two phases: in the first, messengers are sent to the seat of the god to bring back the oracle; in the second, the god's servant is asked to complete the oracle and determine how and with regard to what its orders are to be carried out. The other procedure is essentially judicial: it involves questioning people in order to find out if there are witnesses; of summoning those indicated; of establishing their identity and authenticating their testimony; of putting questions to them and, if necessary, if they refuse to answer, of threatening them at the least with torture. All this is the reproduction of the inquiry ritual as it was applied in the fifth century. It is no doubt not exact to describe the first procedure as "religious" and the second [as] "judicial": in both cases,

---

\* ["Lord" in the English translation; G.B.]

but according to different forms of composition, religious, political, and judicial procedures are involved in determining where defilement exists in the city and how to get rid of the person who is its carrier. The first is more archaic, more linked to traditional practices; the second is more recent, set up in the sixth and fifth centuries, no doubt in correlation with the whole reorganization of the city.

We even find the trace of a third procedure in *Oedipus the King*, which is also well known in the archaic Greek world, but which remained in use fairly late on (at least, it seems, in some cases of relatively little importance), so that we still find its trace in the third century. This is the procedure of the purgatory oath:[55] Do you agree to swear that you are not guilty and thus, should this oath be perjury, expose yourself to the vengeance of the gods you have invoked? This is the old procedure by which Menelaos and Antilochos settle their dispute in *The Iliad*,[56] after the chariot race whose regularity was questionable due to the action of Antilochos. It is the procedure by which Creon wants to put an end to the dispute with Oedipus when the latter accuses him of plotting. In front of witnesses—Jocasta and the Chorus—he makes the solemn oath: "Woe to me, may I die accursed if I have done what you accuse me of" (644-645).[57] It is true that the procedure is not complete here; what is missing is the first and, in truth, indispensable element: that the accuser accepts this form of settlement, and that he himself offers it to the accused, through a set phrase which is at the same time a challenge. Now Oedipus, who raised the suspicions, not only does not offer Creon the test of the oath himself, but he rejects it to start with and accepts it only begrudgingly, at the invitation of Jocasta and the coryphaeus. He has no more faith in this test than in the honesty of the divinations of Teiresias. He feels his power threatened by this procedure of the oath, as by that of divination (658-659).

So *Oedipus the King* stages the three great procedures utilized by Greek "pre-law" and law for removing defilement and for looking for the criminal: oracular consultation, purgatory oath, and, to use an anachronistic expression, "administrative inquiry (*enquête du pays*)."*

---

* This is the term used in the Middle Ages to refer to a procedure of this type, in which people of the country, those thought likely to be "in the know," are asked to say what they know regarding a dispute. (Note by M.F.)

Three procedures which are put to work by the Sophocles tragedy in their historical order of appearance: from the oldest to the most recent. Three procedures which figure also in their respective places, according to the dignity and hierarchy of the characters they involve: consultation when addressing the gods; purgatory oath when it is a confrontation between chiefs (Creon, at 85, is also hailed as *Anax*, and in his dispute with Oedipus emphasizes that he is on equal footing with the king); and inquiry by interrogation and testimonies when common people and slaves are involved.* For each character, according to the power he holds or the place he occupies in the city, and for every level of the hierarchy, from gods to the lowliest mortal, there is a particular procedure and ritualized way of obtaining the truth. Each form of knowledge is therefore linked to the exercise of power brought to bear in accordance with a rite of which it appears to be the effect.

So it is not so much Oedipus's "ignorance" or "unconscious" that appears in the forefront of Sophocles' tragedy. It is rather the multiplicity of forms of knowledge, the diversity of the procedures which produce it, and the struggle between the powers which is played out through their confrontation. There is a plethora of forms of knowledge in *Oedipus*. Too much knowledge. And Oedipus is not someone who is kept in the dark by ignorance: he is the one who plays—or tries to play—with the multiplicity of forms of knowledge.

What position does Oedipus with his power occupy between these three procedures and the forms of knowledge which are their specific effects? As we have seen, Oedipal knowledge, the knowledge of he who "governs" and "pilots," is a knowledge of *gnōmē* and *tekhnē*; a knowledge which discovers by itself, by linking the present to the past, and by relying on what has been seen. Given this, we can understand the mistrust which exists from the start between Oedipus and those who speak to him in the name of the gods. Certainly, the god's answer arrives first through the mouths of Creon and Teiresias. But we should not forget that they were summoned by Oedipus only as last resort: "Know that

---

* One detail among others clearly indicates the judicial character of the final episode of the discovery. The slave, summoned to appear and threatened with torture if he does not speak, presents himself as having always been part of the household of Laius, and so of the household of Oedipus. Now the rule in the fifth century requires that slaves be tortured as a test of truth only with the consent of those to whom they belong (Note by M.F.)

I have ... shed many tears, that my mind, in its restlessness, has sought many means of salvation. The only remedy I have found after long reflection, I have employed ... I have sent [Creon] to the temple" (66-70).[58] And if he then appeals to Teiresias it is because the questions he has asked in order to find witnesses and discover the guilty party by himself have failed. For as soon as he learned of what defilement the city had to be cleansed, he demanded: "In what place are ... the murderers ... ?" "Was it in his palace, in the fields, or in a foreign land? ... Did no companion ... see anything?" Why have you not tried to find out? (108-129).[59] And further on, before the people brought together for this purpose, he declares: "Who among you knows who killed Laius[60] ... I order him to tell me everything" (224-226).[61]* Teiresias reappears only when the people, having declared both their ignorance and innocence, have turned again to the god (276-279).

Divination, which is the first to state the truth in the tragedy, is only the final solution for Oedipus. And he constantly seeks to confront it with what he, the king, can see with his own eyes and grasp through his *gnōmē*: Where did you get your knowledge? (357).[62] "Your ears, mind, and eyes are closed" (371).[63] "My mind worked it out, and the birds did not teach me" (398).[64] Oedipus the tyrant, both sovereign and judge, wants to discover the truth by himself, by finding those who saw and heard. To the old oracular procedures to which the piety and terror of the people have pushed him, to the procedure of the purgatory oath, to which, without his assent, Creon opens himself, Oedipus constantly prefers his own questions: Who did it, who saw it, who can testify about it? If Oedipus turns his back on the oracular procedure, it is through an impulse of pride, of excess, which the Chorus denounces as soon as the guilt of the king begins to dawn. The coryphaeus says so clearly: "The oracles given to Laius are disregarded; nowhere is Apollo honored with splendor; worship of the gods is no more" (906-910).[65] He reproaches the tyrant's pride for this impious state of affairs, his presumption in words and deeds, his culpable negligence with regard to *Dikē*: "May

---

* Commentators used to ask whether it was plausible that Oedipus was entirely ignorant of the death of Laius. In fact, the questions put by Oedipus should not be analyzed in terms of plausibility. They are questions that form part of a regular procedure. The promise of relative impunity for whoever denounces himself, line 227, was also part of the procedure. (Note by M.F.)

he suffer an unfortunate fate" (886).[66] Oedipus (and Jocasta) wanted to avoid what the gods foresaw for them; even now Oedipus refuses to listen to the prophecy of Apollo's priest. Rather than yield before the words of the gods who see everything but threaten his power as tyrant, who knows or believes he is loved by the *plēthos*, but over whom he exercises his sovereign power, he seeks eye-witnesses in the crowd. The two words, *akouein* and *oran*, recur throughout *Oedipus the King*, but with a meaning which shifts from "submission" to the decrees of the gods who "see" all, to hearing the account of those who were present.

Now this new procedure, which listens differently and looks in a different way, reveals the same things that the gods' saw, and makes the same words resound as those they uttered. The scene with the old shepherd is typical. Following the regular forms of inquisitorial procedure, it multiplies the signs of presence, of authentic testimony, of direct hearing, of immediate sight. "I think I see," Oedipus says, "the one we have been seeking for a long time" (*oran dokō*); but "you who saw him" (*idōn*), will be a better judge. "Be sure of it, I recognize him" (*Egnōka gar, saph'iothi*) (1111-1117).[67] Then, turning to the messenger from Corinth, he asks him the same question, and the foreigner replies: "This is he, you have him before your eyes" (*eisoras*) (1120).[68] Then the questioning can begin: but the witness must speak looking in the face (1121, *phōnei blepōn*). Question, pointing: "This man, you knew him there?" (1128, *tonde oistha*)...This one here" (1130, *tond'os parestin*).[69] The other witness joins in: "I know that he knew me" (1133-1134, *oid'oti katoiden*).[70] The second witness questions the first witness: "Do you remember (1142, *oistha*) giving me a child? ...This is he" (1145, *Od'estin*).[71] The second witness replies: "He speaks without knowledge" (1151, [*Legei gar*] *eidos ouden*).[72] The dominant theme of this interplay of looking, pointing, presence, and attested memory is found in the technical expression *historein, historēsai* (1150, 1156, 1165): giving evidence, being questioned as witness to what one has seen. And the only result of listening to all these testimonies subject to conditions of presence and looking is that Oedipus is forced to hear what he did not want to listen to, to see what he did not want to see. "*All'omōs akousteon*" (1170).[73] "*Ta pant'an eksēkoi saphē*" (1182).[74]

Such is the trap Oedipus set for himself: putting to work, against *manteia*, a procedure which rests on *historein*, and to discover here what he did not want to accept from there. The first effect of the "*enquête du pays*" is to confirm point by point everything that the word of the gods and seers had prescribed-predicted. There is an exact correspondence and a faultless match between the oracular *phatis* and everything said by common people (*errētha*). There is an exact "symbolic" relation between divination and inquiry, between old and new procedures,[75] between the way in which leaders, great men, "kings" traditionally questioned the gods, and the way in which the city's judges now question witnesses in accordance with recent laws. The gods' decrees take on a visible form in the city's judicial practices; and in return the new procedures receive a religious seal. The form of the *sumbolon*, which we have seen circulating throughout *Oedipus the King*, ensures the bond between these two ways of seeing, these two ways of hearing, these two ways of submitting—these two socially, politically, and religiously different rituals of knowledge.

The *sumbolon*, which was linked to religious practices, to the exercise of power, but which is now preserved in the new political and social organization of the city—where it retains the same functions of authentication, but at a different level—here lends its form to the fitting together of two procedures of different date, origin, and status, which are thus authenticated by each other.* In this "symbolic" correspondence, the foreseen coincides with the seen; the predicted with the testified; what belongs to the realm of *pronoia* coincides with what belongs to the realm of *gnōmē*; and what the immortal gods uttered coincides with what the city's justice discovers retrospectively.

In looking to the past, justice according to the laws sees the same thing as the gods' gaze that scans the future. The mechanism of the *sumbolon* at work throughout the tragedy shows that human time is also the gods' time. "Time who sees everything" and who has "discovered" Oedipus despite himself (1213):[76] investigation of the past has joined prediction of the future.

But this exact alignment of the gods' decrees with the city's laws, nullifies the tyrant's place. It is nullified because the tyrant cannot avoid resorting to others. It is nullified because, under the threat of torture,

---

* We could also say that the procedure of the oath is also ratified in the end. The inquiry actually shows that Creon did not distort the god's message or plot against Oedipus. The overturning of the accusation brings about an overturning of power and reversal of the penalty of exile. (Note by M.F.)

a slave's voice says the same thing as Phoebus from his Delphic seat. It is nullified because the outcome of human procedures is no different from that of divine decrees. The gods' word is the principle for what rules the city, for what happens to the city, for the evil that befalls it, or for the remedy that is found for it. To govern the city one does not need a specific "*gnōmē*." What must reign over the city are laws, *nomoi*. And these laws are not a human invention, even if this or that person established them in the city. The "sublime laws" were "begotten in the celestial Ether; Olympus alone is their father; the mortal nature of men did not produce them; forgetfulness will never let them sleep; a great god dwells in them, and this god knows no old age" (865-871).[77] Human laws are founded on the gods' decrees; what happens depends on their will; inquiry leads to what was foreseen by divination. It is the gods themselves who rule the *khōra*. What need is there for a tyrant amongst them, or for the *tekhnē* by means of which he hopes to flee the gods? And where will he flee? In the *khōra*, in the land itself. And in search of what other truth? That which the people of the land hide deep in their memory.

Turning his back on oracular methods for those of the inquiry, Oedipus is brought back by the latter to the former. The sovereign who wanted to see with his own eyes finds himself in this unexpected curve, in the position of being seen as guilty by the witnesses. Refusing to hear what was brought to him from elsewhere—from Delphi, from the gods—he wanted to be the king-judge who "heard and saw." Now finally he sees with his own eyes those who saw him with their own eyes, accursed child abandoned by Jocasta, lost child taken in by Polybus. Wanting to see for himself (*autos*), he has seen himself (*eauton*) in the visual testimony of others. He has seen himself as what should never have been seen, he can no longer bear to be seen by anyone, and never again will he be able to see anyone. That sovereign gaze—both instrument and emblem of a tyrannical knowledge which did not want to listen to divine orders or messages—must be extinguished. Doubtless Oedipus would also like to block up those ears which should never have heard what they did; but this is precisely what he cannot do: now and until the end of his days he is doomed to listen. Doomed to hear voices which he does not know from whence they come. Doomed, consequently, to obey.[78] This is how he hears Creon's *krateia* first of all.

When Oedipus asks to be banished (in line with his order when he ruled), Creon condemns him to wait until the decrees uttered by the voice of the gods arrives, finally brought back by messengers. Even the decision by which the tyrant Oedipus unknowingly exiled himself no longer has any force. The city's laws are handed back to the Olympian order. Oedipus is put back under the yoke of listening-submission. Only in *Oedipus at Colonus* will this listening bring him peace of mind.

* * *

Oedipus—not *blazon* of the unconscious, portrait of the subject who does not know himself, but portrait of the sovereign who is the bearer of an excessive knowledge, of a knowledge which wants to shake off measure and the yoke.[79] Between knowledge conveyed by oracles and knowledge reported by regular inquiry, there is no longer any place for "royal" knowledge, for a *gnōmē* that can solve riddles and save cities without calling on anyone—neither on seers and their birds, nor on men of experience who have seen and remember. What is played out in *Oedipus* is a struggle between kinds of knowledge (*savoirs*) and kinds of power, a struggle between forms of power-knowledge. What disappears with the fall of Oedipus is that old oriental form of the expert king (*roi savant*), of the king who controls, governs, pilots, and sets the city right with his knowledge, fending off disasters or plagues; more directly, it is the updated version that Greek "tyranny" tried to give this old form when it wanted to put the cities right by using, diverting, and often twisting the gods' oracles; maybe it is the even more contemporary image that some in Sophocles' own time sought to project, those who "shot their arrows further than the others" and got themselves recognized as "first citizens."[80]

The problem of political knowledge—of what it is necessary to know in order to govern the city and put it right—, a problem of such importance in the second half of the fifth century, no doubt arose from the definitive elimination of this old figure. *Oedipus the King* is its reappearance and elimination anew on the tragic stage.

In a system of thought like ours, it is very difficult to think of knowledge (*savoir*) in terms of power, and so of excess, and so of transgression. We think of it—and precisely since Greek philosophy of the fifth and sixth centuries—in terms of justice, of pure "disinterestedness," of pure passion to know (*connaître*).

We think of it in terms of consciousness. That is why we have negativized Oedipus and his fable. It doesn't matter whether we speak of ignorance and guilt or of the unconscious and desire: in any case, we place him on the side of the lack of knowledge—instead of recognizing the man of power-knowledge whom the gods' oracles and the city's testimonies, in accordance with their specific procedures and the forms of knowledge they produce, drive out as man of excess and transgression. Everything concerning and around Oedipus is too much: too many parents, too many marriages, fathers who are also brothers, daughters who are also sisters, and this man, so excessively given to misfortune and who ought to be tossed into the sea.

1. Recognition and peripeteia (or dramatic turn of events) structuring Greek tragedy according to Aristotle in *La Poétique*, ch. 11, 52a 23-35 and 52b 3-10, trans. R. Dupont-Roc and J. Lallot (Paris: Seuil, 1980); Foucault used the J. Voilquin and J. Capelle edition, *Art poétique* (Paris: Garnier, 1944); English translation by I. Bywater, *Poetics*, in *The Complete Works of Aristotle*, Vol. Two, ed. Jonathan Barnes (Princeton: Princeton University Press, Bollingen Series LXXI, 2, 1984), p. 2324: "reversal of fortune," "reversal and discovery." See also J.-P. Vernant, "Ambiguïté et renversement. Sur la structure énigmatique d'Œdipe Roi'" in J. Pouillon and P. Maranda, eds., *Échanges et Communications. Mélanges offerts à Claude Lévi-Strauss à l'occasion de son soixantième anniversaire* (Paris-The Hague: Mouton, 1970) vol. II, pp. 1253-1273; English translation by Janet Lloyd as "Ambiguity and Reversal: On the Enigmatic Structure of *Oedipus Rex*I," in Jean-Pierre Vernant and Pierre Vidal-Naquet, *Myth and Tragedy in Ancient Greece*, trans. Janet Lloyd (New York: Zone Books, 1988).
2. This was noted already by Plutarch in *De curiositate*, *On Curiosity*, 522c, trans. W.C. Helmbold, in *Plutarch's Moralia*, Volume VI (Cambridge, Mass.: Harvard University Press, Loeb Classical Library, 1970).
3. In 1980—that is to say, in the version of *Oedipus* in which Foucault expresses himself in alethurgic terms—he opposes six halves, present in reality in this exposition. See "Du gouvernement des vivants. Cours au Collège de France, 1979-1980" (in preparation). The material differentiation of knowledge (*savoirs*) is theorized in *L'Archéologie du savoir* (Paris: Gallimard, 1969); English translation by A. Sheridan, *The Archeology of Knowledge* (London and New York: Tavistock/Pantheon, 1973).
4. Sophocle, *Œdipe-Roi* in *Œuvres*, vol. I, ed. and trans. P. Masqueray [reference edition] (Paris: Les Belles Lettres, 1922); English translation by David Grene, Sophocles, *Oedipus the King*, in *Sophocles I, Three Tragedies*, ed. David Grene and Richard Lattimore (Chicago and London: The University of Chicago Press, 1991), p. 14: "the word you bring us from the God."
5. Ibid., 1121-1122, Fr. p. 181: "Oedipus: Answer all the questions I shall put to you"; Eng. p. 59: "...tell me what I ask you."
6. Phoebus Apollo, literally, "luminous and pure (*katharos*)," is equally passionately occupied with murder; the pure and impure alternate in him. See M. Detienne, *Apollon le couteau à la main. Une approche expérimentale du polythéisme grec* (Paris: Gallimard, 1999; republished in series "Tel, " 2009).
7. *Oedipus the King*, p. 21: "Lord Teiresias" followed on the next line by "Lord Apollo."
8. Ibid., p. 25: "Then I warn you faithfully to keep/the letter of your proclamation."
9. Ibid., pp. 28-29: "A deadly footed, doubly striking curse,/from father and mother both, shall drive you forth/out of this land ... Misery shall grind no man as it will you."
10. Ibid., p. 32: "I would never agree/with those that find fault with the king/till I should see the word/proved right beyond doubt."
11. "*Orthon epos*": truthful speech or account; see line 505.
12. *Oedipus the King*, p. 62: "but she within,/your wife would tell you best how all this was."
13. *Œdipe-Roi*, p. 149: "I would not be able to follow the criminal's track for long if you were not to give me some clue"; *Oedipus the King*, p. 19: "For I would not/be far upon the track if I alone/were tracing it without a clue"; *sumbolon*: originally sign of recognition between the holders of each of the halves of an object broken in two, then sign, image. The word is employed by Sophocles in verse 221. See above, p. 199.
14. *Oedipus the King*, p. 20: "Search it out." Knox also develops the hypothesis that Sophocles follows Athenian judicial procedure and tracks down its vocabulary; he does not retain this term but the series *skopein, historein, zetein* to describe different modalities of the inquiry. However, close examination makes it possible to put forward that he was a source for Foucault. See B. Knox, *Oedipus at Thebes* (New Haven and London: Yale University Press/Oxford University Press, 1957).
15. *Oedipus the King*, p. 68 and pp. 70-71: "In such misfortunes it's no wonder/if double weighs the burden of your grief"; "O marriage, marriage!/you bred me and again when had bred/bred children of your child and showed to men/brides, wives and mothers ... "
16. An allusion to René Girard who was then teaching at the University of Buffalo where this lecture was given. This theme was already pointed out by Girard in an analysis of *Oedipus the King*: "Symétrie et dissymétrie dans le mythe d'Œdipe," *Critique*, 249, February 1968,

pp. 99-135; see also R. Girard, *La Violence et le Sacré* (Paris: Grasset, 1972) ch. III: "Œdipe et la victime émissaire," pp. 102-130; English translation by Patrick Gregory as *Violence and the Sacred* (London and New York: Continuum, 2005), ch. Three, "Oedipus and the Surrogate Victim."

17. See J.-P. Vernant, "Ambiguité et renversement ... "
18. *Oedipus the King*, p. 60: "it's a long time ago."
19. See the important article by L. Gernet, "Le temps dans les formes archaïques du droit," *Journal de psychologie normale et pathologique*, LIII (3), 1956, pp. 379-406.
20. *Oedipus the King*, p. 25 and p. 61: "you have made me speak against my will"; "If you'll not talk to gratify me, you/will talk with pain to urge you."
21. Ibid., p. 29: "But it's in riddle answering you are strongest."
22. *Œdipe roi*, 397: *o meden eidos Oidipous*, "me, Oedipus, knowing nothing"; *Oedipus the King*, p. 27: "I came,/Oedipus, who knew nothing."
23. This is also the thesis of Knox, who finds the scientific vocabulary of the fifth century in the words of Oedipus. But Foucault lays more stress on the tyrant's knowledge. Knox picks out fourteen uses of *turannos*, sometimes in the neutral sense of *basileus*, king, for Laius, in lines 799 and 1043, and sometimes in the pejorative sense, of the fifth century, that of despot in lines 541 and 873; he bases an interpretation of the tragedy's meaning on this.
24. Knox emphasizes that Oedipus conducts a private judicial action; the individual and not the State is looking for the murderer, but the victim being the king, Oedipus also acts in parallel as king.
25. *Oedipus the King*, p. 76: "Do not seek to be master in everything."
26. Ibid., p. 76: "Do not seek to be master in everything,/for the things you mastered did not follow you throughout your life."
27. Ibid., p. 76: "who ... was a man most masterful;/not a citizen who did not look with envy on his lot."
28. Ibid., p. 11: "O ruler of my country, Oedipus."
29. Ibid., p. 58: "the months, my brothers, marked me, now as small,/and now again as mighty."
30. Ibid., "brothers."
31. Ibid., "Such is my breeding."
32. See below, note 79.
33. *Œdipe roi*, p. 184; *Oedipus the King*, p. 64: "he shot his bolt/beyond the others."
34. *Oedipus the King*, p. 32: "in that test/he saved the city. So he will not be condemned by my mind."
35. *Œdipe roi*, p. 166: " ... the good road"; *Oedipus the King*, pp. 40-41: "be sure that I would have been proved a madman ... if I should put you away, you who steered the country I love safely when she was crazed by troubles."
36. *Oedipus the King*, p. 38: "I too have some share/in the city; it is not yours alone."
37. Ibid., p. 37: "But yet/I must be ruler."
38. Ibid., p. 48: "begotten in the clear air of heaven,/whose only father is Olympus."
39. Ibid., p. 44: "the fields."
40. *Oida* evokes both *oidanō*, "to inflate, swell," *oidēma*, "swelling" (Oedipus's feet), and *eideō*, *eidō*, to see with one's own eyes.
41. *Œdipe roi*, p. 155: "O wealth, power, superiority of art ... "; *Oedipus the King*, p. 27: "Wealth, sovereignty and skill outmatching skill ... "
42. Oedipus's power is characterized as *skill*—the skills were invented by the gods and then stolen by men—and *knowledge*: *tekhnē* and *gnōmē* - knowledge learned from no one. Herodotus (I, 207-208) employs *gnōmē* to refer to counsel given in political deliberations.
43. *Œdipe roi*, p. 42: " ... without any knowledge from us ... " (p. 42); *Oedipus the King*, p. 12: "You came and by your coming saved our city,/ ... This you did/in virtue of no knowledge we could give you,/in virtue of no teaching."
44. *Oedipus the King*, p. 27: "And yet the riddle's answer was not the province/of a chance comer. It was a prophet's task."
45. Ibid., p. 41: " ... human beings/have no part in the craft of prophecy."
46. Ibid., p. 42: "what God discovers need of, easily/he shows to us himself."
47. Knox recalls that at the time of Pericles the truth of prophecies was a matter of debate. Pericles did not believe in them, unlike Herodotus. Foucault does not raise this debate.

48. "*iketeuomev se pantes oide prostropoi alkēn tin'eurein*"; *Œdipe roi*, 41-42, p. 142: "We all beg you, we beseech you to find some rescue/help for us"; *Oedipus the King*, p. 12: "here falling at your feet we all entreat you,/find us some strength for rescue."

49. "*Oukoun ou taut aristos euriskein ephus*"; *Œdipe roi*, p. 157: "TEIRESIAS: Are you not naturally skillful in finding these riddles?" (In reply to "OEDIPUS: How obscure and enigmatic is everything you say"); *Oedipus the King*, p. 29: "*Oedipus:* How needlessly your riddles darken everything. *Teiresias:* But it's in riddle answering you are strongest."

50. *Oedipus the King*, p. 25: "the truth is what I cherish/and that's my strength."

51. Ibid., p. 22: "in whom alone of mankind truth is native."

52. *Œdipe roi.*, p. 140: "I did not wish to learn it from foreign mouths"; *Oedipus the King*, p. 11: "I did not think it fit that I should hear/of this from messengers but came myself."

53. Ibid., Fr. p. 171: "... until this witness has enlightened you, have hope"; Eng., p. 46: "... until you see this man face to face and hear his story, hope."

54. *Theon manteumata*. Ibid., Fr.: "divine oracles"; Eng. p. 5: "oracles of the Gods."

55. See L. Gernet, "Le temps dans les formes archaïques du droit" in *Droit et Institutions en Grèce antique* (Paris: Flammarion, "Champs," 1982) p. 32: "It is currently said that the oath is a kind of ordeal ... It does not act like an ordeal, one does not wait for the one who swears it to be struck by fire from the sky, it acts like a test. To talk of the judgment of God would not be at all suitable. The word *orkos* designates first of all not the oath in the abstract sense, but a material, a sacred substance with which the one who swears is put in contact. To swear is therefore to enter the domain of [the most fearful] religious forces ... The total wager which signifies a change of state or, to speak more correctly, a displacement of being, is indeed the most important part of the ordeal."

56. See the lecture of 27 January 1971, above p. 74.

57. *Oedipus the King*, p. 38: "That God may never bless me! May I die/accursed, if I have been guilty of/one tittle of the charge you bring against me!"

58. Ibid., p. 13: "know that I have given many tears to this,/gone many ways wandering in thought,/but as I thought I found only one remedy/and that one I took. I sent ... /Creon ... to Apollo,/to his Pythian temple."

59. Ibid., pp. 15-16: "Where are they [the murderers] in the world?" "Was it at home,/or in the country ... /or in another country travelling? ... Was there ... no fellow traveller/who knew what happened?"

60. *Œdipe roi*, p. 149: "... by what man Laius was killed"; *Oedipus the King*, pp. 19-20: "by whose hand Laius ... died."

61. *Oedipus the King*, pp. 19-20: "who so among you knows the murderer/by whose hand Laius ... ,/died—I command him to tell everything/to me."

62. Ibid., p. 25: "And who has taught you truth?"

63. Ibid., p. 26: "... you are blind in mind and ears/as well as in your eyes."

64. Ibid., p. 27: "I solved the riddle by my wit alone./Mine was no knowledge got from birds."

65. Ibid., p. 49: "The oracles concerning Laius/are old and dim and men regard them not./Apollo is nowhere clear in honour; God's service perishes."

66. Ibid., p. 48: "may an evil doom/smite him ... "

67. Ibid., p. 59: "*Oedipus:* ... I think this is the herdsman,/whom we were seeking ... / ... / ... You/perhaps may better me in knowledge since/you've seen the man before./*Chorus:* You can be sure/I recognize him."

68. Ibid., p. 59: "This is he/before your eyes."

69. Ibid., p. 60: "And somewhere there perhaps you knew this man? ... This man here,/have you had any dealings with him?"

70. Ibid., p. 60: "For I know that he well knows."

71. Ibid., p. 60: "Do you remember giving me a child/ ... /here he is ... "

72. Ibid., p. 61: "He speaks out of his ignorance, without meaning."

73. Ibid., p. 62: "And I of frightful hearing. But I must hear."

74. Ibid., p. 63: "... they will all come,/all come out clearly!"

75. What Foucault describes as the law of halves is in a way identified by Knox in terms of mathematical equalization; Knox establishes a series of equations between the object and the subject of the procedure of inquiry; hearing and sight; medical knowledge and mathematical knowledge; divination and the witness. Knox proceeds on the basis of philology, Foucault on the

basis of a formal analysis. Foucault became aware of Knox's book only during this lecture in the United States.

76. *Oedipus the King*, p. 65: "Time who sees all has found you out/against your will."

77. Ibid., p. 48: "laws begotten in the clear air of heaven,/whose only father is Olympus;/no mortal nature brought them to birth,/no forgetfulness shall lull them to sleep;/for God is great in them and grows not old."

78. See 1516: "I must obey, although it costs me"; *Œdipe roi*, p. 196: "It is necessary to obey, though with regret"; *Oedipus the King*, p. 75: "I must obey, though bitter of heart" —which is the reversal, the dramatic turn of 627 (Oedipus to Creon): "Obey your king"; Fr. p. 163: "It is necessary to obey all the same"; Eng. p. 37: "But yet/I must be ruler."

79. "*Hubris phuteutei turannon*" (872); *Œdipe roi*, p. 172: "Pride engenders the tyrant"; *Oedipus the King*, p. 48: "Insolence breeds the tyrant." Mazon's translation: "Excess begets the tyrant"; J. Bollack, *La Naissance d'Œdipe. Traduction et commentaire d'"Œdipe roi,"* Paris: Minuit, 1985): "Violence makes the tyrant."

80. Knox compares Oedipus the King with Pericles, at the time when Athenian hegemony over Greece becomes tyranny, rather than with the oriental expert king. Commentators have traditionally seen the expression "First citizen" (31; *Oedipus the King*, p. 12: "the first of men") as an allusion to Pericles.

## COURSE CONTEXT

# Daniel Defert

THIS COURSE IS INAUGURAL in more than one sense. Recognition of the speaker's new status;[1] entry into the long-term historical process of the ancient beginnings of philosophy, even though the title of the chair, "History of systems of thought," expresses a certain emancipation from philosophy; and even though the *doxa* associates only "the final Foucault" with Greece. Shift of the target of research: at the end of his inaugural lecture of 2 December 1970 (published by Gallimard in 1971 with the title *L'Ordre du discours*,[2] and so not republished in this volume) Foucault announces that if hitherto his analyses had focused on instances of limitation of discourses, what he describes as the "critical aspect," or archeology, henceforth he will be concerned with the "effective formation of discourse … on both sides of the boundary."[3] What he refers to as their "genealogical aspect," the conditions of their emergence and of their transgression: illegalities, perversions and abnormalities, deregulations, confessions, parrhesiastic speech, will be the effective content of the following thirteen years of teaching. The reciprocal implication of language and power, and, as the Hellenist Henri Joly elegantly summarizes it, "that two languages may exist in language, that of truth and that of error,"[4] are so many constraints that subject "discourse to an order."

Inaugural too is the medium to which we have had to resort in order to edit this course: no longer "the thing said," the recorded voice, with its intonations, instant commentaries, and reinterpretations, but "the written thing,"[5] acroamatic manuscripts, that is to say, according to Léon Robin, intended to be heard by a public and not for reading.[6]

Inaugural too, finally, is the obligation this course imposes on us to question again the meaning of the forms of knowledge described by Foucault, the continually displaced historical, empirical forms of knowledge constitutive of our classical reason, of its confrontation with an irreducible other, insanity, knowledge in which, "in the clarity of death," our modern medicine was constructed, a medicine that is itself a paradigm for our human sciences whose rules of transformation Foucault described. What relations do these forms of empirical knowledge maintain with the great tradition of philosophy which, from the origin, presents itself as discourse of truth or theory of knowledge (*connaissance*)? This is what his rereading of Nietzsche seems to clarify.

We cannot fail to be struck by the fact that Foucault's first course, with Nietzsche, thrusts aside Socrates, "the theoretical man," who is certainly barely mentioned, and to whom at the very end of his teaching, 15 February 1984, Foucault devotes a session to reevaluating the nihilist interpretation deplored by Nietzsche[7] and tied to the account of the sacrifice of a cock to Asclepius at the time of Socrates' death.[8] Foucault reinterprets this account through Dumézil, to whom his debt for the analysis of the internal system of a discourse he acknowledged already in December 1970.[9] Thus, all of Foucault's teaching at the Collège de France would have taken place in the interstice of this Nietzschean riddle of Socrates, as if the original title of this course, *The Will to Know*, was self-reflexive.

A secret dramaturgy organizes these lectures: of the slow descent, from the empyrean of the gods, from the word of truth uttered as a lightning flash, finally "to place the sun of truth within man,"[10] that is to say, in the judgment, the report, the testimony of a shepherd which joins together saying and seeing: two major themes of Foucault's preceding works. Halfway on this trajectory, the Sophists: neither speech of the ordeal nor of the report, but speech which mixes words and things, purely tactical speech which wants only to be power, which challenges that "speech-dialogue" whose emergence too with the Greek city Marcel Detienne recounts.[11] Now with speech-dialogue, sixth century Athens invents man who has become a problem for himself:[12] dialogue with the gods, dialogue with the world, and dialogue with oneself get confused; Oedipus is the constantly repeated symbol of this. The *agora* is the site of the emergence of *logos* as well as of tragic feeling.

The inaugural lecture announced a genealogy of knowledge without Foucault employing the expression. In a sense Nietzsche establishes a genealogy of knowledge (*savoir*) which sweeps away all theory of knowledge (*connaissance*) as a faculty, the traditional theory in philosophy. However, he does not distinguish clearly the meaning that he gives to *Erkenntnis* and to *Wissen*. If we put together the aphorisms on which Foucault relies: *The Gay Science*, §110 and §111, *Beyond Good and Evil*, §230, *On the Genealogy of Morality*, III, §12, and *La Volonté de puissance*, Book I, §195 (*The Will to Power*, Book Three, 4, §503), we notice that Nietzsche actually placed genealogy at the heart of knowledge (*connaissance*), treating it as the "knowledge (*savoir*) of science," and did not make it merely a matter of the subversion of moral values. The real theme of this course would therefore be less the possibility of such a genealogy, than its effects on the theory of the subject and object at the foundation of the theory of knowledge, on our conception of truth since Plato, in a word, on philosophy itself.

"In the question of what knowledge is, we are basically asking about truth and its essence ... What is *true* here means that which is. ... The question about the essence of knowledge, as question about what is true and truth, is a questioning about being," writes Heidegger,[13] who is not mentioned in these lectures, but who could be its target, especially since Pierre Klossowski's translation of his *Nietzsche* was planned for the same year, 1971.

Is a Nietzschean genealogy of knowledge still knowledge, or the destruction of knowledge? For knowledge is "linked to the high monarchy of the Subject (sole I, coherent self)" and to "Representation (clear ideas that I run through at a glance ... image that thought formed of itself"[14]—and, as a consequence, of all the metaphysics with which it was constructed. For Nietzsche, is it not rather a question of uncovering the passions, instincts, struggles, challenges, procedures, events, and discontinuities which radically call it into question? How are these conditions so different from the economic determinants, social forces, and dialectic which Marx put at the root of knowledge and from which Foucault had already freed himself with Nietzsche at the beginning of the fifties? The difference is that Marx retained a theory of knowledge, whereas genealogy destroys it. Genealogy retains social forces, but so as to structure them around a theory of power. But Nietzschean genealogy first of all poses the question of value, like all genealogy: Who is speaking? Noble or not noble?

*Beyond Good and Evil* begins thus:

> "The will to truth (*der Wille zur Wahrheit*), which is still going to mislead us into many adventures, that famous veracity of which all philosophers have hitherto spoken with veneration: what problems this will to truth has already set us! What strange, serious, and problematic problems!... Is it surprising... if this Sphinx has taught us too to ask questions? *Who* is it exactly who question us here? What part of us really strives towards 'the truth'?—In fact, we halted for a long time before the question of the reason for this will—until we ended up in suspense before an even more fundamental question. We then asked what the *value* of this will was. Granted that we desire the truth: why *would we not prefer* untruth? And uncertainty? And even ignorance?—The problem of the value of truth presented itself to us—or was it we who presented ourselves to this problem? Which of us here is Oedipus? Which the Sphinx?... And, would you believe it, it seems to me, when all's said and done, that the problem has never been posed until now..."[15]

Apparently returning to the mode of reasoning of *History of Madness*, Foucault does not refer to the division between true and false as a logical division, or an ontological division, or as historical moments of consciousness, "like oil and water, which without mixing are united only externally,"[16] but as an act of exclusion, a social violence which, according to him, is carried out through the exclusion—late on moreover—of the Sophists; an exclusion which Plato described as a moral act, "purgation": "getting rid of whatever has little value."[17]

Foucault does not attribute this division—or, as this course attests, its function as moral division—to Plato; he situates it in a complex prehistory between Hesiod and Plato, formed through a series of shifts between the test of the magical-religious justice of archaic Greece and the juridical-political procedures of the judicial inquiry of classical Greece, abandoning the Hegelian dramaturgy with its share of negativity—still invoked in the great division of *History of Madness*—in favor of a series of displacements and differences between the singular points of great events. However, a truth of the sophistic like a truth of madness continues to haunt our contemporary spaces in new countenances, no longer Hölderlin, Nerval, Artuad,[18] but Roussel, Brisset, Wolfson.

Writing *The Archeology of Knowledge* in 1966, Foucault made it clear that his problem was not language but the limits of possible statements. There is no knowledge without a regulated discursive practice; for him, discourse and knowledge continued to be two forms of a quasi-incorporeal materiality which is describable because it has its rules of construction, historicity, thresholds, discontinuities, and prohibitions limiting its wild proliferation.

From *The Archeology of Knowledge*, Foucault had emphasized that knowledge is identified neither with a cognitive faculty, of which philosophy throughout its history has produced the theory, nor with science. Knowledge ( *savoir* ) surrounds science and does not disappear when a science is constituted. A science is inscribed and functions in the element of knowledge.[19] The territory of knowledge enabled Foucault to describe "epistemes" without having to resort to those divisions of true and false, science and ideology. He called his teaching: "History of systems of thought," which prevented it being confused with the other Collège chair of philosophy, namely, that of the "philosophy of knowledge ( *connaissance* )," held by the logician Jules Vuillemin, who presented Foucault's candidacy to his peers.

If a will to truth is amply present and commented on in Nietzsche, from July 1967 Foucault identified another form of will: "I am perusing Nietzsche; I think I am beginning to see why he has always fascinated me. A morphology of the will to know in European civilization, which has been neglected in favor of an analysis of the will to power."[20] That Foucault's passion for knowledge-*savoir* recognizes itself in the Basel philologist's fascination for knowledge-*connaissance* is understandable, but—accentuating the knowledge-*savoir* here, which the lecture on Nietzsche describes in terms of the singularity of the event, expressing neither identity nor eternity, while knowledge-*connaissance* would be only its idealization, its substantialization—Foucault displaces two dominant interpretations of Nietzschean thought:

1. To start with, that traditional interpretation which rests on an insistent antagonism in Nietzsche between dangerous, mortal knowledge (Empedocles throwing himself into Etna's crater out of an instinct to

know), and life. Nietzsche is the opponent of every manifestation of the egoistic will to know. "Above all necessary: the joy of what exists; to take this taste further, this is the mission of the master."[21] Instinct is a means of preservation for the individual; nothing is more "inconceivable" than the advent of an "honest and pure instinct of truth in men."[22] "The instinct of knowledge, having reached its limits, turns around against itself to arrive at the critique of knowledge (*Kritik des Wissens*), knowledge in the service of the better life. We must will even illusion, that is what is tragic. ... The unlimited and indiscriminate instinct of knowledge (*Erkenntnistrieb*) is a sign that life has grown old."[23]

2. And that, henceforth more influential interpretation of Heidegger, for whom will to knowledge, being, and will to power tend to merge:

> "*Ti estin epistēmē?* 'What is that—knowledge?' Only very late, in the course of the nineteenth century, did this metaphysical question become a subject for scientific inquiry, that is, a subject for psychological and biological investigations. ... In retrospect, stimulated by historical and philological investigation into the past, one discovered that Aristotle and Plato, and even Heraclitus and Parmenides, and then later Descartes, Kant, and Schelling 'too' were in 'pursuit' of such 'theory of knowledge.' ... We could have omitted mention of the twaddle of scholarly 'theory of knowledge' here if Nietzsche, too, had not moved in its sultry air—in part reluctantly, in part eagerly—and become dependent on it.
>
> ... If Nietzsche's thought of will to power is the fundamental thought of his metaphysics and the last thought of Western metaphysics, then the essence of knowledge, that is, the essence of truth, must be defined in terms of will to power."[24]

Thus, Foucault identified a will to know (*savoir*) which cannot be assimilated to knowledge (*connaissance*) or will to truth that Heidegger, following Nietzsche in this, assimilates to the will to power.

## THE TITLE

On the basis of this isolation of a will to know in 1967, Foucault devoted a series of lectures to Nietzsche, first at Vincennes in the winter of

1969-1970 (teaching module 170), then at the New York State
University at Buffalo in March 1970, and then at McGill University at
Montreal in April 1971; lectures whose outcome will be the long article:
"Nietzsche, Genealogy, History."[25]

At Vincennes, Foucault stresses that before *On the Genealogy of
Morality*, Nietzsche had not clearly defined genealogy but that, from
*The Birth of Tragedy*, he identified a will to know—at any rate, what
Foucault translates as "will to know": *Wissensgier*, which Geneviève
Bianquis translates as "greed for knowledge" or "craving for
knowledge."

> "Picture the unheard-of universality of that craving for knowledge
> (*Wissensgier*), spreading to the most distant zones of the civilized
> world where it presented knowledge as the worthy aim of every
> self-respecting man and the extraordinary vogue for which has
> never been completely refuted."[26]

And in an almost contemporary text, the *Theoretical Studies*, Nietzsche
employs the notions *enfesselten Wissenstrieb* (§37, "unbridled instinct to
know") or *Erkenntnistrieb* (§25, "knowledge instinct").[27]

*The Birth of Tragedy* accuses the "theoretical man," Socrates, of having
destroyed tragic knowledge with the dialectic—"we know that he only
understood a single form of art, the *Aesopian fable*."[28] Socrates, "the first
who knew not only how to live but also, which is more, how to die in
conformity with this instinct of knowledge," had however his "great
Cyclopean eye fixed on tragedy, that single eye which never shone with
the sweet madness of aesthetic enthusiasm" and did not even see that
"tragedy might be able to 'tell the truth'."[29]

In a subtle article, Andrew Cutrofello[30] is surprised at the few references of the "genealogist" Foucault to *The Birth of Tragedy*, even though
in his writings one could pick out a veritable theory of tragedy, from
Aeschylus to Euripides, from Shakespeare to Racine. This is to forget
that in Nietzsche the question of tragedy is not primarily an aesthetic
question but one of the major figures of knowledge:

> "O Socrates, Socrates is this then your secret? ... The fact that I suc-
> ceeded in grasping, at that time, this fearful and dangerous fact,

this horned problem which, without necessarily being a bull, was a new problem, I would say today it was *the very problem of knowledge*; for the first time knowledge was envisaged as problematic and suspect ... Now I consider [this book] ... a work of beginning ... with a gaze less young, one hundred times more sharpened, but not cooled, and which has continued to go deeply into the problem which was taken on for the first time by this audacious book, *examining science in the light of art, but art in the light of life ...*"[31]

From *The Birth of Tragedy* there is indeed then the possibility of a genealogy of knowledge, of a knowledge enveloped in avidity, an instinct, which radically destroys the components of our metaphysics of representation, beginning with the categories of reason, truth, subject, and object. Only later will *On the Genealogy of Morality* pose the question of the value of values.

Accentuating this double genealogical agenda, Foucault resorts to the same title, *The Will to Know*, on two occasions: in 1970, for these lectures, and in 1976, for the first volume of his *History of Sexuality*, which is as much a genealogy of the knowledge constitutive of the sexuality *dispositif*, as a genealogy of modern morality. To avoid any confusion between these two studies, this volume has been given the title *Lectures on the Will to Know*, since it includes not only the twelve lectures at the Collège, but a lecture on Nietzsche, which had disappeared from the manuscript, and a lecture with the title "Oedipal Knowledge (*Le savoir d'Œdipe*)," which is both a brilliant development of the last lecture and an epitome of literary analysis which Foucault used six times (even seven, for its schema was already outlined in the article "*Ariane s'est pendue*") as a paradigm of regimes of veridiction.[32]

## CIRCUMSTANCES

That the birthplace of this course is Nietzsche is evident. But three almost simultaneous publications additionally shaped the conjuncture: *The Masters of Truth* by Marcel Detienne,[33] *Difference and Repetition* by Gilles Deleuze,[34] and the translation of Nietzsche's *On Truth and the Lie* by Angèle Kremer-Marietti,[35] a philosopher close to Foucault. A conjuncture which supported Foucault in his desire not to follow in the

steps of Heidegger on the Greek paths of knowledge, although he recognized that, for his generation, Heidegger had reinserted Nietzsche in
the philosophical tradition, rescuing him from literary or psychologistic
interpretations.[36]

First of all, in the historical depths of archaic Greece of the seventh
and sixth centuries, precisely those studied by Nietzsche in his Basel
years, Marcel Detienne rediscovers the question, which became crucial
at the end of the sixties, of "who is speaking, by what right, and according to what rituals?" in a prehistory in which he found the mythical-
religious structuring couple of *Alētheia* and *Lēthē*, on the basis of which
he was able to trace the transformations of speech with the effectiveness
and constraint of truth back to the birth of the Greek City-State.

In *Difference and Repetition*, Deleuze revisits the whole history of metaphysics in an anti-Platonic fashion. Foucault produced two enthusiastic
reviews of the book in an almost mimetic style.[37] Deleuze, in fact, dis-
rupted the codes of the history of philosophy, importing the technique
of collage from painting; this, shortly before *The Archeology of Knowledge*,
itself a meticulous description of the rules specific to discursive practices,
which refuses to "plunge [discursive objects] into the common depth of
a primal soil."[38] The *Archeology* is a book on the dispersion and infinite
re-implantation of statements, *Difference and Repetition* is a book on the
intensities and ontological differences, and the eternal return of the same
always at a remove; two key works in the journeys of both philosophers,
two outcomes, and probably two turning points in their thought whose
trajectories continued to confront each other over more than ten years.
In fact, Deleuze seemed to have inverted the Heideggerian problematic:
the Swabian philosopher interpreted Nietzsche on the basis of his own
thought of being as difference; Deleuze surreptitiously rewrote *Being and
Time* on the basis of Nietzschean ontology.

Finally, to close this triangle, together with her translation of
Nietzsche's text, Angèle Kremer-Marietti contributed a close study of
the relations between language and truth, this stake being at the heart of
the location of the sophistic effect in language developed in the lectures
of 6 and 13 January. Foucault made a fragment from *Truth and Lie* the
starting point of the lecture on Nietzsche missing from the manuscript,
of the version of this lecture given at McGill University in April 1971
(that is to say, just after this course), and of his lecture at Rio de Janeiro

with the title "Truth and Juridical Forms":[39] "In some lost corner of this universe whose blaze pours forth innumerable solar systems, there once was a star on which some intelligent animals invented knowledge. This was the moment of the greatest lie and supreme arrogance of universal history."[40]

Deleuze's work fixed the difference and singularity of the event in a same pluralist ontology, and nonetheless its repetition and eternal return at a remove. This book is in fact inserted in the long labor of elucidation of Nietzschean thought undertaken in France after 1945 by Bataille, Blanchot, Jean Wahl,[41] and Klossowski. The large French edition of the Colli and Montinari *Complete Works* of Nietzsche—with which Foucault and Deleuze were initially associated—must have contributed a final point to this research, getting rid of the two posthumous compilations bearing the title *The Will to Power*, a contested montage on which Heidegger's interpretation relies. For sure, this work of philosophical elucidation had been strongly marked by the lectures delivered by Heidegger between 1936 and 1939 in a supposed moment of retirement, that is to say after his sinister rectorial address. Deleuze had in fact offered two rewritings of Heidegger: the serious *Difference and Repetition*, and the ironic "An unrecognized precursor to Heidegger: Alfred Jarry" or pataphysics as the overcoming of metaphysics.[42]

The task that Deleuze, following others, assigns to philosophy is, Foucault recalls, overturning Platonism, which could even be the definition of philosophy since Aristotle, or since the Sophists. "The whole of Platonism," Deleuze writes, "is dominated by the idea of drawing a distinction between 'the thing itself' and the simulacra [dream, shadow, reflection, painting, phantasm]. Difference is not thought in itself but related to a ground, subordinated to the same and subject to mediation in mythic form."[43] Now when it is a matter of thinking the ground, Plato resorts to myth. What *Difference and Repetition* refers to as Plato's game (*jeu*):

> "It is as though division, once it abandons the mask of determining species and discloses its true goal ... is ... relayed by the simple 'play' (*jeu*) of a myth. ... *The Statesman* invokes the image of an ancient God who ruled the world and men ... The procedure in the *Phaedrus* is the same: when it becomes a question of

distinguishing the different 'madnesses', their incarnation, along with the memory which they carry of the Ideas they have been able to contemplate."[44]

It is in the *Sophist*, the third great Platonic text concerning division, that division is carried out without myth, by isolating the Sophist, the false claimant par excellence, who brings everything to the condition of the simulacrum. Because the supreme end of the Platonic dialectic[45] is not division but the selection of difference, that is to say, evaluation, the installation of a mythical circle.

## FOUCAULT'S GAME

At the start of this course, despite the institutional solemnity of the Collège and the intellectual rigor expected from the new recipient of its honors, Foucault invokes "the game he wants to play here." The expression doesn't cease to surprise unless one links it to the mythical-ontological or theological-ontological game described by Deleuze as the ground of Platonic metaphysics. And what if "Foucault's game" was precisely to respond to this through history?

In *The Archeology of Knowledge* he advanced the main lines of a new historiography, or rather recalled the main lines of the new historiography of historians: not local history, or event-based history, or total history, but series of series, an already Nietzschean historiography. In the Introduction he stated the characteristics of the contemporary historiography in which he inserted himself:

> "...the theme and possibility of a *total history* begin to disappear, and we see the emergence of something very different that might be called a *general history*. The project of a total history is one that seeks to reconstitute the overall form of a civilization, the principle—material or spiritual—of a society, the significance common to all the phenomena of a period, the law that accounts for their cohesion...These are the postulates that are challenged by the new history when it problematizes series, divisions, limits,...chronological specificities...The problem that now presents itself—and which defines the task of a general history—is to determine what

form of relation may be legitimately described between these different series ... what 'series of series'—or in other words, what
'tables' it is possible to draw up."[46]

It is to this history that he resorts here, not on the basis of unknown
archives whose exploration he undertakes himself, but by referring to
a corpus still recognized by the corporation of historians of Antiquity:
from Louis Gernet to Gustave Glotz, at the start of the century, to
Edouard Will, whose then very recent works, supported by the latest
discoveries of Corinthian archeology, had just been published. Foucault
never set out either to repeat or comment on Nietzsche, but to put his
philosophical intuitions to the test of "the rope ladder"[47] of history.
Nor let us forget that Heidegger inscribed Nietzsche's ambivalences
concerning history in his own distinction between history-*Geschichte*
and history-*Historie*, that is to say, the distinction between the event and
its reading by historical science, which has the same essence as technology. Thus, to the theological-ontological game denounced by Deleuze,
Foucault opposes this game characterized by Eugen Fink not as divine
game, but as "intra-mundane game," or the game of anybody, the social
relation to the world, the game of men when exposed to the appearance
of the world.[48]

Given these premises, and so as to understand not only the historical but also the profoundly philosophical stake of this course, we pro-
pose reading, one after the other and in order, Foucault's two articles on
*Difference and Repetition* (and, of course, the work itself), the 1970-1971
course, and finally the article "Nietzsche, Genealogy, History," published in homage to Jean Hyppolite, his predecessor in the same chair at
the Collège de France, and written in the same year, 1971. Then you will
be invited to the Foucault-Deleuze Symposium, a symposium which
was so discreet in the life and so meticulous in the reciprocal reading and subsequent philosophical development of each of these great
contemporaries.[49]

In "Nietzsche, Genealogy, History," Foucault begins by describ-
ing genealogy as grey—a quotation of Nietzsche taken from a phrase by
Goethe quoted by Hegel: "theory is grey." Genealogy is documentary,
relentless in its erudition; it locates the *singularity* of events where it was
thought there was no history, for example in the domain of sentiments,

conscience, instincts, the body, and love. It grasps the recurrence of events in distinct roles. There is indeed then a distinction to be made between history and genealogy. The object of genealogy is not defined by the search for the origin, or *Ursprung*, but for the *Herkunft*, that is to say, provenance, the ancient affiliation to a group, and for the *Entstehung*, the emergence, or arrival of forces on the scene. Provenance refers to the proliferation of events, that is to the *"disparate"* of Deleuze in *Difference and Repetition*. Emergence, on the other hand, is the placeless theater where the same play of dominators and dominated *is repeated*. Thus is born the differentiation of values, the *Entstehung* being at the same time the singularity of the event and its repetition always at a remove. That is to say, in his article, Foucault in turn rewrites, in his own vocabulary, on the basis of considerable work of historical inquiry, the intensities, material, and stake of *Difference and Repetition*: "The different emergences that we may locate are not the successive figures of an identical meaning; they are so many effects of substitutions, replacements and displacements, disguised conquests... If interpretation were the slow exposure of a meaning buried in the origin, then only metaphysics could interpret the becoming of humanity";[50] we see Plato's game and the game of history resurfacing here and confronting each other. For Nietzsche, genealogy transcribed what was still without history, because it was a matter of sentiment, soul, body, and instinct, which we suppose to be unchanging in man. Philosophical anthropology would be only the contemporary, positivist form of metaphysics.

Archeology as method, and *The Order of Things* in particular, are in fact a preparatory introduction to genealogy. Genealogy, as Foucault presents it, is not therefore the crisis of archeology; they mutually support each other. In the same article, Foucault recalls that one can do the genealogy of history: the genealogy of the historical sentiment (this is the absence of œuvre) as the genealogy of the historian's profession (this is writing so as to no longer have a face). In "Nietzsche, Genealogy, History," written on the same impulse as the 1970-1971 course, Foucault proposes as genealogy what Deleuze had presented as a differentialist ontology.

\*   \*   \*

It will be objected that this purely theoretical conjuncture is surprising in the recent posterity of May 1968, in which Foucault was setting up the

Information Group on Prisons (*Groupe d'information sur les prisons*) and discussing future "Truth and Justice committees." But the question posed by Nietzsche through Oedipus—"who is speaking?"—is *the* question of the seventies. In the final analysis, "politics" is the actuality in which the young people who flocked to Foucault's lectures think and act. Politics in the final analysis is the rise of individuation, no longer as ideological effect of law, but in the transformation of the mystical–religious forms of power; it is the emergence of asceticism as popular struggle against the extravagant displays of the aristocracy, or that of the democratization of immortality of the soul, or of the place of the sage (of the sage who knows) in relations of power; it is the appearance of an ethic of purity as the condition for disclosing order, and this is no longer thought of as the effect of the moralism of Platonic philosophy, but as the effect of the constitution of the *nomos*; finally, it is the presence of popular power in all these processes of transformations.

This ascent to archaic Greece served, as it had already served the young Wagnerian Nietzsche, as metaphor of actuality.

## A NIETZSCHEAN GREECE

History or philosophy? The answer is in the cut (*découpe*): archaic Greece is Nietzschean Greece. To approach Greece philosophically on the basis of Nietzsche was no longer self-evident in 1970. Philosophical Hellenism was no longer Hegelian or Nietzschean but, in France at least, "à la Heidegger."[51]

Charles Andler, in his *La Dernière Philosophie de Nietzsche*, reports:

"The great revelation for him was the sixth century before Christ. At that moment a new spirit passed through Greece. Babylonian civilization fell apart, an immense need of reform, an unusual spiritual fervor spread from the depths of Asia Minor. The philosophers of Ionia, of Magna Graecia are affected by its last repercussions. The mystical feeling with which they are filled suddenly finds a language in which to express itself. In the oriental age in which religious delirium seizes hold of the Greek people, it finds the *logos*, which translates it and checks it at the same time. Europe is detached by them from Asia and becomes aware of its different originality ... As a result, the epic, the poetry of the aristocratic classes, comes apart and fades into lyricism ... Barely established custom (*nomos*) breaks up. The crowd outside demands its revision ... This disordered chorus also wants its coryphaeus, which will be the tyrant ... [The tyrants] prepare the advent of democracy."[52]

Nietzsche's enthusiasm: "The greatest fact in the cultivation of Greece remains that Homer became pan-Hellenic so early. All the spiritual and human freedom the Greeks attained to goes back to this fact."[53] Foucault's course gaily covers all the territories of Greece, from Ionia to Corinth and Sicily—Athens has no privilege, we are before the city-state or in the nascent city-state which irritates Hesiod, whom Nietzsche calls the genealogist—and the course comes to an end on *Oedipus the King* or *turannos*, in which some commentators have wanted to read a metaphor for the tyranny of Athens over its empire: "Early Greek philosophy is a philosophy of statesmen ... This is what most distinguishes the Pre-Socratics from the Post-Socratics. In them there is not 'that hideous claim to happiness' which begins with Socrates. Everything is not yet reduced to the state of the individual soul. Later the meaning of Apollo's *gnōthi seauton* was unknown."[54] Foucault will reinterpret this Delphic precept starting from the lecture of 6 January 1982.[55] Foucault's archaic Greece is neither commentary on nor repetition of Nietzsche but documented entirely by the work of historians, that is to say, tested against knowledge.

With regard to Nietzsche's approach, Foucault seems to cover some of the essential points of Heidegger's study.

First, the thesis according to which the thought of justice dominates Neitzsche's reflections on truth: "It can be demonstrated historically that [the Greek thought of *dikē*] came to him from his meditation on Pre-Platonic metaphysics—in particular on Heraclitus. ... The rare main thoughts on 'justice' were not published."[56] Now Foucault traces the history of *dikē* between the Apollonian Homer and the Dionysian Sophocles.

Second, Heidegger rethinks the arbitrary and posthumous composition of *The Will to Power*, edited in 1906 and 1911, in order to reconstruct the secret of this itinerary towards the will to power and especially, supported by many aphorisms, to show that the notion of knowledge is a structure of it; the will to power itself corresponding to an interpretation of the destiny of being, which nullifies its Nietzschean truth—at no point does Foucault follow him in this.

Third: "If the thought of the Will to power is the fundamental thought of Nietzschean metaphysics and the last thought of Western metaphysics, then it is on the basis of the Will to power that the essence of knowledge, that is to say the essence of truth, should be defined. ... That is why in all his behavior man sticks to what is true in some way or other."[57] Thus, representing aphorism 515 of *The Will to Power*, which became [14 (152)] in the Colli-Montinari edition:[58] "Will to power as *knowledge*, not 'to know' but to schematize, to impose on chaos enough regularity and form to satisfy our practical needs." Heidegger comments on this aphorism in this way: "Not 'to know' but to schematize ... This means: to know is not 'to know' in the supposed sense of receptive, imitative reproduction ... this conception of knowledge as schematization is situated in Platonic-Aristotelian thought in the same domain of decision, even though Nietzsche did not 'take' the concept of schema from Aristotle *historically*, in the course of an examination of past opinions."[59]

That is to say, for Heidegger, Nietzsche is inscribed in the tradition of metaphysics and is its outcome, whereas Foucault contrasts two paradigms of the will to know, Aristotle and Nietzsche. Again, on page 398, Heidegger recalls that "the definition of truth which, since Plato and Aristotle, dominates and penetrates not only the whole of Western thought, but the history of Western man in general,"[60] is defined as "correctness ( *Richtigkeit, rectitude* )," *homoiōsis* or *adaequatio*.[61] Against this definition of truth he opposes a new interpretation of *Alētheia*,[62] on the basis of the privative *a*, as un-forgetfulness, dis-occultation, as an etymologically negative concept.

To this Foucault replies:

1. by displacing this Heideggerian division of philosophy;
2. by analyzing the relations between *Dikē* and the emergence of an order of the *kosmos*, not on the basis of Heraclitus—the beginnings of Western metaphysics according to Heidegger—but of Hesiod (the philosopher is Hesiod, Deleuze wrote in his *Nietzsche and Philosophy*),[63] and above all the introduction of measure through the social struggles of Greece: measure of time and money as measure.

3. Foucault does not start from philology but from history, in particular from the works of Vernant and Detienne, who himself completely bypasses Heidegger in *The Masters of Truth*, a work which unquestionably nourished Foucault's reflections.

4. The Pre-Socratics are practically absent, apart from references made by Aristotle in his history of truth. It is the analysis of the Sophists here which makes it possible to think the relations of language to truth, and not to being. The notes preserved by Hélène Politis show that Foucault made this displacement explicit orally. But it is in the lecture at McGill University that he develops his opposition to the "ideology of knowledge as effect of freedom" most clearly. The essence of truth is not freedom in Foucault. He comes back to this assertion that "the truth is not by nature free" in *The Will to Know*, the first volume of the *History of Sexuality*.[64]

## ESTABLISHING THE TEXT

1. The *Lectures on the Will to Know* have been established on the basis of the acroamatic manuscripts, the pagination indicated in the margin to the left of the text.* The punctuation and spatial arrangement—which sometimes has the form of a list of points to be developed—have been modified to make for smoother reading. Additions by the editor are few and in square brackets. The Greek characters of the manuscript have been respected,† but the texts were often quoted from memory by Foucault, who, as a student of the *École normale supérieur* of his generation, was quite comfortable in that language.

In *Oedipus at Thebes*, B. Knox recalls that at that time [1957; G.B.] a scholarly text had to respect the Greek characters and he, wanting to address the "Greekless reader," had shocked the profession.[65] In the eighties, Foucault used Latin as well as Greek characters when he was writing his lectures. (On the basis of the recording of the course delivered, its editors adopted Latin transcription.)

2. In 1970, it was not customary to record courses at the Collège de France, which are the speaker's property. Mini-cassettes were not in use;

---

* [See "Translator's note"; G.B.]
† [Not in this edition; see "Translator's note"; G.B.]

however, a partial recording of some lessons was made on a Nagra by Gilbert Burlet,[66] with Foucault's agreement. The tapes were erased after transcription, so it is unfortunately impossible to authenticate them. Some fragments of transcriptions have been used in the critical apparatus when they contributed a clarification; they are indicated by an asterisk in the notes.

3. On the occasion of a repeat of the lecture abroad, Foucault removed from the manuscript of his 1970-1971 course the lecture devoted to the Nietzschean paradigm of the will to know, delivered in the sessions of 23 December 1970 and 6 January 1971. It has disappeared from his archives.

Compensated for by several references to the Nietzschean conception of knowledge and truth, this gap does not radically unbalance the organization of the course. However, the late discovery of precise notes by Hélène Politis revealed the importance of this lack. Foucault having always displayed reservations with regard to the publication of auditors' notes, we have preferred to include a lecture he delivered in April 1971, and so immediately after the course, which takes up its main elements.

Only a quarto sheet of headed paper from his Montreal hotel listing the leitmotiv that he was going to develop, an aide-memoir which he often put on top of his lectures, makes it possible to place this lecture at McGill.

An editor's note indicates the main differences, mainly of a philosophical order, from the notes preserved of the Paris lectures of December 1970 and January 1971.

4. The last component of the *Lectures on The Will to Know* is a lecture written in the summer of 1972 and delivered with the title "Oedipal Knowledge (*Le savoir d'Œdipe*)" at the State University of New York at Buffalo, and then at Cornell University the same year, and then repeated at Rio de Janeiro in 1973, and of which there are a total of seven different versions in the Foucault archive.

This lecture develops the twelfth lecture of the 1970-1971 course. Formally, in relation to this course it plays something like the role played by *Las Meninas* in relation to the theory of representation in *The Order of Things*. In fact, it identifies and pieces together all the constitutive elements of the transformation of the juridical-religious truth-test in archaic Greece into the political-juridical truth-report of classical Greece, thus reconstructing one of the most important processes, according to Foucault, in the history of the production of truth. It brings together in this way the two stages on which, according to Foucault, Deleuzian representation was played out, metaphysics and the theater: metaphysics of the phantasm, of the "liberated simulacrum [which] is carried out or mimes itself, on two privileged stages: psychoanalysis, which, dealing with phantasms, will one day have to be understood as metaphysical practice; and theater, multiplied, polyscenic, simultaneous theater broken up into scenes that ignore each other and signal to each other and where, without any representing (copying, imitating), masks dance, bodies cry, and hands and fingers gesticulate."[67]

Philosophically, it is hard not to bring together *Oedipal Knowledge*, with its law of halves, and Hegel's reading, when he makes the *Phenomenology of Mind* both the real tragedy of the human mind whose final unveiling is self-consciousness or "I always knew," and the history of domination and servitude: of the tyrant and the slave.

It is in fact through the law of verbal halves—the magical-religious words of gods and seers, the words of sovereigns, and the words of shepherds—that the truth is revealed, less by intercommunication, as in Hegel, than by the hierarchical conflict of interpretations at the end of which the articulation of saying and seeing summons all the powers of the body, all the social forces, the lower parts of the people. *Pudenda origo*. In Hegel language substituted for God, the God still required by Descartes to establish his certainties. Here, it is the seeing of shepherds, objectivized truth that supplants the veracity of the god Apollo and his prophet: testimony which is linked less to perception (and its rediscovery by phenomenology), than to the judicial and political history of procedures of veridiction. Were these procedures already forgotten by Aristotle as they were by Plato? It is not forgetfulness however, but the status of the tyrant, that Foucault foregrounds as constitutive of Oedipal knowledge. If there is forgetfulness, it is much less forgetfulness of being than occultation of the history of power by the philosophical tradition.

## THE SOURCES

It is generally difficult to reconstruct the immense documentation on which Foucault always relied. It is incorporated in his manuscripts only at the final stage of publication, and never exhaustively. Of his preparatory research, Foucault preserved only precise quotations with their sources on separate cards in the 21/14 format he adopted during his years of study and then abandoned, except for this course apparently. Usually, one quotation per card, apart from those for this year's teaching. These have made it possible to reconstruct the bibliography, which is never referred to in the body of the text.

However, neither Detienne nor Moulinier figure in Foucault's documentation. The notes in the margins of *Masters of Truth* attest to their use; with regard to Moulinier[68] (to whom we refer in the notes), if the quotations of Homer follow their order of appearance in *Le Pur et l'Impur*, the author's insufficient differentiation of Greek and Christian defilement no doubt explains why Foucault copied out nothing from it.

The *Aristote* of Aubenque,[69] who was very familiar with the Heideggerian interpretation, underlies many of Foucault's comments on the Stagirite. Aubenque maintains that Aristotelian philosophy is less a derivative branch of Platonism than a response to the Sophistic beyond Plato.[70] Some people have thought that they could detect in *Oedipal Knowledge* the contribution of *Oedipus at Thebes* by Bernard Knox. This book was not used by Foucault; he read it later in the United States, on the suggestion of his auditors. For Knox, the decisions taken by Oedipus are the expression of his character, his "self-made rules" (lines 65, 69, 72, 77, 145, 287) have the stamp of both tyranny and, equally, his psychology. For his part, Foucault eliminates any psychologistic interpretation linked to the tradition of the tragic hero. In this tragedy we have the formalization of the succession of magical-religious and judicial regimes of veridiction whenever Oedipus sees a threat to his power.

According to the notes of the auditor [Hélène Politis], Heidegger's name was uttered in the course, and he is mentioned in the lecture on Nietzsche given in Canada. His name does not appear anywhere in the manuscript. Of course, there is the notion of unconcealment (*dévoilement*), referring to a moment of truth: it is when the world has been put in order by measure that this order discloses itself to the truth, as *kosmos* and not as *phusis*. As Werner Jaeger had already written: "*Kosmos* is a word with a political meaning. It is the reign of justice. Afterwards *kosmos* referred to the life of nature; but it is always a question of justice and not of the chain of causes and effects."[71]

1. *Le Monde* generally gives an account of inaugural lectures at the Collège de France and of welcoming addresses at the Académie Française. See J. Lacouture, "Le cours inaugural de M. Michel Foucault. Éloge du discours interdit," *Le Monde*, 4 December 1970.

2. M. Foucault, *L'Ordre du discours* (Paris: Gallimard, 1970); English translation by Ian McLeod, "The Order of Discourse," in Robert Young, ed., *Untying the Text* (London: Routledge and Kegan Paul, 1981).

3. Ibid., Fr. p. 67; Eng. p. 71.

4. H. Joly, *Le Renversement platonicien, logos, epistémè, polis* (Paris: Vrin, "Tradition de la pensée classique," 1974), p. 140.

5. *L'Ordre du discours*, p. 10; "The Order of Discourse," p. 52.

6. L. Robin, *Aristote* (Paris: PUF, 1944) p. 13 (see *akroasis*; *akroamatikos*).

7. F. Nietzsche, *The Gay Science*, trans. Walter Kaufmann (New York: Random House, Vintage, 1974), p. 272: "I wish he had remained taciturn at the last moment of his life."

8. M. Foucault, *Le Courage de la vérité. Le gouvernement de soi et des autres II. Cours au Collège de France, 1984*, ed. F. Gros (Paris: Gallimard-Seuil, 2009) lecture of 15 February, p. 68, p. 84, and pp. 87-107; on the interpretation of Nietzsche, see p. 89; English translation by Graham Burchell, *The Courage of Truth. The Government of Self and Others II. Lectures at the Collège de France 1983-1984*, English series editor Arnold I. Davidson (Basingstoke: Palgrave Macmillan, 2011), pp. 74-75, p. 91, and pp. 95-116 and pp. 98-99.

9. M. Foucault, *L'Ordre du discours*, p. 73; "The Order of Discourse," p. 73.

10. M. Foucault, "Theatrum philosophicum," (1970), in *Dits et Écrits, 1954-1988*, ed. Daniel Defert and F. Ewald, with the collaboration of J. Lagrange (Paris: Gallimard, 1994), vol. II, 80, p. 77; "Quarto" ed., vol. I, p. 945; English translation by Donald F. Brouchard and Sherry Simon (slightly amended by the editors) "Theatrum Philosophicum," in *Essential Works of Foucault 1954-1984. Volume 2: Aesthetics, Method, and Epistemology*, ed. Fames Faubion, (New York and London: The New Press/Allen Lane the Penguin Press, 1998) p. 345.

11. M. Detienne, *Les Maîtres de vérité dans la Grèce archaïque*, with a Preface by P. Vidal-Naquet (Paris: Maspero, 1967; English translation by Janet Lloyd as *The Masters of Truth in Archaic Greece* (New York: Zone Books, 1996).

Marcel Detienne, with Jean-Pierre Vernant, had then begun to publish in the *Journal de psychologie normale et pathologique*, led by Ignace Meyerson, who also had a real influence on Foucault, who saw him frequently in the years when he was studying psychology. According to Meyerson, psychological functions have something of the nature of the changes and incompleteness of knowledge. They are themselves subject to change, incomplete, and unable to be completed. See I. Meyerson, *Les Fonctions psychologiques et les Œuvres* (Paris: J. Vrin, 1948).

12. J.-P. Vernant, "Le sujet tragique. Historicité et transhistoricité," in *Mythe et Tragédie en Grèce ancienne 2* (Paris: Maspero, 1986) p. 85; English translation by Janet Lloyd, "The Tragic Subject: Historicity and Transhistoricity," in Jean-Pierre Vernant and Pierre Vidal-Naquet, *Myth and Tragedy in Ancient Greece* (New York: Zone Books, 1988).

13. M. Heidegger, *Nietzsche*, ed. and trans. P. Klossowski (Paris: Gallimard, 1971), vol. I, Book III: "The Will to Power as Knowledge," p. 388; English translation by John Stambaugh, David Farrell Krell, and Frank A. Capuzzi, *Nietzsche. Volume III. The Will to Power as Knowledge and as Metaphysics*, ed. David Farrell Krell (New York: Harper & Row, 1987) p. 24: "In the question of what knowledge is, we are basically asking about truth and its essence.... Here, what is *true* means what *is*.... The question about the essence of knowledge, as the question about what is true and truth, is a question about beings."

14. M. Foucault, "Ariane s'est pendue" (1969) in *Dits et Écrits*, vol. I, 64, pp. 768-769; "Quarto" ed., vol. I, pp. 795-796.

15. F. Nietzsche, *Par-delà le bien et le mal*, ed. and trans. H. Albert (Paris: Mercure de France, 1948) §1, pp. 11-12; English translation by R. J. Hollingdale, *Beyond Good and Evil* (Harmondsworth: Penguin Books, 1973), p. 15: "The will to truth, which is still going to tempt us to many a hazardous enterprise; that celebrated veracity of which all philosophers have hitherto spoken with reverence: what questions this will to truth has already set before us! What strange, wicked, questionable questions! ... Is it any wonder ... this Sphinx should teach us too to ask questions? *Who* really is it that here questions us? *What* really is it in us that wants 'the truth'?—We did indeed pause for a long time before the question of the origin of this will—until finally we

came to a complete halt before an even more fundamental question. We asked after the *value* of this will. Granted we want truth: *why not rather* untruth? And uncertainty? Even ignorance?— The problem of the value of truth stepped before us—or was it we who stepped before this problem? Which of us is Oedipus here? Which of us sphinx? ... And would you believe it, it has finally almost come to seem to us that this problem has never before been posed ... ?"

16. G.W.F. Hegel, *La Phénomenologie de l'esprit*, trans. J. Hyppolite (Paris: Aubier-Montaigne, 1939), vol. I, p. 35; English translation by J.B. Baillie, *The Phenomenology of Mind* (London/ New York: George Allen and Unwin Ltd./Humanities Press Inc., 1971) p. 99: "[That 'in very case of falsity there is something true' is an expression] in which they are taken to be like oil and water, which do not mix and are merely united externally."

17. Platon, *Le Sophiste*, 227d, in *Œuvres complètes*, ed. and trans. L. Robin (Paris: Gallimard, "Bibliothèque de la Pléiade," 1969) vol. II, p. 273; English translation by F.M. Cornford, *Sophist*, in *Plato: Collected Dialogues*, ed. Edith Hamilton and Huntington Cairns (Princeton: Princeton University Press, Bollingen Series LXXI) p. 97: "purification ... to cast out whatever is bad."

18. M. Foucault, *History of Madness*, trans. Jonathan Murphy and Jean Khalfa (London and New York: Routledge, 2006) p. 511: "Since the late eighteenth century, the life of unreason has only manifested itself in the lightning flash of works likes those of a small number of writers such as Hölderlin, Nerval, Nietzsche and Artaud—works that could never be reduced to these alienations that cure ... " (translation slightly modified).

19. M. Foucault, *The Archeology of Knowledge*, trans. A.M. Sheridan Smith (London: Tavistock Publications, 1972) Part IV, ch. 6, "Science and knowledge." The notion of the materiality of knowledge was already developed by Husserl.

20. M. Foucault, letter of 16 July 1967, *Dits et Écrits*, vol. I, p. 31; "Quarto" ed., vol. I, p. 41.

21. F. Nietzsche, *Introduction aux leçons sur l'Œdipe-Roi de Sophocle (été 1870)*, followed by *Introduction aux études de philologie classique (été 1871)*, trans. F. Dastur and M. Haar (La Versanne: Encre Marine, 1994) p. 94.

22. F. Nietzsche, *Le Livre du philosophe. Études théorétiques*, trans., introduction and notes, A. Kremer-Marietti (Paris: Aubier-Flammarion, 1969) § 37, p. 53.

23. Ibid., §25, p. 45.

24. M. Heidegger, *Nietzsche*, Vol. Three, pp. 22-24.

25. M. Foucault, "Nietzsche, la généalogie, l'histoire. Hommage à Jean Hyppolite," (1971), *Dits et Écrits*, vol. II, no. 84, pp. 136-156; "Quarto" ed., vol. I, pp. 1004-1024; English translation (slightly amended by editors) by Donald F. Brouchard and Sherry Simon, "Nietzsche, Genealogy, History" in *Essential Works of Foucault 1954-1984*, Vol. Two, pp. 369-391.

26. F. Nietzsche, *La Naissance de la tragédie*, ed. and trans. G. Bianquis (Paris: nrf/Gallimard, 1949) §15, p. 78; English translation by Ronald Spiers, *The Birth of Tragedy and Other Writings*, ed. Raymond Guess and Ronald Spiers (Cambridge/New York: Cambridge University Press, 1999), pp. 73-74: "Consider for a moment ... how an unimaginable, universal greed for knowledge, stretching across most of the cultured world, and presenting itself as the true task of anyone of higher abilities, led science on to the high seas, from which it could never again be driven completely."

27. F. Nietzsche, *Le Livre du philosophe*, p. 52 and p. 44.

28. F. Nietzsche, *La Naissance de la tragédie*, §14, p. 72; *The Birth of Tragedy*, p. 68: "We know that the only genre of poetry Socrates understood was the *Aesopian fable*."

29. Ibid., §15, Fr. p. 78; Eng. §15 p. 73: "Socrates ... appears to us as the first man who was capable, not just of living by the instinct of science, but also, and this is much more, of dying by it"; §14, p. 67: "Socrates' one great Cyclopian eye turned on tragedy, an eye in which the lovely madness of artistic enthusiasm never glowed" and p. 68: "But the art of tragedy did not seem to Socrates even to 'tell the truth'."

30. A. Cutrofello, "Foucault on tragedy," *Philosophy and Social Criticism*, 31 (5-6), 2005, pp. 573-584.

31. F. Nietzsche, *Essai d'autocritique* (1886), in *La Naissance de la tragédie*, pp. 128-129; "An Attempt at Self-Criticism" in *The Birth of Tragedy*, pp. 4-5: "O, Socrates, Socrates, was that perhaps *your* secret? ... What I had got hold of at that time was something fearsome and dangerous, a problem with horns, not necessarily a bull, but at any rate a new problem; today I would say that it was the *problem of science (Wissenschaft)* itself, science grasped for the first time as something problematic and questionable ... I shall not suppress entirely just how unpleasant it

[the book] now seems to me … standing there before me sixteen years later—before eyes which are older and a hundred times more spoiled, but by no means colder, nor grown any more of a stranger to the task which this reckless book first dared to approach: *to look at science through the prism of the artist, but also to look at art through the prism of life.*"

32. See M. Foucault, *Le Gouvernement de soi et des autres. Cours au Collège de France, 1982-1983,* ed. F. Gros (Paris: Gallimard-Seuil, "Hautes Études," 2008), "Situation du cours," pp. 357-358; English translation by Graham Burchell, *The Government of Self and Others. Lectures at the Collège de France 1982-1983,* English series editor, Arnold I. Davidson (Basingstoke: Palgrave Macmillan, 2010), "Course context," pp. 385-386.

33. M. Detienne, *Les Maîtres de vérité dans la Grèce archaïque* (1967); Eng., *The Masters of Truth in Archaic Greece.*

34. G. Deleuze, *Différence et Répétition* (Paris: PUF, 1968); English translation by Paul Patton, *Difference and Repetition* (London: Athlone Press, 1994).

35. F. Nietzsche, *Le Livre du philosophe;* English translation by Walter Kaufmann as F. Nietzsche, "On Truth and the Lie in an Extra-moral sense" in *The Portable Nietzsche* (New York: Penguin, 1976). A. Kremer-Marietti published the first overall analysis of Foucault's work in *Michel Foucault. Archéologie et généalogy* (Paris: Seghers, 1974).

36. See E. Bertram, *Nietzsche. Essai de mythologie,* foreword by P. Hadot (Paris: Éd. du Félin, 1990).

37. "Ariane s'est pendue" (1969) and "Theatrum philosophicum" (1970).

38. M. Foucault, *The Archeology of Knowledge,* p. 48.

39. M. Foucault, "La vérité et les formes juridiques" (1974), *Dits et Écrits,* vol. II, no. 139, pp. 538-646; "Quarto" ed., vol. I, pp. 1406-1490; English translation by Robert Hurley, "Truth and Juridical Forms" in *Essential Works of Foucault 1954-1984. Vol. 3. Power,* ed. James D. Faubian (New York: New Press, 2000).

40. See above, "Lecture on Nietzsche," p. 220 note 1.

41. In 1946-1947 Foucault followed the course of Jean Wahl, outstanding objector, on the relationships of Heidegger to Plato, Jean Wahl himself taking inspiration from a course by Heidegger on Nietzsche (1925 and 1936) and the *Holzwege* (course notes preserved by Foucault).

42. G. Deleuze, "Un précurseur méconnu de Heidegger, Alfred Jarry," in *Critique et Clinique* (Paris: Minuit, 1993); English translation by Daniel W. Smith as, "An unrecognized precursor to Heidegger: Alfred Jarry" in G. Deleuze, *Essays Critical and Clinical,* trans. Daniel W. Smith and Michael A. Greco (London: Verso, 1998).

43. G. Deleuze, *Difference and Repetition,* p. 66.

44. Ibid., pp. 60-61.

45. Ibid., p. 67.

46. M. Foucault, *The Archeology of Knowledge,* pp. 9-10 (translation slightly modified).

47. F. Nietzsche, *La Naissance de la philosophie à l'époque de la tragédie grecque,* ed. and trans. G. Bianquis (Paris: nrf/Gallimard, 1938) p. 75: "Heraclitus grasped by intuition instead of scaling [the truth] by the rope ladder of logic"; English translation by Marianne Cowan, *Philosophy in the Tragic Age of the Greeks* (Chicago: Gateway, 1962) p. 69: "truth grasped in intuitions rather than attained by the rope ladder of logic."

48. See E. Fink, *Das Spiel as Weltsymbol* (Suttgart: W. Kohlhammer, 1960); French translation by H. Hildenbrand and A. Lindenberg, *Le Jeu comme symbole du monde* (Paris: Minuit, 1966), ch. IV, "The worldliness of the human game."

49. On the Foucault-Deleuze relationship, read Judith Revel, *La Pensée du discontinu. Introduction à une lecture de Foucault* (Paris: Fayard/Mille et une nuits, 2010); E. Bolle, *Macht en verlangen, Nietzsche en het denken van Foucault, Deleuze en Guattari* (Amsterdam: 1981); G. Deleuze, *Foucault,* trans. Seán Hand (Minneapolis: University of Minnesota Press, 1988); A. Sauvagnargues, *Deleuze. L'Empirisme transcendental* (Paris: PUF, 2009).

50. M. Foucault, "Nietzsche, Genealogy, History," *Essential Works of Foucault,* Vol. Two, p. 378 (translation modified slightly).

51. M. Foucault, "Prisons et asiles dans les mécanismes du pouvoir" (1974), *Dits et Écrits,* vol. II, no. 136, p. 521; "Quarto" ed., vol. I, p. 1389.

52. C. Andler, *Nietzsche, sa vie et sa pensée,* vol. VI: *La Dernière Philosophie de Nietzsche. Le renouvellement de toutes les valeurs* (Paris: Bossard/Gallimard, 1931), pp. 369-370.

53. F. Nietzsche, *Human, All Too Human. A Book for Free Spirits*, trans. R.J. Hollingdale (Cambridge: Cambridge University Press, 1986) §262, p. 125.

54. F. Nietzsche, *La Naissance de la philosophie à l'époque de la tragédie grecque*, p. 211. [The quotation comes from a fragment (1875) entitled—in the French translation—"The Conflict between Science and Wisdom." It is not included in the English translation of *Philosophy in the Tragic Age*; G.B]

55. See M. Foucault, *L'Herméneutique du sujet. Cours au Collège de France, 1981-1982*, ed. F. Gros (Paris: Gallimard-Seuil, "Hautes Études," 2001) pp. 4-6 et passim, notably p. 164; English translation by Graham Burchell, *The Hermeneutics of the Subject. Lectures at the Collège de France, 1981-1982*, English series editor, Arnold I. Davidson (Basingstoke: Palgrave Macmillan, 2005) pp. 2-5, pp. 170-171.

56. M. Heidegger, *Nietzsche*, (French) vol. I, Book III, p. 490; English, Vol. Three, Part One, p. 137: "It can be historiologically shown that it [the thought of justice (*Gerechtigkeit*)] dawned on him in his reflections on pre-Platonic metaphysics, especially that of Heraclitus. ... These few main thoughts on 'justice' were not published."

57. Ibid., Fr. p. 388; Eng. p. 24: "If Nietzsche's thought of will to power is the fundamental thought of his metaphysics and the last thought of Western metaphysics, then the essence of knowledge, that is, the essence of truth, must be defined in terms of will to power. ... Thus in all relating man somehow keeps to what is true." (See above, p. 267.)

58. F. Nietzsche, *Œuvres philosophiques complètes*, ed. G. Colli and M. Montinari, trans. J.-Cl. Hémery (Paris: Gallimard, 1977) Vol. XIV, p. 116; English translation by Walter Kaufmann and R.J. Hollingdale in F. Nietzsche, *The Will to Power* (New York: Vintage Books, 1968) §515, p. 278: "Not 'to know' but to schematize—to impose upon chaos as much regularity and form as our practical needs require."

59. M. Heidegger, *Nietzsche*, Fr., Vol. I, Book III, p. 431; Eng., Vol. Three, Part One, p. 71: "'Not "to know" but to schematize.' ... This means that to know is not 'to know'—namely, in the supposed sense of a receptive, imitative copy ... this interpretation of knowledge as 'schematizing' abides with Platonic-Aristotelian thought in the same region of decision, even though Nietzsche did not 'get' the concept of schema *historiologically*, by looking up past opinions, from Aristotle."

60. Ibid., Fr. p. 398; Eng. p. 34: "The essential definition of truth that since Plato and Aristotle dominates not only the whole of Western thought but the history of Western man in general."

61. Ibid., Fr. p. 399; Eng. p. 35.

62. See in particular, M. Heidegger, "Le retour au fondement de la métaphysique," trans. R. Munier, *Revue des sciences phiosophiques et théologiques*, XLIII, 3 July 1959, p. 413: "*Alētheia* might be the word which would give an indication as yet untested, on the unthought essence of the *esse*. If this is so, it is clear that the thought by representation of metaphysics could never arrive at this essence of truth. The truth of being remains hidden from metaphysics throughout its history, from Anaximander to Nietzsche."

63. G. Deleuze, *Nietzsche and Philosophy*, trans. Hugh Tomlinson (London: Athlone Press, p. 1983) p. 2.

64. M. Foucault, *The History of Sexuality. Vol. 1: An Introduction*, trans. Robert Hurley (London: Allen Lane, 1979) p. 60 et seq.). See "Lecture on Nietzsche" above, p. 223 note 41.

65. B. Knox, *Oedipus at Thebes* (New Haven: Yale University Press/London: Oxford University Press, 1998), "Preface to the New Edition," p. x.

66. In Foucault's circle, Gilbert Burlet, a rare personality, was the first to have suggested recording the lectures at the Collège de France; Jacques Lagrange took over from him in this. It is thanks to them that the Collège de France and then the Centre Foucault have had at their disposal several years of recordings which have served as the basis for these editions. Gilbert Burlet, a West Indian born in Vietnam, studied theology at the Papal University of Jesus at Rome, then moved to the École nationale d'administration before becoming a doctor in Paris Hospitals and being engaged as researcher at the Pasteur Institute in Tokyo and Peking. He also took part in the seminar on Pierre Rivière. The person who saw to the transcription, Jacqueline Germé, also born in Vietnam, did not attend the lectures and studied Chinese at the Langues Orientales; she was one of Paco Rabanne's stylists.

67. M. Foucault, "Theatrum philosophicum": Fr. p. 80; "Quarto" ed., p. 948; Eng. p. 348 (translation modified; G.B.).

68. L. Moulinier, *Le Pur et l'Impur dans la pensée des Grecs d'Homère à Aristote* (Paris: Librairie C. Klincksieck, 1952).

69. P. Aubenque, *Le Problème de l'Être chez Aristote* (Paris: PUF, 1966).

70. Ibid., p. 96.

71. W. Jaeger, *The Theology of the Early Greek Philosophers* (Oxford: Clarendon Press, 1947) p. 35 (Foucault's translation); English translation for the Gifford Lectures from the German manuscript by Edward S. Robinson, pp. 35-36: "In the life of politics the Greek language refers to the reign of justice by the term *kosmos*; but the life of nature is a *kosmos* too, and indeed this cosmic view of the universe really begins with Anaximander's dictum... Some writers have tried to read our idea of the laws of nature into Anaximander's words, but what we have found is something else altogether. Here is no sober rehearsal of the regular sequence of cause and effect in the outer world, but a world-norm that demands complete allegiance, for it is nothing less than divine justice itself."

# INDEX OF NOTIONS
Compiled by Sue Carlton

# INDEX OF NAMES
Compiled by Sue Carlton

Page numbers followed by n refer to the notes